Rethinking Langu
in Digital Africa

NEW PERSPECTIVES ON LANGUAGE AND EDUCATION
Founding Editor: Viv Edwards, *University of Reading, UK*

Series Editors: Phan Le Ha, *University of Hawaii at Manoa, USA* and Joel Windle, *Monash University, Australia.*

Two decades of research and development in language and literacy education have yielded a broad, multidisciplinary focus. Yet education systems face constant economic and technological change, with attendant issues of identity and power, community and culture. What are the implications for language education of new 'semiotic economies' and communications technologies? Of complex blendings of cultural and linguistic diversity in communities and institutions? Of new cultural, regional and national identities and practices? The New Perspectives on Language and Education series will feature critical and interpretive, disciplinary and multidisciplinary perspectives on teaching and learning, language and literacy in new times. New proposals, particularly for edited volumes, are expected to acknowledge and include perspectives from the Global South. Contributions from scholars from the Global South will be particularly sought out and welcomed, as well as those from marginalized communities within the Global North.

All books in this series are externally peer-reviewed.

Full details of all the books in this series and of all our other publications can be found on http://www.multilingual-matters.com, or by writing to Multilingual Matters, St Nicholas House, 31–34 High Street, Bristol BS1 2AW, UK.

NEW PERSPECTIVES ON LANGUAGE AND EDUCATION: 92

Rethinking Language Use in Digital Africa

Technology and Communication in Sub-Saharan Africa

Edited by
Leketi Makalela and Goodith White

MULTILINGUAL MATTERS
Bristol • Blue Ridge Summit

DOI https://doi.org/10.21832/MAKALE2309
Library of Congress Cataloging in Publication Data
A catalog record for this book is available from the Library of Congress.
Names: Makalela, Leketi, editor. | White, Goodith, editor.
Title: Rethinking Language Use in Digital Africa: Technology and Communication in
   Sub-Saharan Africa/Edited by Leketi Makalela and Goodith White.
Description: Bristol, UK; Blue Ridge Summit, PA: Multilingual Matters, 2021. |
   Series: New Perspectives on Language and Education: 92 | Includes bibliographical
   references and index. | Summary: "This book challenges the view that digital
   communication in Africa is relatively unsophisticated and questions the assumption
   that digital communication has a damaging effect on indigenous African languages. It
   offers a paradigm of language merging that provides a blueprint for the decolonization
   of African languages through digital platforms"— Provided by publisher.
Identifiers: LCCN 2021004707 (print) | LCCN 2021004708 (ebook) |
   ISBN 9781800412293 (paperback) | ISBN 9781800412309 (hardback) |
   ISBN 9781800412316 (pdf) | ISBN 9781800412323 (epub) | ISBN 9781800412330
   (kindle edition)
Subjects: LCSH: Multilingualism—Africa, Sub-Saharan. | Translanguaging
   (Linguistics) | Digital communications—Africa, Sub-Saharan. | Digital media—Social
   aspects—Africa, Sub-Saharan. | Language policy—Africa, Sub-Saharan.
   Classification: LCC P115.5.A357 R48 2021 (print) | LCC P115.5.A357 (ebook) |
   DDC 306.4460967—dc23 LC record available at https://lccn.loc.gov/2021004707
LC ebook record available at https://lccn.loc.gov/2021004708

British Library Cataloguing in Publication Data
A catalogue entry for this book is available from the British Library.

ISBN-13: 978-1-80041-230-9 (hbk)
ISBN-13: 978-1-80041-229-3 (pbk)

Multilingual Matters
UK: St Nicholas House, 31–34 High Street, Bristol BS1 2AW, UK.
USA: NBN, Blue Ridge Summit, PA, USA.

Website: www.multilingual-matters.com
Twitter: Multi_Ling_Mat
Facebook: https://www.facebook.com/multilingualmatters
Blog: www.channelviewpublications.wordpress.com

The policy of Multilingual Matters/Channel View Publications is to use papers that are
natural, renewable and recyclable products, made from wood grown in sustainable
forests. In the manufacturing process of our books, and to further support our policy,
preference is given to printers that have FSC and PEFC Chain of Custody certification.
The FSC and/or PEFC logos will appear on those books where full certification has been
granted to the printer concerned.

Typeset by Nova Techset Private Limited, Bengaluru and Chennai, India.
Printed and bound in the UK by the CPI Books Group Ltd.
Printed and bound in the US by NBN.

Contents

Contributors   vii
Introduction   xi

Part 1: Multilingual Practices

1   Multilingual Literacies and Technology in Africa:
    Towards Ubuntu Digital Translanguaging   3
    Leketi Makalela

2   Translanguaging in the Rwandan Social Media: New Meaning
    Making in a Changing Society   19
    Epimaque Niyibizi, Cyprien Niyomugabo and Juliet Perumal

Part 2: Linguistic and Cultural Maintenance

3   Creating Translated Interfaces: The Representations of African
    Languages and Cultures in Digital Media   51
    Elvis ResCue and G. Edzordzi Agbozo

4   Mdocumentation: Combining New Technologies and Language
    Documentation to Promote Multilingualism in Nubian Heritage
    Language Learners of the Diaspora   73
    Kirsty Rowan

Part 3: The Effects of Communication Outside Africa

5   A Network of Anger and Hope: An Investigation of
    Communication on a Feminist Activist Facebook
    Website, the Network of Eritrean Women (RENEW)   99
    Sarah Ogbay and Goodith White

6   Identity, Language and Literacy in an African
    Digital Landscape   118
    Bonny Norton

7   Networked Poetics: WhatsApp Poetry Groups and Malawian
    Aesthetic Networks   137
    Susanna Sacks

Part 4: Language Change

8   Human–Agent Interaction: L1-mode Intelligent Software
    Agents Instructing Nigerian L2 Speakers of English During
    Assembly Tasks   157
    Abdulmalik Yusuf Ofemile

Conclusion   188
Index   196

Contributors

G. Edzordzi Agbozo is a PhD candidate in Rhetoric, Theory and Culture at Michigan Technological University, graduating in May 2021. He received a Master of Philosophy degree from the Norwegian University of Science and Technology (NTNU) and a Bachelors from the University of Ghana. His research interests include Language Policy, Language Acquisition, Critical Discourse Studies, Digital Rhetoric and Technical Communication. His most recent publications and reviews appeared in the *Applied Linguistics Review, Current Issues in Language Planning, African Journal of Rhetoric, Multicultural Shakespeare* and *Programmatic Perspectives*. His poems also appeared in *Prairie Schooner, North Dakota Quarterly, Dunes Review*, and elsewhere.

Leketi Makalela is full professor and founding Director of the Hub for Multilingual Education and Literacies (HuMEL) at the University of the Witwatersrand, South Africa. He is a Distinguished Visiting Professor at City University of New York. His research areas include translanguaging, multilingual education and literacies. He is a rated researcher and holder of an Endowed Chair (South African Research Chairs Initiative) on Multilingual Education for Social Inclusion and Access. His academic citizenship includes being a Research Convenor for the National Reading Coalition of South Africa and an Executive Committee member of Umalusi Council for Quality Assurance and an Editor-in-Chief of the *Journal of Southern African Linguistics and Applied Language Studies*.

Epimaque Niyibizi is a senior lecturer at the University of Rwanda – College of Education. He is currently the Deputy Dean in the School of Education and Head of Nyagatare Campus. He holds a PhD in Applied Languages and Literacy Education from the University of the Witwatersrand (South Africa), a master's degree in Applied Linguistics, a master's degree in Educational and Social Research Methods and a Postdoctoral fellowship in Educational leadership and management. He has published journal articles and book chapters in the area of Applied Linguistics, language policy in education, language education, language management in multilingual settings and educational leadership.

Cyprien Niyomugabo was the Dean of the School of Education at University of Rwanda-College of Education and the Chairman of the Rwanda Academy of Language and Culture until October 2019, when he became a Senator at the Parliament of Rwanda/the Senate representing Public Institutions of Higher Education in Rwanda. He holds a PhD in Linguistic Science Education and a Post Graduate Certificate in Teaching and Learning in Higher Education. His area of research is mainly on Bilingual Education, Mother Tongue and Second Language Education, Glottopolitics in Education and Lexicography with application to the teaching and learning of African languages.

Bonny Norton (FRSC) is a Professor and Distinguished University Scholar in the Department of Language and Literacy Education, University of British Columbia, Canada. Her primary research interests are identity and language learning, digital storytelling and open technology. A Fellow of the Royal Society of Canada and the American Educational Research Association, she was given the BC CUFA 2020 Academic of the Year Award for her work on the Global Storybooks project (https://globalstorybooks.net/).

Abdulmalik Yusuf Ofemile holds a PhD (English) University of Nottingham, UK; an MA (TESOL & ICT) University of Leeds, UK; and a BEd in Language Arts (English) from ABU Zaria, Nigeria and Associate Fellowship (Advanced-HE, UK). He is the Director of Quality Assurance FCT-COE Zuba with teaching and research experience in Nigeria and the UK. Abdulmalik's research straddles language, linguistics, multimodality, computer science, ELT, and contributes to the understanding of linguistic and communicative issues surrounding Human–Computer Interaction in real-world application and contexts. Abdulmalik's recent article appeared in *African Journal of Social Sciences and Humanities* research and he contributed a chapter to the *IGI Global Handbook of Research on Curriculum Reform Initiatives in English Education*.

Sarah Ogbay completed her doctoral degree in Applied Linguistics at Lancaster University in the UK. She taught at the University of Asmara, Eritrea, for 26 years, both at undergraduate and post graduate levels In addition she served as the Head of the Department of English and many other capacities and responsibilities for the University of Asmara. Sarah taught at the British Council Eritrea for 11 years. Currently she is working for the University of Manchester Language Centre as a freelance English language examiner and tutor. Sarah is co-founder of the registered Network of Eritrean women and has served on the board of directors. She has worked in different organisations as a community worker and a professional interpreter for a number of psychologists and medical professionals.

Juliet Perumal is Professor in the Department of Education Leadership and Management at the University of Johannesburg. She is a Visiting Professor at the University of Nsukka, Nigeria. Perumal has taught at various schools and universities throughout South Africa. She has published in the field of critical, and feminist pedagogies; transformative curriculum, educational leadership; and qualitative research methodologies. Perumal is a South African National Research Foundation Rated Researcher; and the recipient of the Joyce Cain Award Winner for outstanding research on peoples of African descent.

Elvis ResCue (PhD) is a Lecturer at the Department of English, Kwame Nkrumah University of Science and Technology, Ghana. He holds a PhD and MA in Applied Linguistics from Aston University, UK, and a BA in Linguistics with English from the University of Ghana, Legon. His research interests lie in the area of Discourse Analysis, African and General Linguistics, Language Contact/Sociolinguistics, Media Language, and Language Policy and Planning. His most recent publication (co-authored) on language attitudes to language-in-education policy in Ghana appeared in the journal *Current Issues in Language Planning* and he has also published a chapter in *The Routledge Handbook of African Linguistics*.

Kirsty Rowan is a Senior Teaching Fellow in the School of Languages, Cultures and Linguistics at the School of Oriental and African Studies (SOAS), University of London, United Kingdom. She is a member of the Anthropology and Language Committee of the Royal Anthropological Institute (RAI) and a Fellow of the RAI and the Royal Geographical Society (RGS with IGB). She conducts endangered language documentation on Nile Nubian languages, toponymy and culture and works with African heritage and diaspora communities towards the maintenance of languages.

Susanna Sacks is Assistant Professor of English at the College of Wooster in Ohio, where she has taught since receiving her PhD from Northwestern University in 2019. Her research investigates the relationship between transnational institutions, poetic forms and aesthetic networks in Africa. Her current book project draws on anglophone, Chichewa and isiXhosa literary traditions to map the interactions between embodied and digital literary forms and institutions. Sacks has published work on hashtag poetry, poetry spectacles and the development of slam poetry networks in southeastern Africa.

Goodith White retired as Director of the Applied Language Centre, University College Dublin in 2016, and is currently a Senior Research Fellow for the University of Nottingham Malaysia. She has served as

Chair of the British Association for Applied Linguistics Language in Africa SIG, and besides her interest in language use in Africa, has published widely in the areas of sociolinguistics, language pedagogy and the use of technology in political and educational contexts. Her most recent books focused on technology-assisted language learning (OUP) and literature in language learning (Palgrave Macmillan).

Introduction

At the time of writing (August 2020) the world is in the grip of a major pandemic. We are all living in unprecedented times, having to socially distance and unable to travel far. One of the significant effects of the pandemic has been to propel us, in Africa as everywhere elsewhere, into using digital connectivity in ways and amounts we would not have believed possible only six months ago. It seems timely, in a volume focusing on digital communication in Africa, to start off this introduction with some current, living examples of how individuals and governments are communicating virtually in Africa in these challenging times, and to discuss the priorities, difficulties and innovative practices they seem to reveal. Many of these factors were already present before the pandemic, and are reflected in the chapters of this book, which were written before the world went into lockdown. We asked the contributors to the volume, as well as the current Chair and Secretary of the *Language in Africa Special Interest Group*, British Association of Applied Linguistics, which provided the inspiration for the project, to send us some 'snapshots' of how digital communication is currently being used to fight the pandemic and support citizens in their African contexts. The comments are of course personal but made by keen and qualified observers.

Their snapshots reveal how longstanding problems, such as language choice, persist in new modes of digital communication, how the pandemic has highlighted the digital divide between rich and poor in the same country, but also how the pandemic is forcing change and development. Some African countries seem to be quite well connected already, and importantly there is a willingness on the part of the government to improve digital connectivity. The government in Nigeria seems to have reacted very similarly to the global North in terms of desired and ambitious measures, although the infrastructure is not totally up to the task. However, local inventiveness and creativity are evident. Abdulmalik Ofemile emailed the following:

> 'The pandemic has forced people and policy makers in Nigeria to emphasise digital communication in tertiary education, government, commerce and personal interaction.
>
> The Minister of Education directed that all tertiary institutions should start delivering lectures online. The academic staff replied that he has

not provided the required infrastructure to make full scale online teaching a reality that is effective in the institutions. They pointed out that power outages, inadequate hardware, lack of trained personnel, classrooms/lecture hall that are not designed to align with online teaching and learning, lack of digital libraries to support learning, and expensive broadband costs inhibit online education. In addition, the majority of students do not have digital devices and adequate digital literacy to enable them attend lectures effectively. However, the government and some private organisations are now organising lessons for primary and secondary school students in various subjects that are presented on television, radio and some locally produced interactive web-based learning management systems as well as Zoom.

The President and state governors now hold council meetings with their executive committees using digital devices and online platforms.

Business is getting more digitised. For example, banks and other utility service providers are rolling out more online platforms to enable consumers carry out transactions from the comfort of their homes/offices without meeting physically. This ensures that social distancing is not violated.

Due to the lockdown and restriction on movement across the country, family members who are stranded in different parts of the country communicate using digital devices and platforms such as smart phones, tablets and computers using WhatsApp, Facebook Messenger and WeChat to make voice and video calls as well as sending text messages. Furthermore, awareness regarding Covid-19 is propagated more through digital devices, content and platforms by government, groups and individuals.

On the whole, communication among Nigerians is becoming profoundly digital at all levels however, a lot of work still needs to be done to bring this up to the accepted standards. In addition, the pandemic provides huge opportunities for multidisciplinary knowledge and skill development to enhance digital communication in Nigeria.

As for as how languages are being used in digital communication in the pandemic, for official interaction, the President, Governors and most government officials are using English in official communications. Their official Twitter handles all communicate in English too. However, during the pandemic, government officials such as the Presidential Task Force on Covid-19 now give out information using English, Hausa, Igbo, Yoruba and Nigerian Pidgin during press conferences when journalists and other members of the audience ask questions in these languages. For education, all lessons and learning materials provided for all categories of learners online, on tv and radio are presented in English except for teaching other languages. Radio and tv stations now use multilingual anchor systems for Covid-19 programmes. They also have similar multilingual social media teams to handle online communication which often co-occurs with live programmes. The lockdown has led to a remarkable increase in online chat groups on WhatsApp, Facebook etc as well as the use of Zoom for personal interaction.

The language of communication on these platforms is not strictly regulated and is a matter of personal choice. So members use multilingual strategies to communicate'.

Multilingual Practices

It is interesting that in Abdulmalik's observations, formal online instruction for learners appears to be focused on English, in contrast to the multilingual practices in other forms of digital communication. Leketi Makalela has also noticed this phenomenon in South Africa, where home schooling has been taking place:

'The (learning) materials are in English when the majority of the parents are themselves not proficient in English. The need for African languages was apparent, but no resources were available during the pandemic crisis. Absence of indigenous African languages for learning and teaching and by extension to online resources is the case in point why students are not coping so far with online learning and why parents are not able to engage with online content for their children'.

However, Epimaque Niyibizi has noticed a more multilingual approach:

'At the University of Rwanda, where I teach, we are now holding faculty virtual meetings using Zoom, WebEx and Microsoft Teams; our students are studying from home using e-learning platforms, radio and TV; and I have to say that social media like WhatsApp are now being used by students not only to exchange chats and information, but to exchange learning materials as well. You find that every unit/department has created a WhatsApp group for easy and quick communication.

On the aspect of mixing languages in such digital communication, it is also a frequent practice. We use four official languages in Rwanda, namely Kinyarwanda, English, French and Kiswahili, and they are used in various fora, but with frequent mixing of those languages, particularly on social media'.

These comments resonate with a major theme in our chapters :

• **How does digital communication support the multilingual practices of Africans (or not)?** For example, In the case of Nigeria and South Africa, multilingual practices do not seem to be happening in education online, but does seem to be taking place on social media, in official and personal communication and for disseminating information about Covid 19.

Social and Political Change

A number of our contributors have noted how digital communication has linked the diaspora to those living in a particular African country, often with a politically subversive or corrective effect. For example,

Seraphin Kamden, the current Chair of the Language in Africa SIG, makes the point that the pandemic has encouraged close communication between the diaspora and those living in Cameroon, with the diaspora providing accurate information and negating the effects of false news:

> 'Going from the point of digital communications as including social media information and the digital online tools and platforms such as WhatsApp and Facebook, I would say that the Covid-19 pandemic has brought much more importance to mobile technologies and phone communications between rural Africa and the African diaspora in Europe, but has also helped fill an information gap: between established local media networks trapped in political propaganda and hidden corporate advertising and diasporic Africans who have access to some more up-to-date information about the Covid-19 pandemic and who try their best to feed back that useful medical information to their families back in Africa. Again, this pandemic has created a new landscape in digital communications in terms of a new layer of data and information flows that somehow does bypass the traditional and government-controlled channels – something unimaginable just three decades ago where political propaganda and any useful information were mostly generated by state-controlled media, and most of it on local press and radios and TV networks'.

Sarah Ogbay reports much the same phenomenon for Eritrea, where households are not allowed access to the internet, and where individuals can theoretically only receive information via state controlled television and media. However ordinary people (if they can afford it) are accessing information by phone from relatives in the diaspora and TV channels from outside Eritrea via satellite dish. Similarly, Abdulmalik Ofemile observes for Nigeria that:

> 'One other trend emerging is that Nigerians in the diaspora are using online media to hold the government to account for the handling of Covid-19 and other issues as well as make meaningful contributions for improvement. Nigerian interest/pressure groups in the diaspora are using digital media, particularly Zoom, to organise virtual interactive town hall meetings with Ministers and government officials. Participants ask government officials questions on pressing issues while government officials provide answers. Nigerians in the diaspora also pass on their experiences in their host countries as well as relevant professional input to the government officials. These meetings are held using English but you still see some use of Nigerian pidgin and a sprinkling of Nigerian languages during interaction.'

These comments echo another theme in the volume, which addresses the question:

• **How does digital communication put African countries in contact with ideas and influences from the wider world, and what effects might this have?** As we have seen from the above examples, information flows and political practices are being affected by the ease of digital connections with the outside world, a trend which some of the chapters in this book were already researching before the pandemic, but which has perhaps become more marked in the current global emergency.

African Languages and Culture

On a rather brighter note, Susanna Sacks has noted a blossoming of the arts in the digital sphere in Africa during the lockdown:

'My sense is that the pandemic has focused and concentrated energy towards digital networks and communities. I haven't come across anyone doing anything totally new (yet!), but what I have seen is all energy turn towards the digital. Because more people are online for more of the day, this focus has paid off, with more engagement and faster turn-arounds than usual. I have a sense this might indicate a major shift in how poetry and the arts are shared, especially as workshop-style projects are being published open source online. A sort of bright spot in this terrible time. The work I've come across has largely been promoted in English, but the performances themselves vary in language a great deal.

So, for example, Afrolit Sans Frontieres are running a virtual literary festival featuring African writers in French, English and Portuguese. In Harare, Zimbabwe, The Book Café has been sharing their '#Lockdown sessions' on Facebook. In a further example in South Africa, the poet and playwright Siphokazi Jonas is organizing a #slam4urlife digital poetry slam on Instagram".

These comments reflect the third theme which is addressed by many of the contributors to this volume:

- **How does digital technology help maintain African languages and cultures?**

The final theme of this book encompasses all the others:

- **How does digital technology provide new ways of recording and researching language use and change?**

The ways in which the chapters this volume focus on these four themes are outlined below.

How does digital communication support the multilingual practices of Africans (or not)?

Although we have problematised the situation in institutionalised online education, in the informal digital platforms described in this book, people move seamlessly, naturally and easily between languages, and there is no expectation that sites such as the Facebook groups described by ResCue and Agbozo or the WhatsApp groups described in Niyibizi *et al.*'s paper should use one language only. All languages are equal in such spaces, replacing a situation where some languages, often colonial ones, exert more power. Makalela has a uniquely African and innovative take on the multilingual communication which is facilitated in digital spaces, defining it as different from code switching or translanguaging but instead characterising it as Ubuntu translanguaging, a communicative practice where input and output are exchanged in different languages to signal that one language is incomplete without the other. Makalela and Niyibizi *et al.* describe the positive effects of this multilingual translanguaging, which boosts social cohesion, encourages freedom of expression and generates a sense of community and togetherness.

How does digital communication put African countries in contact with ideas and influences from the wider world, and what effects might this have?

As Castells (2015) points out, digital technology can disrupt traditional power structures. It does this by facilitating the creation of autonomous spaces which are beyond the control of governments and corporations who usually monopolise channels of communication. In these freer spaces, participants can grow and develop because they are given agency. They can also communicate on a global level, receiving ideas and input from far flung places and people. Ogbay and White argue that the Facebook group they have researched, which was created by Eritrean women refugees in the diaspora, helps the members to become both politically active and more aware of their rights as women. Norton writes about the ways in which digital communication has made education a more democratic process, enabling learners themselves to both access and contribute to global knowledge production. She is interested in the extent to which identities shift as language learners and teachers engage with digital technology in diverse African communities. Her chapter contains a powerful description of The African Storybook project, whose main goal is to promote mother tongue literacy. It provides over 1000 illustrated open-access digital children's stories with over 5000 translations, in over 170 African languages, as well as the official languages of English, French and Portuguese. Users can read, download, translate, adapt and create stories for local use, using a range of mobile devices. She notes how the project developed the digital skills and social power of both teachers and learners, and enabled them to develop new identities as poets, writers, trainers and global citizens. Sacks has researched a WhatApp group in Malawi who write, share and critique poetry, creating new postcolonial poetic forms of expression. Because they operate in a digital space, the group are not reliant on western or African publishing houses for the dissemination of their work, giving them freedom of expression about topics which might otherwise be censored.

How does digital technology help maintain African languages and cultures?

Social media are providing a powerful way of maintaining African languages, of encouraging people to use them in communication, and of ensuring their vitality and transmission to the next generation of speakers. This also means that the important cultural concepts and customs embodied in a particular language are passed on. ResCue and Agbozo describe the creativeness of Ewe users on Facebook in improvising new lexis and orthography to communicate and represent their culture. Rowan illustrates how the use of digital technology is a much better and more holistic way compared with traditional print methods for documenting the multilingual and sociocultural contexts in which endangered languages such as Nubian are used. She also shows how digital technology empowers the language users themselves, rather than foreign 'experts', to keep records through smartphones, and how technology connects the diaspora of Nubian speakers, enabling Nubian to remain a living language.

Digital technology provides new ways of recording and researching language use and change

The chapters in this book all consider some aspect of the ways in which languages in an African context are being influenced and changed by digital communication. Digital communication provides new spaces in which language use and language rules are freer and more fluid; communicating one's message is more important than whether one adheres to conventional notions of correctness which may apply in some non-digital contexts. We've noted already that language mixing or translanguaging is a common feature of digital communication in African contexts. Crystal (2006) has pointed out that the language of digital communication merges written and spoken genres, creates neologisms and makes use of visual and spatial possibilities of meaning making. Many of the chapters in this book (for example, ResCue & Agbozo and Ogbay & White), describe how images, photos, video, emoticons and other visual affordances combine with words to produce complex layers of connotation, emotional expression and cultural reference. These analyses require new research methodologies. For example, taking as his starting point the fact that there is an increasing use of software agents in learning contexts, and therefore a need to understand how these agents interact with learners, Ofemile has found an innovative methodology for researching visual information. He analyses data recording spontaneous facial actions and uses it to understand patterns of listenership behaviour for Nigerian L2 English speakers taking instructions from L1 English-mode devices.

Organisation of this Book

We have organised the chapters of the book around these four themes – multilingual practices, linguistic and cultural maintenance, the effects of communication outside Africa and language change – while bearing in mind that the reader will find that the themes are often echoed by different contributors over the entire book.

References

Castells, M. (2015) *Networks of Outrage and Hope: Social Movements in the Internet Age*. Cambridge: Polity Press.
Crystal, D. (2006) *Language and the Internet* (2nd edn). New York: Cambridge University Press.

Part 1
Multilingual Practices

1 Multilingual Literacies and Technology in Africa: Towards Ubuntu Digital Translanguaging

Leketi Makalela

Introduction

'Where [the] government has failed, technology is bringing hope to the people,' says the Makalela. 'African languages were probably going to die, were it not for technology, social media and popular culture. Technology is going to take African languages forward and these languages are going to evolve to fit into the digital age and any future world shift [s].' (Physig.org, online)

The author had an intensive interview with a Communications Officer after she had received numerous reports about the negative effects of technology in the development and standardized use of indigenous African languages. In particular, concerns were raised around how the social media platforms produce non-standard versions of these languages and how they become vulnerable to the dominant former colonial languages such as English, French and Portuguese. Unlike these dominant languages with a high ICT coverage and use, African languages have very few online resources and their presence as the media of communication via ICT tools is still negligible (Jantjies & Joy, 2014; Mabweazara, 2016; Osborn, 2006). This conversation is reminiscent of what was an old-age linguistic dilemma on whether changes signify decay or progress. The sentiments expressed in the above quote go against the conventional view that predicts doom and extinction. Rather, it regards the ICT advances as a positive development to save indigenous African languages from extinction and move them through digital migration platforms.

Although there is a need for advances in technology for literacy in African languages in Southern Africa, the usefulness of technology and its impact on the development of African languages does not have a universal agreement (Shanglee, 2004; Tassé, 2003). As demonstrated in the report above, there are two contesting views: the most dominating one is that the use of technology will 'decay' the pristine models of African languages and that the strong international languages like English will dominate over the digital space in a manner that will eventually result in the extinction of the less dominant languages. The second view is that technology will fasten development trajectories of these languages as platforms such as social media will give them coverage and use by their speakers across a wider spectrum of nationalities and ethnic divides that were historically based on languages.

The result of the divergent views on the impact of digital technologies has been that the resources outside of classroom spaces cannot be leveraged to support the cultural competence of multilingual encounters and e-literacy opportunities. Where attempts are notable in selected areas, there has been scepticism on the full use of available resources both outside and inside of the classrooms. This scepticism ironically includes the view that technology will 'corrupt' the standards of the languages if technology encourages a linguistic cross-over or what is generally referred to as translanguaging (Makalela, 2018; Otheguy *et al.*, 2018). Worth noting, however, is that there is very little research on the use of technology for African language development. In this chapter I report on the success of technology induction in a classroom project, which was tailor-made to have leverage outside of the classroom multilingual resources. In conclusion I discuss how technology can respond to ways of knowing peculiar to African cultural competence and literacy initiatives that cut across a number of languages. A model for multilingual e-education and literacy, referred to as digital translanguaging, will be highlighted and significant areas of good practice will be shared at the end of the chapter.

African Languages as Media for Technology Communication

It is axiomatic that many parts of the world have experienced a wave of technological developments as the world exponentially gravitated towards information economies. Concomitantly, digital learning and teaching have become a constant and normal feature in many classrooms as societies advance, among other things, through machine learning and the 'internet of things' (Hayward, 2018). A scant survey of the use of technology generally and among African languages in particular shows that Sub-Saharan Africa has been lagging behind since the dawn of the information society era (Janties & Joy, 2014; Osborn, 2006; Tassé, 2003). Notably, many African governments have developed policies and started several projects, which to date remain incomplete and under resourced for a meaningful fourth industrial revolution to take effect. Shanglee (2004), for example, argues that the developments of Human Language Technologies (HTL) have not sufficiently addressed African languages party due to lower level of awareness and lack of interest in HLT among African language scholars.

Research on the use of technology in African languages shows that Africa is lagging behind in a variety of ways. First, the developments in voice interfaces where searches can be carried out via voice have left nearly all African languages behind. Even Kiswahili, which has about 98 million speakers, does not have the options for voice interfaces as yet. One of the technological devices is mobile learning (Jantjies & Joy, 2014). Jantjies and Joy (2014) developed a framework for using mobile technology in low-income communities. However, the multilingual nature of Africans means that the developers are not producing multilingual models where more than one language is used at the same time. These technological advances and many others fail to take root as they were designed for 'ideal' monolingual speakers. There is therefore a research and development gap that is not being addressed to advance African languages as the media for communication in the digital platforms.

Multilingualism, Translanguaging and African Cultural Competence

One of the ways in which new technologies will take effect in Sub-Saharan Africa is the material effect of addressing multilingual nature and epistemological pathways that are authentic to speakers of African languages. It is conventionally accepted that multilingualism is a norm in many African states, but the ways of knowing that are often introduced through educational packages and technological advances reflect monolingual bias that disproportionately disadvantages speakers of African languages (Brock-Utne, 2015; Makalela, 2017). Even more poignantly, practices of multilingualism are also rejected in favour of foreign language monolingualism despite a plethora of research pointing to the need of these languages for sustainable development (Prah, 1998).

Research is replete with the recommendations for disrupting monolingual bias and allowing divergent voices to come into contact. One of these includes looking back at the sociolinguistic background of the African people prior to colonialism (Makalela, 2018; Makoni & Pennycook, 2007). The history of Mapungubwe – a cultural heritage site at the border of South Africa, Zimbabwe and Botswana – and its linguistic repertoire becomes the obvious point of reference for Southern Africa to reclaim its linguistic and cultural heritage. I have elsewhere (Makalela, 2018) shown that the African value system of Ubuntu is a heuristic for African multilingualism where the use of more than one language through porous interaction is a norm that can be cultivated strategically in contemporary platforms. To this end, the concept of *Ubuntu translanguaging* accounts for a communicative practice where input and output are exchanged in different languages to signal that one language is incomplete without the other. As will be discussed below. the main idea of Ubuntu translanguaging is its paradox found in the saying: *I am because you are; you are because I am*. The complex interface of 'I' and 'we' offers a window through which individuality and collectivism co-exist in a shared identity space.

To date, translanguaging as a social and cultural practice has been studied elsewhere in the world as a discourse where linguistic input and output are alternated in different languages (Creese & Blackledge, 2010; García, 2009, 2011; García & Li Wei, 2014; Li Wei, 2018). In the African context, the use of languages goes beyond alternation where complex interfaces within and between languages could involve more than two named languages in the same communicative event. In our research in complex multilingual settlements in South Africa, we found that there is both vertical and horizontal translanguaging discourse practices in classrooms (Nkadimeng & Makalela, 2015). For example, teachers who teach different subjects have a tendency of using languages of their preference with a similar group of learners who interact and respond in any of the named languages in the process of meaning making. In other words, we found situations where six teachers choose different named languages for input–output exchange to respond to questions from their learners. It is in this connection that these overlapping ways of meaning making mirror larger sociocultural practices that are, however, not reflected in the emergent technologies.

Viewing multilingualism from a complex array of translanguaging and meaning-making practices provides opportunities for an epistemological shift from what languages look like to what speakers do with languages. Research shows that the missionary linguists' development of African languages orthographies often without a central coordination system form the basis of invented artificial languages (e.g. Makoni, 2003). For example, a language variety called Sesotho was written down by three different missionary groups who wrote the spelling systems differently according to their own languages. In the northern part of South Africa, the German missionary group founded and developed an orthography of the language they called Northern Sotho (which later became Sepedi); the London Missionary group worked in the western part of the country and named their language, Western Sotho (which later became Setswana); and then the Roman Catholic missionary group were in the south where they wrote down a language they called Southern Sotho (which is known today as Sesotho). Here, one language that should have one writing system and more readers has been divided into three different languages (see Makalela, 2009).

The translanguaging approach in the context of Ubuntu provides policy makers with measures to question the validity of current boundaries among African languages. Under Ubuntu translanguaging, notions such as first language, mother tongue and second language are questioned as these do not account for complex translingual discourse practices in many African contexts (García, 2011; Makalela, 2018). Instead, they suggest a sequential view of language acquisition (i.e. one language at a time) and they tend to favour monoglossic discourse patterns. In this context, multilingualism is viewed as separated and bounded languages, as is widely believed. On the contrary, multilingualism from the translanguaging point of view does not place emphasis on enumeration of languages; rather it is the degree to which simultaneous use of the languages in line with the linguistic competence of the speakers is valorized. In the same vein, technology and literacy based on this fluid system offers African languages with a digital platform to cross over language boundaries.

Ubuntu Translanguaging Model and Digitization

A translanguaging model based on Ubuntu principles, referred to here as Ubuntu translanguaging, shifts the attention from African language divisions to complex repertoires that are fluid in everyday meaning-making interactions (Makalela, 2017, 2018). It also reflects a dialectic disruption of linguistic boundaries and simultaneous recreation of new ones, which digitization of the languages needs to take into account. Published in several outlets, it is presented in Figure 1.1.

The *Ubuntu* translanguaging (UT) model in Figure 1.1 shows a fluid relationship between languages, which operate in tandem with the African human logic of I × We: *I am because you are; you are because I am.* The use of a multiplication sign suggests an existential and complex relationship between these entities that look separate, but yet are tied together. This identification of the self and others in a complex web of being is at the core of Ubuntu where humaneness binds matters into an infinite bond

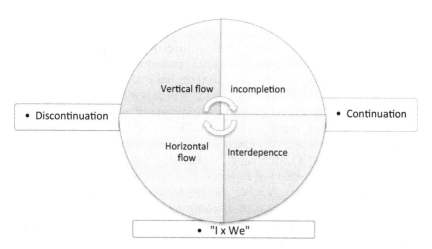

Figure 1.1 Ubuntu translanguaging model (Makalela, 2018)

of collectivity (Khoza, 2013; Makalela, 2015). Languages, like people, are a representation of this logic of being together as opposed to separated entities that are capable of being placed in sealed boxes (Makalela, 2015). Because of their endowment with Ubuntu, language encounters in multilingual communities show a constant process of disruption and cohesion – dialectic processes that occur simultaneously.

The notion of *incompletion* shows that no language is complete without the other in complex multilingual encounters. Both the 'I'ness and 'We'ness do not form a coherent whole when they stand alone, as is relatively well known in the African folklores and idioms such as '*moeng etla ka geso re je ka wena*' for 'visitor please come to my place so that I am complete' (Makalela, 2015). This sense of incompletion renders monolingual meaning making incomplete among speakers of more than one language. It is the desire to be complete that forces multilingual speakers to draw from rich communicative resources from other languages in a process that may be implicit for hearers to deduce and unconscious for the speakers to pre-meditate.

Ubuntu translanguaging's third pillar is *interdependence*, which refers to co-existence of two or more named language entities in the process of meaning making. Because these languages are typically acquired at the same time, the world view and self-concept of the speakers are formed from this plural nexus of one language depending on the other. In this connection, the consistent state of being incomplete becomes a necessary condition for completing the cycle of meaning making. This means that the speakers use communicative resources from different varieties to make sense of the world around them. African languages, in particular, have responded to this sociolinguistic reality of interdependent multilingualism as opposed to the treatment of languages as separated entities cognitively and socioculturally.

The fourth pillar of UT shows a multilayered flow of information where both the *horizontal and vertical* axis points simultaneously become the beginning and end points of the flow direction. The plus–minus signs show that this complex flow has a push–pull effect with backward and forward movements that render the terminal end of information flow unpredictable, uncertain and indefinite. Whereas it is common for interlocutors to hear input in one language and give out a response (output) in a different language, many African multilingual speakers have the tenacity to carry on input in more than one named language and output in more than one language (Nkadimeng & Makalela, 2015).

It is in this connection of flow complexity that the pillars of Ubuntu translanguaging, namely '*I* × *We*', *incompletion, interdependence, vertical* and *horizontal* axis, create discontinuation continuation: constant disruption of language and literacy boundaries and simultaneous recreation of new ones. In everyday speech, the journey of multilingual speakers is to cross boundaries of named languages, overlap, disrupt features of one language by constantly drawing from and replacing with features of other languages without losing focus of the meaning-making process – making sense of the world around them and of who they are. It would seem that the challenge for technology innovations in African languages is not only how to assume multilingual character (Janjies & Joy, 2014), but also how to enhance multilingual performance. There is, therefore, a need for digital technologies that disrupt African languages boundaries while at the same time enhancing cohesion in meaning making as explored in the multilingual model above.

The Study

The Hub for Multilingual Education and Literacies (HUMEL) was founded by the Makalela in 2017 at the Wits School of Education, University of the Witwatersrand in South Africa. Among other strategic objectives, the Hub was created to modernize African languages via technological devices and make them accessible to the current users of these languages. Realizing that there was still a systematic exclusion of African languages in education and in all domains of prestige, a programme was developed for digital and social media inclusion of African languages. To this extent, a multilingual laboratory was repurposed to archive good digital practices outside of the formal schooling environment for in-service and pre-service teachers as well as for raising awareness of the practical nature of using African languages in digital spaces for transformation.

This study reported in this chapter involved use of technology as a tool to acquire and use African languages from resources outside of classrooms. A group of 30 second-year students at the University of the Witwatersrand were enrolled for Sepedi (one of the 11 official languages in South Africa) as a second or additional language in order to meet the African language requirement for their Bachelor of Education degree. The students were multilingual speakers of Nguni languages: isiZulu, siSwati, isiXhosa and isiNdebele language varieties.

The students were introduced to translanguaging as a pedagogical strategy and asked to participate in collection of digital artefacts in Sepedi as the target language. Particularly, the students were asked to create language blogs in which they would list new vocabulary items in Sepedi and equivalents in their home languages and English. Digital dictionaries were generated and stored online for analysis. The overall aim of this section of the course was to increase and assess the possibility of using an African language as the medium of communication on the internet and in digital platforms.

The second part of the digital assignment tasks was to find cultural events recorded online from YouTube. These included traditional weddings, stand-up comedy, music and poetry. To stimulate more interest, the researcher collected and brought to class evidence of African language soap operas that could be played back on YouTube channels. These programmes included *Muvhango, the Generations* and *Skeem Saam*, which had been national television evening programmes for at least five years. The students had to develop PowerPoint slides for presentations to the whole class and parts of their presentations were digitally archived as instructional materials in the newly repurposed multilingual laboratory.

In order to increase a pool of the vocabulary items for the students, digital social networks were used to get the students interested in using the language via technology. A Sepedi Facebook group, '*A re boleleng*', was used as an open multilingual space to extend language use beyond the classroom. While Sepedi was the main medium of writing in the group, an array of other languages the students knew were encouraged and used in the group. Moreover, at the end of each week, each student was expected to fill up a vocabulary list of 15 words acquired from any encounters they have had and place this in their individual blogs. The multilingual blog had a secondary function to help the students chart their intellectual journeys through the use of Sepedi, their home languages and English. The students were also encouraged to draw from examples from other related African languages they knew to expand linguistic repertoires.

In order to use the students' language background, the instructor's teaching approach approximated 'Ubuntu translanguaging' where languages such as isiZulu, isiXhosa, siSwati and isiNdebele were used for communication in the discussion groups. The main language of communication verbally and digitally remained Sepedi, with English and other local African languages mentioned above embedded sufficiently in the first semester. English was gradually released in the second part of the year except for vocabulary items and isolated pockets of conversations. Their home languages were preferred to English, with the instructor directly calling for use of other languages to explicate concepts such as greetings and their meanings. This practice was meant to produce both creative and critical assessments of the own-learning process through use of all languages available to them as resources.

The study relied on data collected from three sources: Facebook interactions, self-reflections and interview schedule. With regard to the interview schedule, regular conferencing with each of the students was conducted to assess their understanding of the course content and their acquisition development trajectories of Sepedi as a new language.

Analysis of the data followed both inductive and deductive thematic analyses to guide thematic development and allow for emergent themes. Verbal quotes were used as necessary to support the themes developed.

Results

The results of the study showed a successful integration of Sepedi and related African languages into digital information technologies. Specific results are classified and discussed under the following themes: using Facebook for writing about habits, blending English and African languages, deeper engagement with contents and moving out of boxes.

Using Facebook for writing about habits

The results of the study showed that the students were comfortable to create African language content using the platform of Facebook. From an assignment that asked them to place the content in the Facebook group, *A re boleleng* (let us talk), the students produced content that was less academic but nonetheless comprehensible in Sepedi – the target African language. The Facebook group showed a range of postings that were about the routines as expressed in Extract 1:

(1)   Ka le tsatsi le lengwe le le lengwe ke dumedisa batsawadi baka ke re 'thobelang bo mme le tate'. [one day I greeted my parents saying 'good day mom and dad]

(2)   Ke dula ke sa diso tse a pealego ke moratiwa wa ka mme wa sechaba.[I eat food cooked by my love...]

(3)   Ke hlwa ke theeleditse mmeno wa Maskandi le ditaba tse di sa felego, ke tshebe di movie [I spend time listening to local music called Maskandi, news and watch movies]

(4)   Ge ke tla sekolong, ke dula ke namela taxi [when I come to school, I use a taxi for transportation]

(5)   Ke dula ke raloka gwele ya maoto le bagwera baka ka SABATHA (Saturdays) [on Saturdays I play soccer with my friends].

In this extract the Facebook entry shows a speaker who is learning to write and speak Sepedi fluently. In the first line, the writer reports on how she was able to greet strangers in the community using Sepedi. The next lines details habits which include taking a taxi to go to school (line 3), cooking (line 2), listening to music (line 4) and playing soccer (line 5). From expression of ideas, this entry represents a successful and coherent depiction of habits or routines carried out outside of school. These words are recognizable as Sepedi words despite notable spelling errors, which are phonologically induced by the students' home languages. This reveals that the digital use of African languages allows them to leak into each other and mesh the original boundaries that would otherwise be restricting in ordinary classrooms.

Second, the extract shows a tendency to expand a repertoire of words taken from sister languages. For example, a blended word such as 'thebe' (line 3) for 'shebe', which means 'watch' as in watching movies within the context of the writing has its origin from Sesotho – a sister language to Sepedi. Two points worth noting about use of African languages within the digital and social media platforms is that the traditional versions of correctness are overlooked in favour of the meaning-making equivalents. The second observation is that the social media platforms allows disruption of the boundaries created among varieties of the same language as in the case of Sepedi and Sesotho. It is evident therefore that digitization and the use of technology offer agency for speakers to disrupt African languages boundaries in favour of cross-language repertoires for meaning making. In this connection, non-standard use of written conventions shows that digital platforms are positioned to offer new experimental ways of re-standardizing the language beyond traditional borders.

Blending English and African languages

The second observation from the data is that the African languages leveraged on English for words and concepts that are not familiar. A typical example is in Extract 2 below:

Extract 2a

Dumelang !! Maikemisetso aka ke go bapala bolo ya maoto,ke bapalle sethlopa sa afrika borwa,engwe ya di toro tsa ka ke go godisa abuti waka omonyani ebile ke month bone Agwetsa degree ya gagwe. [Greetings!! My goal is to play soccer and play for the national South African team. My next dream is to raise my younger brother until the month he graduates for his degree]

Extract 2b

Dumelang baithuti! Gosasa ke tla be ke swaragane ka lebaka la baeng ba rena. Ke kgopela gore le se tle classeng (I will be tied up tomorrow due to our visitors' programme on and around campus. Let's cancel the class and I will do catch ups when we meet on Monday. Tuesday too may be a problem, but I'll advise on Monday. Le be le weekend ye monate!

Both segments of the Facebook entry reveal blended use of English and African languages. In the first segment, a student talks about the participant's goals that include playing football for the national team and raising his brother till he gets his degree. In this instance the recognizable borrowed word is 'degree'. Although the reason for this may be that the student has not yet acquired an equivalent word in Sepedi, degree has come to be too familiar and commonly used in conversations among Sepedi speakers.

The second part of the extract (Extract 2b) reveals an announcement by the instructor who intentionally uses Sepedi first and repeats the message in English. He empathically uses Sepedi in closing, but with an English word, 'weekend' in *Le be le weekend ye monate* [have a good weekend]. It is also noticeable that the first version of the message in Sepedi shows borrowing of English word, *class*, with a locative marker- / *eng*/ for 'to class.' The social media and use of digital platforms allow forms that may not be accepted in classroom situations despite their prevalence outside of the classroom environment. Here, the pristine models of both Sepedi and English usages are disrupted in favour of utterances that are meaning-driven. That is, the speakers are concerned with meaning making instead of the aesthetics of the language and proceeded fluidly in this digital platform without restrictions. The important note here is this digital platform enables movement of of words into African languages, a natural sociolinguistic process.

Deeper engagement with content

The results of the study show that the use of Sepedi in the social media platform offers dialogues that clarify messages and promote deep and independent learning. Extract 3 demonstrates this finding:

Extract 3

Bagwera, ke na le putso. Ge motho a ngoala lebitso le 'sepedi' o dira bjang? Ana o ngoala 'Sepedi' kapo 'sePedi'? Ke otlwa ke thothomela ge motho a ntsoara ka dipolelo tse tsa se Kgowa are 'Pedi' eupsa a sa se ngole sintle. I think this is the most prominent problem I have in language, I have too many changes I'd like to see. [friends, I have a question. What is the correct version of the name, Sepedi? Do you write Sepedi or sePedi? I tremble when someone use the English version Pedi but not using appropriate orthography.]

This extract also breaks the writing conventions in the Sepedi language even though the message is lucidly clear. The speaker uses the medium of Sepedi to ask questions without fear of criticism from peers. She would like to know the correct spelling of Sepedi and sees value in having it spelled correctly. As noted above, it is worth noting here that a number of lexical items such as putso (question), lebitso (name), sintle (good) are not traditionally Sepedi words, but they are words borrowed from its sister language, Sesotho. To close the message for this utterance, the speaker makes a bold English pronouncement: 'I think this is the most prominent problem I have in language, I have too many changes I'd like to see.' The speaker is concerned with the orthography of Sepedi and she would like to see some changes. Points worth making here are manifold. First, there is a cross-over meaning that cuts across sister language boundaries (Sepedi and Sesotho) and between these language varieties and English. What one sees is a disruption of orderliness represented through single language codes to one that is accommodative and versatile while not losing the logic and cohesion of the meaning conveyed. This balance between disruption of boundaries through technology and stability epitomizes a development journey of African languages which is volatile, unpredictable, complex and ambiguous (VUCA) (Hayward, 2018). As discussed elsewhere, translanguaging enhanced by technological platforms goes beyond 'artificial' boundaries that often become a barrier for modernization and use of the languages.

Moving out of boxes

Themes that emerged from the interviews centred around the notion of 'moving out of linguistic boxes' (Makalela, 2015). Analysis of various data segments show a gravitation to step outside of the conventional boundaries – a point already mentioned above. The following extract is prototypical:

Extract 5a

Using Sepedi in A re boleleng has gave me independent space to use the language without anyone correcting us. I have seen more similarities between many languages- um just like out own.

Extract 5b

I don't know if I could have learned another African language so easily without the Facebook page. It allowed me to grow from one point to the next. Plus we did not have any one correcting us when we made mistakes.

Extract 5c

I start to see more commonalities and appreciate African languages more. We were told they are difficult to learn. Thanks to Facebook, we did not have to struggle. I can identify with Bapedi people better now.

In the three extracts above, there is a recurrent theme of relief and shaking off boundaries that looked real at first, but artificial after exposure. Extract 5a is particular about how the social media mode freed the participants from over-correction typically realized in classrooms. This idea of self-correction is carried further in Extract 5b while Extract 5c stresses realization of commonalities among sister languages and how exposure through social media and use of technological devices has made it possible to access the messages and express high sense of self. But even more importantly, the interconnectedness of the languages and the speakers resonate with the value system of Ubuntu where no one language is complete without the other (Makalela, 2018). The teaching of Sepedi in the context of this study has thus shown an interwoven network of cultural continuity beyond learner language boundaries. It appears that segmentation of identities according to home languages will, in this particular case, limit the holistic and broadened sense of self within intercultural fluidity of expressions (García, 2011). The finding revealed in this extract tallies with earlier observations that indigenous African languages have in fact been 'disinvented' (Makoni, 2003) and that their perceived boundaries are 'artificial' (Makalela, 2005). It is therefore through the advances in technology that translingual practices and re-organization of African languages become possible.

Digital Translanguaging and Implications

One of the findings of the study is that the participants used technology and social media spaces offered to them to extend language use beyond the traditional boundaries of discrete languages. The students' positive attitudes towards the Sepedi Facebook page and their active use of the platform to talk about their habits and goals are strong indicators of how well the digital divide between languages of wider communication such as English and indigenous local languages such as Sepedi can be closed over time. Using Sepedi and vocabulary from sister languages showed that the students are aware of the interconnections between sister language varieties: Sepedi, Sesotho and Setswana. This observation resonates with a long-held view of higher degrees of mutual intelligibility among African languages that were historically divided into artificial and exaggerated linguistic entities (Alexander, 1989; Makalela, 2005, 2009; Nhlapo, 1944). However, in the context of the current study, mutual intercomprehensibility is enhanced and magnified by the use of less-formal digital and social media platform. It is therefore fitting that bounding languages into boxes is not supported in heteroglossic environments as represented by the students when granted opportunities explore uses of information technologies in African languages.

The results of the study point out the need to reconceptualize our view of African languages standards in line with the recent scholarship on translanguaging (e.g. García & Li Wei, 2014; Makalela, 2019; Li Wei, 2018). Once the shift is towards meaning making, there is a natural cross over between various forms of different languages that cohere around meaning making. This epistemological shift aligns with the value system of Ubuntu, which disrupts the traditional view of African languages based on external models that favour territorial inclusion or exclusion of the speakers (Makalela, 2016). It also makes it possible for gravitation from linguistic division of the past through full utilization of technology for African language development, modernization and use on a large scale. This inclusive Ubuntu lens recognizes the wealth of multilingualism and the linguistic continuum of African languages while debunking the old ways of using African languages from models that were borrowed wholesale from monolingual approaches. It is in this context that digital translanguaging provides richer opportunities for disrupting old boundaries between African languages and simultaneous recreation of new ones: discontinuation continuation. When stated differently, the use of translanguaging strategies revealed through technologically infused use of African languages disrupts etho-linguistic divisions based on language differences and creates opportunities for re-integration through digitization. This integration is liberating for historically excluded languages and affirms the fluid linguistic identities of their speakers.

Conclusion

In concluding the chapter, it is useful to return to the interview recording reported in the introduction part of the paper. The results of this preliminary work by the HUMEL in South Africa, coincide with the author's reaction when asked to assess the status of African languages versus technological advances within a chorus of discord about standards:

> 'Where government has failed, technology is bringing hope to the people,' says the author. 'African languages were probably going to die, were it not for technology, social media and popular culture. Technology is going to take African languages forward and these languages are going to evolve to fit into the digital age and any future world shift.' (Physig.org)

It seems possible to agree with the sentiments of the interview: technology is bringing hope to the people where government and language policies failed to enhance the development of African languages for use in the domains of high prestige. The study has revealed that a dynamic multilingualism can be harnessed through the use of technology and less restrictions on the standards of writing and acceptance of meaning as the driving force for African language communication. The use of technology has also unveiled an African cultural competence where there is complex input and output exchanges between a variety of languages. I have referred to this meaning-making process as *Ubuntu translanguaging*, which reveals more of a unitary and dialectic interactions between various language systems.

A corollary to the languaging phenomenon enhanced through use of technological devices is the second message in the interview: the possibility of African languages going into extinction if they do not adapt to changing ecosystems of meaning making. This technology ecosystem is replete with social media platforms, digitization and the 'internet of things' and it is largely characterized as volatile, unpredictable, complex and ambiguous (Hayward, 2018). The conclusion derived from the analysis in this chapter is the need for non-linear and fluid intersection of African languages, on the one hand, and African languages and dominant languages such as English, on the other hand, through a *discontinuation continuation* of discourse practices. This means a dialectic process where there is both disruption of linguistics forms and rigid boundaries between languages as well as simultaneous drive for cohesion based on the principle of meaning making. This evolution through what I termed *digital translanguaging* is the central point of whether these languages can be saved into the future. This viewpoint of Ubuntu translanguaging and its discontinuation continuation aligns with complexity theory where non-linear and dynamic relationships between constantly changing entities are nurtured and understood as the new normal in the fourth industrial revolution (Larsen-Freeman, 2017; Manson, 2001).

While this scope for growth and advancement of African languages through valorization of technological devices is vital for the future, there is a need for more research to explore opportunities for digital translanguaging for African languages as a precursor for social transformation and linguistic development.

References

Alexander, N. (1989) *Language Policy and National Unity in South Africa/Azania*. Cape Town: Buchu Books.

Brock-Utne, B. (2015) Language, literacy and democracy in Africa. In L Makalela (ed.) *New Directions on Language and Literacy Education for Multilingual Classrooms in Africa* (pp. 15–33). Cape Town: CASAS.

Creese, A. and Blackledge, A. (2010) Translanguaging in the bilingual classroom: A pedagogy for learning and teaching? *The Modern Language Journal* 94, 103–115.

García, O. (2011) From language garden to sustainable languaging: Bilingual education in a global world. *Perspectives* 34 (1), 5–9.

García, O. (2009) *Bilingual Education in the 21st Century: A Global Perspective*. Miden, MA: Wiley/Blackwell.

García, O. and Li Wei (2014) *Translanguaging: Language, Bilingualism and Education*. London: Palgrave Pivot.

Hayward, S. (2018) *The Agile Leader: How to Create an Agile Business in the Digital Age*. New York: Kogan Publishing Limited.

Is Tech killing African languages? (2017) Pyscs.org. See https://phys.org/news/2017-09-tech-indigenous-african-languages.html

Jantjies, M. and Joy, M. (2014) A framework to support mobile learning in multilingual environments. A Paper presented at the International Conference on Mobile Learning 2014 (10th, Madrid, Spain, Feb 28–Mar 2, 2014).

Khoza, R. (2013) *Let Africa Lead: African Transformational Leadership for 21st Century Business*. Johannesburg: Vezubuntu.

Larsen-Freeman, D. (2017) Complexity theory: The lessons continue. In L. Ortega and Z. Han (eds) *Complexity Theory and Language Development* (pp. 11–50). Amsterdam: John Benjamins.

Li Wei (2018) Translanguaging as a practical theory of language. *Applied Linguistics* 39, 9–30

Li Wei (2011) Moment analysis and translanguaging space: Discursive construction of identities by multilingual Chinese youth in Britain. *Journal of Pragmatics* 43, 1222–1235.

Mabweazara, H. (ed.) (2016) *Digital Technologies and the Evolving African Newsroom: Towards an African Digital Journalism Epistemology*. Abingdon: Routledge.

Makalela, L. (2005) We speak eleven tongues: Reconstructing multilingualism in South Africa. In B. Brock-Utne and R Hopson (eds) *Languages of Instruction for African Emancipation: Focus on Postcolonial Contexts and Considerations* (pp. 147–174). Cape Town and Dar-es-salam: CASAS and Mkuki n Nyota Publishers.

Makalela, L. (2009) Unpacking the language of instruction myth: Towards progressive language in education policies in Africa. In K. Prah and B. Brock-Utne (eds) *Multilingualism: An African Advantage* (pp. 170–194). Cape Town: Casas.

Makalela, L. (2014) Teaching indigenous African languages to speakers of other African languages: The effects of translanguaging for multilingual development. In L. Hibbert and C. van der Walt (eds) *Multilingual Universities in South Africa: Reflecting Society in Higher Education* (pp. 88–104). Bristol: Multilingual Matters.

Makalela, L. (2015) *New Directions in Language and Literacy Education*. Cape Town: CASAS.

Makalela, L. (2018) *Shifting Lenses: Multilanguaging, Decolonization and Education in the Global South*. Cape Town: CASAS.

Makalela, L. (2017) Bilingualism in South Africa: Reconnecting with Ubuntu translanguaging. *Encyclopedia of Bilingual and Multilingual Education* (pp. 297–309). New York: Springer.

Makoni, S. (2003) From misinvention to disinvention of language: Multilingualism and the South African Constitution. In S. Makoni, G. Smithermann, A. Ball and A. Spears (eds) *Black Linguistics: Language, Society and Politics in Africa and the Americas* (pp. 132–149). London and New York: Routledge.

Makoni, S. and Pennycook, A. (eds) (2007) *Disinventing and Reconstituting Languages*. Clevedon: Multilingual Matters.

Manson, S.M. (2001) Simplifying complexity: A review of complexity theory. *Geoforum* 32 (3), 405–414.

Nhlapho, J. (1944) *Bantu Babel: Will the Bantu Languages Live?* Cape Town: The African Bookman.

Nkadimeng, S.P. and Makalela, L. (2015) Identity negotiation in a superdiverse community: the fuzzy languaging logic of high school students in Soweto. *International Journal of the Sociology of Language* 234, 7–26.

Osborn, D.Z. (2006) African languages and information technologies: Literacy, access and the future. *Proceedings of the Annual Conference on African Linguistics* (pp. 86–96). Somerville: Cascadilla Proceedings Project.

Otheguy, R., García, O. and Reid, W. (2018) A translanguaging view of the linguistic system of bilinguals. *Applied Linguistics Review*, doi.org/10.1515/applirev-2018-0020.

Prah, K. (1998) *Between Extinction and Distinction. Harmonization and Standardization of African Languages*. Johannesburg: Witwatersrand University Press.

Ricento, T. (2000) Historical and theoretical perspectives in language policy and planning. *Journal of Sociolinguistics* 4 (2), 196–213.

Shanglee, R. (2004) Localization in African languages: translators face linguistic challenges as they localize modern technology. *Multilingual Computing and Technology* 61 (Vol. 15, Issue 1), 37–38.

Shohamy, E. (2006) *Language Policy: Hidden Agendas and New Approaches*. London: Routledge.

Tassé, E. (2003) The first steps of African languages on the internet. *iConnect Africa*, 1 (5). See http://www.uneca.org/aisi/IConnectAfrica/v1n5.htm

2 Translanguaging in the Rwandan Social Media: New Meaning Making in a Changing Society

Epimaque Niyibizi, Cyprien Niyomugabo and Juliet Perumal

Though translanguaging is being explored from different angles world-wide, we still observe a paucity of studies that investigate its use across translingual literacies in African languages. Its effects on social media are also under-researched, particularly on social dynamics, which, in our chapter, refer to social behaviours/attitudes or relationships change resulting from monolingual, bilingual and multilingual interactions among individual group members. This chapter reports on an investigation of translanguaging practices that are used on social media, specifically among the selected WhatsApp groups. It investigates the WhatsApp users' perceptions on the extent to which translanguaging practices on social media boosts positive social dynamics, namely friendship, familiarity, social cohesion, freedom in language choice, freedom of expression per excellence and togetherness among communicators, by pairing them with unsocial dynamics such as unfriendliness, unfamiliarity, inhibition of social cohesion and freedom of self-expression, and linguistic isolation or oneness, to compare. Three WhatsApp groups with 600 members were investigated, using a four-item Likert scale for the quantitative part of the study and interviews for the qualitative approach. WhatsApp posts were analysed through the lenses of Ubuntu translanguaging and translingual practices model. The key finding is that several types of translanguaging practices such as vertical/horizontal languaging; poly-languaging; metro-languaging; code-meshing; translingual, transnational and translocal language practices were found to be practiced on WhatsApp as they are practised in other multilingual settings like classrooms. The study revealed that those translanguaging practices boost positive social dynamics among communicators at a higher level than unsocial dynamics. From the new literacies perspective and Ubuntu translanguaging among African communities, we argue for the use of various translanguaging practices on social media in multilingual interactions for new meaning making. Its implications for multiliteracies and multilingualism in African multilingual settings are offered at the end of the chapter.

Introduction: Digital Technology and Translanguaging Practices on Social Media

This chapter explores digital technology and language use in an African endoglossic but multilingual country, and their effects on social media in a changing society. It investigates the extent to which the use of translanguaging on social media such as WhatsApp groups contributes to reinforcing social dynamics, social cohesion, peace-building spirit and digital literacy, in African multilingual contexts, with a focus on Rwandan social media. In Africa and in different parts of the world, the current generation uses various digital forums in today's communication, including social media such as WhatsApp, Facebook, YouTube, Twitter, Instagram, Skype, LinkedIn, Imo and Messenger, We Chat and many others. As a user and reader of some of these social media, it is observed that various translanguaging practices are used on these social media. However, only a few studies (e.g. Huaman & Stokes, 2011; Jørgensen, 2008; Jørgensen *et al.*, 2011; Stæhr, 2014; Zappavigna, 2012) have explored their effects. Hence, this chapter contributes to addressing this gap by investigating the types of translanguaging practices and their effects in reinforcing social versus unsocial dynamics among WhatsApp users. Specifically, the chapter is closely linked with the theme of the book on how digital communication among Africans supports the multilingual practices. The chapter sheds light, with practical evidence, on how digital communication in African multilingual countries is in contact with ideas and influences from the wider world, and the effects it manifests in the debate on translanguaging practices.

Context: Translanguaging and Social Media in Rwanda, Africa and the World

Various studies on language use in societies have been carried out worldwide, but studies which have investigated the effects of translanguaging in boosting social dynamics, social cohesion and peace-building spirit are still few. Here, we agree with Makalela's (2015: 190) observation that 'research on translanguaging and translingual literacies in African countries is still in its infancy'. In Rwanda, we observe the frequent use of translanguaging between Kinyarwanda, English, French, Kiswahili and some other languages (Gafaranga, 2015; Habyarimana, 2014; Kagwesage, 2013; Niyibizi, 2015; Niyomugabo, 2012), but very limited studies have been conducted on the effects of these language practices. Furthermore, limited studies have been conducted on the use of translanguaging in Rwandan social media, with a focus on WhatsApp groups and the extent to which it reinforces social dynamics. Hence, this study seeks to fill in this gap by investigating the extent to which the use of various types of translanguaging practices among the selected WhatsApp groups promotes positive social dynamics, like friendship, familiarity, social cohesion, peace-building interactions, freedom in language choice and togetherness. Those positive social dynamics are paired with unsocial dynamics, like unfamiliarity, unfriendliness, inhibition of social cohesion, freedom of self-expression, linguistic isolation and oneness among communicators, for comparison. This chapter is therefore a contribution in the domain of digital literacy, digital communication in African multilingual settings and language use on social media as it portrays how linguistic strategies like translanguaging practices contribute to boosting social dynamics in a changing society.

To contextualize this study, we built on Canagarajah's (2013: 6) argument that 'Languages are not necessarily at war with each other; they complement each other in communication'. We also built on Alexander and Von Scheliha's (2014: 35) argument that 'Language is a uniquely powerful instrument in unifying a diverse population.' It supports Bamgbose (2000) and Barnes's (2003) viewpoint that the Rwandan and the Somali situations lend weight to this argument. Building on these arguments, this study also argues that in a post-conflict situation, like the Rwandan post-genocide era, where the society is changing and transforming for better, language plays a central role in almost all aspects of life, include the reconciliation process, peace building, social cohesion education and media. That is why this chapter investigates different forms of translanguaging practices that are used on social media and the extent to which they affect social dynamics among communicators, specifically among the selected WhatsApp group users. More specifically, it seeks to answer the following research questions:

(1) What forms of translanguaging practices are used on the three WhatsApp groups?
(2) What effect, if any, do these translanguaging practices have on social dynamics?
(3) To what extent do those translanguaging practices used on the three WhatsApp groups promote digital literacy and multiliteracies?

Literature Review

Translanguaging, translanguaging practices and social dynamics

Translanguaging practices and their effects on social dynamics constitute the focus of this chapter. Social dynamics, in this chapter, are explored from Durlauf and Young's (2001: 13) perspective as 'the behavior of groups that results from the interactions of individual group members as well to the study of the relationship between individual interactions and group level behaviors'. They are applied to translanguaging in this chapter, to refer to social behaviours / attitudes or relationships change resulting from monolingual, bilingual and multilingual interactions among individual group members.

Translanguaging in this chapter is viewed from Williams (2000), Makalela (2013), García (2009) and Li Wei and Hua's (2013) perspectives, as a form of language communication which involves receiving input in one language and providing output in another language. The contribution of this chapter is that it has compiled and broadened the translanguaging features in what we have termed 'forms or types of translanguaging practices'. Our 'forms or types of translanguaging practices' are built on other scholars' terms for various translanguaging components such as code-meshing (Canagarajah, 2011); translingual practices (Canagarajah, 2013); translocal language practice (Makoni & Pennycook, 2007); transglossia (García, 2009; Dovchin, 2015; Dovchin et al., 2015; transidiomatic practices (Jacquemet, 2005); multimodality practices (Kress, 2010; The New London Group, 2000); poly-languaging or polylingual languaging (Jørgensen, 2008; Jørgensen et al., 2011); vertical languaging and horizontal languaging (Nkadimeng & Makalela, 2015); metro-languaging (Otsuji & Pennycook, 2010; Pennycook & Otsuji, 2014) and some others such as code-switching and code-mixing (Moodley & Kamwangamalu, 2004; Moodley, 2013), code-translation and code-alternation (Auer, 2005; Gafaranga, 2015; Georgalidou et al., 2008). All these terms have been coined at a different phase of translanguaging evolution but they are clearly defined in the findings section, where they are paired with examples from the three WhatsApp groups investigated. These terms are being debated among linguists, and we have categorized them all as 'forms or types of translanguaging practices' to engage and contribute to the debate. We describe them as 'forms or types of translanguaging practices' to insinuate their role in contributing in meaning-making in multilingual settings. That is why this chapter mainly explores their effects in promoting social dynamics in a quadrilingual society.

Translanguaging practices and their effects on social interactions and social dynamics, globally and continentally

Language as a communication tool uses some strategies that are said to be boosters of social dynamics among interlocutors or communicators. We all use language in our daily lives, to convey educative peaceful and social reinforcing messages or non-educative and peace inhibiting messages. Wolff (2014) and Alexander and Von Scheliha (2014: 11) describes language as having hegemonic power, with 'language policy as a means of peace building and conflict management'. Hence, language use and its mixing on social media may promote both social or unsocial dynamics. In this study, positive social dynamics are viewed from Paxton's (2009) perspective, who views components of translanguaging as an enabler of interlocutors to explore ideas and concepts in a familiar environment, implying familiarity, friendship, closeness and cohesiveness. They are also viewed from Makalela's (2015) 'togetherness', which is embedded in Ubuntu translanguaging philosophy, and this is believed to promote social cohesion, peace building and harmony in the society. They promote social justice and interconnectedness (Cioè-Peña & Snell, 2016) and linguistic free movement in new social spaces (Li Wei & Hua, 2013). On the other hand, unsocial dynamics are viewed from the lenses of interactions that limit sociability, like unfamiliarity, unfriendly interactions, limited language choice leading to sociolinguistic injustice, inhibition of freedom of expression as well as Makalela's (2015) 'oneness' or what we described as 'linguistic isolation'.

Globally, the 21st-century debates on language mixing or translanguaging show that people can no longer hold static views of autonomous and separate languages, but rather integrate language practices coming from different communities with various languages and distinct language ideologies, drawing from different semiotic codes. As García (2009) and García and Leiva (2014) have observed, 'translanguaging' acknowledges this new orientation within the emerging multilingual world of interactions, where the usage of two or multiple languages is practiced as a normal mode of communication. In Sub-Saharan Africa, about 1500 to 2500 languages (Makalela, 2016; UNESCO, 2010) are used, enabling cross-border and cross-lingual mobility. The advent of migration between nation states has resulted in super diverse communities where various languages intermingle, giving space to translanguaging and translingual interactions (Makalela, 2015).

On social media, studies have indicated that translanguaging is used. Stæhr (2014) who explored online language practices among university students in Mongolia observed how online and offline speakers from diverse linguistic and cultural environments used whatever linguistic features were at their disposal and those features were blended in complex linguistic and semiotic forms. Similarly, Huaman and Stokes (2011) argued that people are using various languages on social media as well as on radio, television and print to amplify their voices and expand their collective power locally, regionally, nationally and internationally.

Translanguaging practices in Rwandan social media and Rwandan education

In Rwanda, translanguaging practices are found not only on social media, but in education as well. In this regard, Niyibizi (2014) found that primary school teachers and students in Grade 1 to Grade 3 rely heavily on translanguaging in their lessons and in their classroom interactions. Similarly, Habyarimana (2014) found that Rwandan primary Grade 6 teachers and learners were using translanguaging between English and Kinyarwanda to promote the learning of content and the target language. University students also use translanguaging because Kagwesage's (2013) study revealed that students at the University of Rwanda were using translanguaging in the three languages (English, French and Kinyarwanda) in their group discussions in order to successfully deal with complex academic tasks, which were offered in English. Also, Niyomugabo (2012) coined 'Kinyafranglais' – a mixture of languages that were being used by the students of Kigali Institute of Education. In a nutshell, translanguaging drivers are used at various education levels in Rwanda. In this chapter, 21st-century translanguaging is not limited to language use in education only, but also in other strata of life, including social media. That is why this chapter explores forms of translanguaging practices that are used in social media and the extent to which they boost social and unsocial dynamics.

Contextualized Theoretical/Conceptual Framework for Translanguaging Practices

This study is guided by two theoretical frameworks, namely 'Ubuntu translanguaging' or the 'Ubuntu Languaging Model' (Makalela, 2014) and the 'Translingual practices model' (Canagarajah, 2013). Ubuntu translanguaging is premised on the ancient African value system called 'Ubuntu', which existed even before colonialism. Ubuntu is embedded in African culture, the African way of life and African humanism (Makalela, 2015). Makalela's model of 'Ubuntu translanguaging' is founded on the African sayings '*I am because you are*'; '*You are because we are*'; or '*Stranger please come to my house so I become complete*' (Makalela, 2015: 6). The overall argument conveyed in this model, as Makalela (2015: 6–7) explains, is that

> African multilingualism should be interpreted from this value system to appreciate the plural logic that one language is incomplete without the other. In Ubuntu languaging discourse practices, interdependence is preferred over independence in tandem with this traditional communication system that is porous, overlapping and versatile.

Hence, as Makalela (2015: 7) concludes, the key point is that 'language should no longer be viewed as being bound to space and time, but that they are fluid discursive systems in a continuous state of flux: from language to languaging'. In this chapter, Ubuntu translanguaging is viewed from Makalela's (2015) 'togetherness' versus 'oneness'. On the one hand, togetherness is linked with positive social dynamics, which are also viewed from Paxton's (2009) perspective, who views some translanguaging drivers as an enabler of interlocutors to explore ideas and concepts in a familiar environment, implying familiarity, friendship, closeness and cohesiveness (Paxton, 2009), social justice and interconnectedness (Cioè-Peña & Snell, 2016) and linguistic free movement in new social spaces (Li Wei & Hua, 2013). On the other hand, Makalela's (2015) 'oneness' is also linked with unsocial dynamics, which are viewed from the lenses of interactions that inhibit sociability, including unfamiliarity, unfriendly interactions, limited language choice leading to sociolinguistic injustice, inhibition of freedom of expression as well as linguistic isolation.

As for Canagarajah's (2013) translingual practices model, it views language speakers as transnational members, and not as members of homogeneous languages, who use texts that are meshed and mediated by diverse semiotic codes, and who integrate all available codes as a 'repertoire' in their everyday communication. That is why he advocates for 'code-meshing' as a practical way of bringing 'different codes within the same text rather than keeping them apart' (Canagarajah, 2013: 112–113). Canagarajah's (2013) code-meshing is in agreement with Jacquemet's (2005) social indexicalities and semiotic codes, because they both accept the mixing of languages and their semiotic codes. They both recognize that the current linguistic practices are not dominated by monolingual orientation, but by integrated semiotic codes from various languages. However, Canagarajah's (2013) code-meshing and Jacquemet's (2005) social indexicalities and semiotic codes tend to be in disagreement with Jørgensen et al.'s (2011: 33) ideology, which supports the linguistic purity, meaning that 'any language should be spoken 'purely', i.e. without being mixed with another language'– otherwise, the local language is in danger of foreign imperialism. In addition to code-meshing in translingual practices, Canagarajah (2013) proposes 'translingual interaction' as a strategy of alignment, which is described as 'ways in which interlocutors match the language resources they bring with people, situations, objects, and communicative ecologies for meaning-making' (Canagarajah, 2013: 82). The analysis of discourse in this study has been drawn from 'translingual interactions'.

To apply these two theories to this study, we found it appropriate to design a conceptual framework, which adapts and connects the investigated forms or types of translanguaging practices to the two theories. While McMillan and Schumacher (2006) and Bock and Mheta (2013) define a conceptual framework as concepts that are placed within a logical and sequential design, we have brought on board selected forms or types of translanguaging practices, which we described as 21st-century concepts and linked them with each of the two theories as well as each of the social dynamics components explored in this study. Table 2.1 links the two theories, namely 'Ubuntu languaging model' (Makalela, 2014) and 'translingual practices model' (Canagarajah, 2013) with translanguaging drivers and social dynamics components.

Table 2.1 Linkage between the two theories and forms of translanguaging practices and social dynamics components

Theoretical framework	Theory 1: Ubuntu languaging model or Ubuntu translanguaging	Theory 2: Translingual practices model
Forms or types of Translanguaging practices	1. Poly-languaging 2. Vertical/horizontal languaging 3. Metro-languaging	4. Code-meshing 5. Code-mixing & code-switching 6. Transnational language practice 7. Translocal language practice
Social interaction strategy	Translingual interactions (in oral or written discourse)	
Social or unsocial dynamics components	Social dynamics versus Unsocial dynamics	
Ultimate effect	Familiarity, friendship, social cohesion, free language choice, freedom of expression per excellence	Unfriendliness, unfamiliarity, limited language choice, inhibition of freedom of expression per excellence

Source: Authors' own design building on other scholars' concepts (2019).

Table 2.1 links the two theories to forms of translanguaging practices applied to this chapter. Theory 1, called the 'Ubuntu languaging model', is linked to three forms or types of translanguaging practices, which are drawn from various scholars. These are poly-languaging or polylingual languaging (Jørgensen, 2008; Jørgensen et al., 2011); vertical/horizontal languaging (Nkadimeng & Makalela, 2015); and metro-languaging or metrolingual multi-tasking (Otsuji & Pennycook, 2010; Pennycook & Otsuji, 2014). The common denominator among the three translanguaging drivers is the 'languaging' aspect, which is described as differentiated ways or a wide range of resources, a variety of linguistic repertoires, multiple literacies and numerous modalities that language users refer to in order to make sense of their actions and their social world (García, 2009; García & Wei, 2014; Makalela, 2015). Their effects are transmitted through translingual interactions in the discourse, then they lead to either social dynamics or unsocial dynamics, whose ultimate effect is togetherness or oneness.

Theory 2 called the 'translingual practices model' is linked to four forms or types of translanguaging practices, namely code-meshing (Canagarajah, 2011a), code-mixing and code-switching (Moodley & Kamwangamalu, 2004; Moodley, 2013), transnational language practices (Canagarajah, 2013) and translocal language practices (Pennycook, 2007). The common feature here is the cross-language and cross-national border aspect. Their effects in promoting social dynamics versus unsocial dynamics are weighed against togetherness and oneness.

Methodological Perspectives and How Technology is Used in this Study

This study applied digital technology, particularly the cell phone and its WhatsApp application. The preference of WhatsApp was motivated by its usage by a great number of all categories of the Rwandan population due to the great increase of telephony penetration in Rwanda and in Africa. WhatsApp is one of a number of social media forums, where users chat and share texts or audio-visual messages. As Internet World Stats (2018) reports, 172 million out of 191 million active social media users (12%) were using WhatsApp application by the end of 2017, in Africa. In Rwanda, the Ministry of Information Technology and Communication (2016) reported that in that year the mobile phone penetration rate was at 79.2% equivalent to 8,921,533 of the Rwandan population, while the penetration of internet was at 35.38% of the population. This confirms that a great number of the Rwandan population use WhatsApp and it raised our curiosity to explore the effects of mixing languages, the forms of translanguaging practices and translingual interactions they use on this social media.

Six hundred adult participants who were using WhatsApp on their cell phones participated in this study, which analysed their views on the effects of translanguaging practices in promoting their mere literacy, as well as their digital literacy and multiliteracies. We assumed that such translanguaging practices were within out-of-school literacy practices, but the nature of the study could not put in place measures to ensure that the participants were not at school at the time they encountered the translanguaging performance in the social media. That is why the analysis focused on mere literacy, digital literacy and multiliteracies. The 600 participants were divided into three WhatsApp groups as follows: the first group was a WhatsApp group of the University of Rwanda – College of Education staff members. This is a social media platform where these staff members exchange views, chats and share information, and 150 staff members were on this platform. The second group is the WhatsApp group of the alumni of Groupe Scolaire Saint Joseph Kabgayi. It numbered 390 members who graduated from this secondary school; they share views, information and chats and they are located anywhere in Rwanda and in other countries. The third group is a WhatsApp group which was created during the International Seminar for University Teachers from Developing Countries, which was held in Changchun, China, on 8–28 July 2016. This WhatsApp group was created to keep the network between 60 participants from various developing countries from all the continents. These three WhatsApp groups altogether consisted of 600 group members at the time of data collection. One author belongs to all these three WhatsApp groups, the second author belongs to one group while the third author did not belong to any group and this facilitated cross-checking.

As WhatsApp group users are located anywhere in Rwanda and in different parts of the world, only using their cell phones to post messages on WhatsApp groups, they represent different virtual sites based on what McMillan and Schumacher (2006: 27) and Bo Sanchez (2011) described as 'several entities' (where multi-sites are explored in the study) as opposed to 'one entity' (where exploration is done within one site of the study).

To select the written posts or WhatsApp messages that were analysed in this study, we used purposive and convenient sampling techniques, where we purposively selected WhatsApp messages that embedded translanguaging and translingual interactions. Hence, 60 WhatsApp messages which embedded translanguaging and translingual interactions were selected among those posted by 600 members from the three WhatsApp groups. Thereafter, 60 participants who posted those selected WhatsApp messages were contacted physically, telephonically and by email to fill in the survey questionnaire, which was analysed quantitatively. The selection of quantitative sample followed what Cresswell (2012: 609) described as making an educated guess such as 10% of the sample population.

To analyse their WhatsApp posts in depth, the study has adopted a mixed methods design, embedding both qualitative and quantitative approaches, which were used consecutively to collect and analyse data. Firstly, qualitative data were collected and analysed through the analysis of written WhatsApp messages, guided by Canagarajah's (2013) translingual interaction strategy highlighted in conceptual framework. Here, qualitative methods were used to identify social interactions or topics and texts posted on WhatsApp groups, embedding translanguaging practices. The authors based their data search methods on Canagarajah's (2013) 'translingual interactions' strategy to scrutinize the social interaction topics that displayed translanguaging practices; then, they categorized them using 'Ubuntu translanguaging' (Makalela, 2014) and 'translingual practices model' (Canagarajah, 2013) as reflected in the theoretical and conceptual framework.

After scrutinizing the forms of translanguaging practices and the corresponding examples from written WhatsApp messages, the authors analysed them quantitatively to indicate the extent to which they boost both social and unsocial dynamics, as well as mere literacy, digital literacy and multiliteracies. Here participants assessed the effect of translanguaging practices on social dynamics and unsocial dynamics or mere literacy, digital literacy and multiliteracies by weighing up each variable on the five Likert scales: 5 = very high; 4 = high; 3 = average; 2 = low; and 1 = very low. It was a survey questionnaire, which was filled in by 60 selected participants and analysed quantitatively. Participants assessed their literacy at three levels, name mere literacy, digital literacy and multiliteracies. Simple descriptive statistics were used, where the summation for each variable's scores were computed to show the selected WhatsApp group users' perceptions on the extent at which the use of translanguaging practices promote social dynamics and unsocial dynamics or mere literacy, digital literacy and multiliteracies. We are cognizant that the quantitative sample of 60 participants does not constitute a representative sample for generalization, and it is one of the limitations of the study.

Regarding the scope in time and space, the researchers analysed the WhatsApp group posts for eight months, that is from 1 December 2016 to 1 August 2017, because the posts on the selected three WhatsApp groups were many. Since Rwanda is located both in the Great Lakes Region and in the East African Community, the forms of translanguaging practices mainly focused on the linguistic and semiotic codes of four languages, namely Kinyarwanda, English, French and Kiswahili, even though a few examples were drawn from other languages.

Results: Forms of Translanguaging Practices and their Effects on Social Media

As qualitative and quantitative data were analysed consecutively but in an integrated manner, and their results are presented following the same pattern, starting with the results from the qualitative data, and followed by findings from the quantitative data. Qualitative results were presented following the types of translanguaging practices and topics that were identified among WhatsApp group interactions. The identified forms of translanguaging practices were presented in relation with their linkage to the Ubuntu Languaging Model (Makalela, 2014) and translingual interactions strategy (Canagarajah, 2013), following the theoretical framework pattern. The researchers identified the forms of translanguaging practices and matched them with the topics, objects and situations under discussion, in relation with social dynamics components. Seven forms of translanguaging practices were identified, together with their symbolisms and illustrative examples from WhatsApp groups. These are (a) poly-languaging as a symbol of solidarity in difficult times like death and stressful situation; (b) vertical and horizontal languaging as a symbol for social support, sensitization and financial collaboration; (c) metro-languaging as a symbol for jokes with words for entertainment; (d) code-translation and code-switching as boosters of the spirit of togetherness, festive season wishes and distant greetings among international friends; (e) code-meshing as a symbol of togetherness and friendship from distant greetings among WhatsApp group users; (f) transnational language practices as a provider of opportunities to learn and use languages across national borders; and (g) translocal language practices as a symbol of political rally, togetherness and confidence in leadership. One example on each of the seven forms of translanguaging practices is illustrated below.

Forms of translanguaging practices related to the Ubuntu languaging model

Poly-languaging as a symbol of solidarity in difficult times like death and stressful situation

Poly-languaging is defined from Jørgensen (2008), Jørgensen *et al.* (2011) and Makalela's (2016) perspective as an instance of language use where speakers use linguistic features that are related to different languages or from Makalela's (2016) perspective of hybrid interlingual interactions in superdiverse contexts. In this regard, poly-languaging as a form of translanguaging practice was identified in WhatsApp translingual interactions that were posted on 6 July 2017 by WhatsApp Group 1 members. The topic which was being discussed was that one of the WhatsApp group members has lost her close relative. Other members were using poly-languaging to comfort her, to express condolences and solidarity in that difficult time, as Excerpt 1 indicates:

> *Oooh non et non…!! Sad news & Pole kabisa family J..... Mwihangane cyane kandi Imana ikomeze umuryango wanyu…*[Oooh no and no….!! Condolences to family J….Be strong and may God strengthen your family….] [My translation].

In this excerpt, poly-languaging involves four languages, starting with French '*Oooh non et non…!!*', followed by English '*Sad news*', then a general semiotic code '*&*', which is followed by the Kiswahili phrase '*Pole kabisa*'. The next is English '*family J….*', which is followed by the Kinyarwanda sentence '*Mwihangane cyane kandi Imana ikomeze umuryango wanyu….*'. Here, poly-languaging features tend to be in line with Makalela's (2016) description of hybrid interlingual interactions in superdiverse contexts, but again the feeling of sadness expressed in the utterance seems to have prevented the speaker from relying on one language but pushed him to draw from the whole set of his linguistic repertoire. Hence, poly-languaging features in the excerpt above tend to be in line with the description given by Jørgensen (2008), Jørgensen *et al.* (2011) and Makalela (2016) of poly-languaging as an instance of language use where speakers use linguistic features that are related to different languages.

Vertical and horizontal languaging as a symbol for social support, sensitization and financial collaboration

Vertical and horizontal languaging are viewed by Nkadimeng and Makalela (2015), who argued that they are particularly used in the classroom context. In this regard, Nkadimeng and Makalela (2015: 20) distinguish them as follows: vertical languaging refers to the classroom spaces that create multilingual spaces, 'i.e. when a teacher chooses different languages within the same lesson and/or the same subject area'. For horizontal languaging, they indicate that it occurs 'when different teachers choose to use different languages between different subject areas'. Their argument on vertical and horizontal languaging is that they allow quick linguistic exchanges and minute negotiation of multiple identities, which demonstrate a language and identity contact that is fuzzy, but with the logic of getting the pedagogical task moving quickly (Nkadimeng & Makalela, 2015).

In addition to their use in the classroom context, this chapter demonstrates that vertical and horizontal languaging are practiced on social media as well. Excerpt 3 below, which was retrieved from WhatsApp Group 2 posted on 12 June 2017 is an illustrative example. The theme that was under discussion was that WhatsApp group members were exchanging ideas for a social project of constructing a vocational school for one community; and they were encouraging one another to participate in raising funds for construction, but mixing languages as follows:

> *Participant A: Salama ndugu, ndabona utwibutsa ko project yacu isa n'iyahagaze. Ubonye iyo iriya linteau ibasha kurangira, ko n'inzu yamara na 10 ans ntacyo yaba....!*[Hello brother, I can see you are reminding us that our project has almost stopped. If we had managed to finish the lintel, we could be confident that the building can stand for 10 years without any problem....]

> *Partcipant B: You are right, ariko contributions zabaye nkeya, et la construction est au point mort!!*[You are right, but contributions are very few, and the construction has stopped completely]

> *Participant C: Kabisa contribution ya buri wese irakenewe* [Everyone's contribution is really needed]

> *Participant D: Supported!* [My translation].

This excerpt displays vertical languaging because participants A, B, C and D discuss the same topic (about construction), but each participant sends a WhatsApp message that embeds various languages. For instance, participant A starts her interaction with Kiswahili '*Salama ndugu*'; she switches to Kinyarwanda '*ndabona utwibutsa ko*', then she borrows an English word '*project*'; and switches back to Kinyarwanda '*yacu isa n'iyahagaze. Ubonye iyo iriya*'; she borrowed now a French word '*linteau*', goes back to Kinyarwanda '*ibasha kurangira, ko n'inzu yamara na*', she inserts French again '*10 ans*' and ends with Kinyarwanda '*ntacyo yaba....!*'. Similarly, participant B talks about the same topic and his interaction involves English, Kinyarwanda and French. Participant C starts with a Kiswahili word '*kabisa*', followed by French or English '*contribution*' and ends with Kinyarwanda '*ya buri wese irakenewe*'. As participant D, he used signs or symbols (which are not familiar in alphabetic writing) to confirm his support.

Based on example above, we claim that vertical languaging on WhatsApp occurs when a participant chooses to interact with others in different languages on the same topic, in a particular domain, like construction in the excerpt above. We also claim that horizontal languaging on WhatsApp take place when various participants interact by using different languages while discussing different topics in various domains. This is the case for participants A, B, C and D in the example above, even if the domain was mainly limited to construction.

Rather, the theme, the context and the translingual interactions that are displayed in the excerpt above tend to support García (2009), García and Li Wei (2014), Mkhize (2016) and Guzula *et al.* (2016) argument which views language as a verb 'languaging', whereby language is viewed as being always in motion, dynamic and unbounded, but not as a noun or an entity with fixed structure. This term 'languaging' refers to differentiated ways that language users apply for meaning making and for performing cognitive and social actions (García & Li Wei, 2014), or a wide range of resources, a variety of linguistic repertoires, multiple literacies and numerous modalities that language users refer to in order to make sense of their actions and their social world (Makalela, 2015; Guzula *et al.*, 2016).

Metro-languaging as a symbol for jokes with words for entertainment

Metro-languaging is described from the perspective of Jørgensen *et al.* (2011), Pennycook (2007), Pennycook and Otsuji (2014) and Makalela's (2016) as different degrees of language alternation in superdiverse communities, especially in cities and urban areas, with no clear meaning to the usual form or grammar, but rather with hybrid emergent interlingual interactions. A typical example of WhatsApp group messages that display metro-languaging is in Excerpt 2 below, which was retrieved from WhatsApp Group 2, posted on 29 July 2017:

> What is **KISIRANI?** KISIRANI is when you give a lift to a girl and she faints in your car. You take her to hospital and when you get there, the doctor says that the girl is pregnant and congratulates you that you are going to be the father soon. You shout that you are not the father and the girl says you are the father. Things are now getting **KISIRANIFUL**. You require a DNA test to prove you are not the father. Things are now getting **KISIRANISTIC** when the doctor comes with results saying that you cannot be the father because you are infertile. You are relieved, but on your way home you remember you are married with three kids at home! Now you are extremely **KISIRANIOUS**. You begin to ask yourself who is the father of those kids. You get home to find out that the gateman is their real father. You are now **KISIRANED**. You decide to travel home to complain to your mother about the situation and your mother also tells you 'my son, I am sorry, your dad was not really your father...Then

*you know that things are now **KISIRANICATED**. If you don't forward,
then you are **KISIRANICLOSIS**.*

From this excerpt, the Kiswahili word 'KISIRANI' which means
'bad luck, misfortune, bad omen or unfortunate' is expanded to
KISIRANIFUL, KISIRANIOUS, KISIRANED, KISIRANICATED and
KISIRANICLOSIS. We have attributed this example to metro-languaging
or metrolingual multi-tasking based on the way this expansion is created
by fusing a Kiswahili word with English morphemes. These Kiswahili–
English mixed words present different degrees of language alternation in
superdiverse communities, especially in cities and urban areas, with no
clear meaning to the usual form or grammar, but rather with hybrid emergent interlingual interactions, as Jørgensen *et al.* (2011), Pennycook
(2007), Pennycook and Otsuji (2014) and Makalela (2016) have argued.

Forms of translanguaging practices related to the translingual practices model and their effects

Code-translation and code-switching as a booster of the spirit of togetherness, festive season wishes and distant greetings among international friends

Excerpt 4 below is a typical example of code-alternation or code-
translation or even code-switching, because they displayed the mixing and
alternation of different languages at intersentential and intrasentential
levels. It was Christmas, on 25 December 2016, when WhatsApp Group 3
members had the following translingual interactions, exchanging
Christmas wishes:

Participant A: *'feliz navidad a todos' I would love to hear Christmas
wishes in your various languages…!!*
Participant B: *In English, we say 'Merry Christmas'*
Participant C: *In Kinyarwanda (Rwanda), we say 'Noheli nziza'*
Participant D: *In Kiswahili (East Africa), we say 'Noeli njema'*
Participant E: *In French: 'Joyeux Noel'*
Participant F: *In Chinese pinyin: 'shengdan kuaile!' Can we hear it in
your languages? Have a wonderful Christmas!*

In this excerpt, international friends expressed the same Christmas
wishes in six languages, namely Spanish, English, Kinyarwanda,
Kiswahili, French and Chinese. This is a sign of togetherness and friendship expressed in various languages. Those six code-alternations or code-
translations are displayed at intersentential level, because each translation
is embedded in its own sentence or clause. Hence, their features are
closely related to intersentential code-switching, as supported by
Kamwangamalu (1994), Moodley and Kamwangamalu (2002) and
Moodley (2013).

Code-meshing as a symbol of togetherness and friendship from distant greetings among WhatsApp group users

Code-meshing or 'a meshing of codes' is described from Canagarajah (2011a, 2015) perspective as instances of translanguaging in writing, which is added to translanguaging in speech, where various semiotic codes, that contribute to meaning making, are added to normal written form we are familiar with. Excerpt 5 below, which was retrieved from WhatsApp Group 3 posted on 23 May 2017, displays code-meshing features based translingual interactions. Here, WhatsApp group users were exchanging greetings as international friends:

A: Hello friends from Kenya

B.

C. Pls we want to hear from u!

D. We are doing great and we

E. Parfait !

This excerpt shows how code-meshing enriches interaction on social media such as WhatsApp. It tends to be a common practice these days and it is believed to be effective in various domains, including education. The five participants in the interaction above expressed their views not through the normal written form we are familiar with, but also through various semiotic codes, that contribute in meaning making. English and French are used in the interactions, but these semiotic codes are drawn from different languages, no single language can claim to own these codes. Hence, it is evident that code-meshing attribute a special image and special meaning to written interactions. We observed that code-meshing was commonly practiced on WhatsApp.

Transnational practices as a provider of opportunity to learn and use languages across national borders

Transnational practices stress the opportunity of using various languages, especially gaining knowledge from different languages, across borders. Excerpt 6 below, which embeds transnational practices, was retrieved from WhatsApp Group 2, posted on 10 March 2017. The theme that was under discussion was about the opportunities offered by the use of various languages, even if the mastery might be limited:

Participant A: *Kiswahili siyo lugha yangu! Lakini ni njia nzuri ya kujifunza.* [Kiswahili is not my language! But it is the best way for self-learning].

Participant B: *Uragerageza et puis nibyo bikenewe.* [You are trying and that is what is needed].

Participant C: *Baravuga mu Kirundi ngo 'biriko biroza'* [In Kirundi, they say 'it is coming, you are improving'] [My translation].

This interaction displays the message that crosses the linguistic and national borders, from Kiswahili which is spoken in East African countries, to Kinywarwanda, which is spoken in Rwanda; and to Kirundi, which is spoken in Burundi, and French, which is spoken in the Great Lakes Region. It starts with participant A's Kiswahili utterance *'Kiswahili siyo lugha yangu! Lakini ni njia nzuri ya kujifunza'*; participant B switches to Kinyarwanda *'Uragerageza .... nibyo bikenewe'* by inserting French phrase *'et puis'*. Then participant C switches to Kirundi *'Baravuga mu Kirundi ngo biriko biroza'*.

The use of various language, as revealed in the example above, reflects the nature of the Sub-Saharan Africa region, which is one of the linguistically complex regions in the world with about 1500 to 2500 languages, making up 13% of the world's total population (Makalela, 2016; UNESCO, 2010). Those translingual and transnational language practices allow cross-nations and cross-borders interactions, using a variety of languages. Li Wei and Hua (2013) argue that transnational practices give room to the creation of transnational space, which is done through flexible multilingual practices, across nations. This tends to be in line with Makalela's (2016) logic of Ubuntu translanguaging, whereby notions such as first language, mother tongue and second language are questioned because they do not necessarily account for complex translingual and transnational discourse practices in many African contexts, but rather supports fuzzy and fluid interactions across languages, boundaries and nations.

Translocal language practices as a symbol of political rally, togetherness and confidence in leadership

Translocal language practices allow free interactions among local and indigenous languages, including the varieties of the same language. Excerpt 7 below reflects translocal language practices, stemming from the political rally, during the Rwandan presidential campaign of July–August 2017. The object is the song called 'NDA NDAMBARA YANDERA UBWOBA', as written on the T-shirt below. This song gained fame during the 2017 presidential campaign in Rwanda because it expresses a high level of confidence in the leadership, expressed in a regional sociolect of Kinyarwanda, which sounds somewhat funny and entertaining for listeners. The picture of the T-shirt and accompanying words were retrieved from WhatsApp Group 2, posted on 28 July 2017. The words on this T-shirt mix different spoken forms of local languages, based on translingual writing or transgraphic forms of local languages:

'Nda ndambara yandera ubwoba'. Uyu munyamuryango anyibukije ya ndirimbo ejobundi twaririmbye ngo Nda ndambara yandera ubwoba' [No war can frighten me. This member reminds me the song we sang yesterday, saying that 'No war can frighten me] [My translation].

This translocal practice is based on free transformation of a standard Kinyarwanda utterance '**Nt**a **nt**ambara ya**nt**era ubwoba', which is adapted to the regional dialect spoken in the northern part of Rwanda, where they transform the writing of cluster '**NT**' into '**ND**' based on their spoken form. Hence, this translocal practice was adapted to these Northerners' way of speaking '**Nd**a **nd**ambara ya**nd**era ubwoba', to convey a particular meaning, and it became a famous music slogan which was used in the Rwandan presidential election campaign to show a high level of support, togetherness and confidence among the political party members.

Here, translocal language practices allow free interactions among languages, but this time around African local and indigenous languages. This example shows that a translingual third space cannot be limited to international or national or cross-borders languages, but must include local languages as well, including those languages and varieties that do not have written forms. Rwanda is an endoglossic country, meaning that the majority of the population (99.4%) use Kinyarwanda as their mother tongue and Standard Kinyarwanda has one written form, while its spoken form presents some varieties that are described as dialects, regiolects and sociolects (Niyomugabo, 2012; Niyibizi, 2015). Rwanda is not like many other African countries which have several or many local languages, with various written forms, reminding us of Motlhaka and Makalela's (2016) 'translingual writing' and 'transgraphic procedures' in a South African context, whereby students wrote in different languages as a mediating technique to boost their abilities to move strategically between different rhetorical conventions of various languages in their academic writing; and translingual writing showed more benefits than monolingual writing practices. In this chapter, the use of translocal practices on social media has social benefits and social impact as well.

To sum up, these are seven forms of translanguaging practices picked from 60 examples, to respond to research question 1: 'What forms of translanguaging practices used on the three Whatsap groups investigated?' The next section presents findings from quantitative data, responding to research questions 2 and 3.

The extent to which translanguaging practices promote social dynamics, unsocial dynamics and literacies

The quantitative analysis of answers to research questions 2 and 3: 'What effect, if any, do these forms of translanguaging practices have on social dynamics?' and 'To what extent do those forms of translanguaging practices used on the three WhatsApp groups promote digital literacy and multiliteracies?', respectively, was based on the sample of 60 participants, who were sampled from a pool of 600 WhatsApp users investigated. The argument around social and unsocial effects of translanguaging on WhatsApp groups was motivated by the pessimistic argument attributed to Albert Einstein on the effects of social media, that the time where technology has replaced human interactions has arrived, and it has created a generation of idiots [My translation], as shown in Figure 2.1.

Although we are not quite sure if Einstein said this, this pessimistic argument pushed us to cross-check it against WhatsApp users' views on its effects in promoting social or unsocial dynamics. Such pessimistic view reflected in Figure 2.1 is linked with unsocial dynamics, which is

Figure 2.1 Pessimistic view attributed to Albert Einstein about the effects of social media

Source: Posted on WhatsApp Group 3 on 22 December 2016, but original source unknown.

represented by 'oneness or linguistic isolation' stemming from Makalela's (2015) Ubuntu translanguaging, as opposed to positive social dynamics, represented by 'togetherness', also stemming from Makalela's (2015) Ubuntu translanguaging. Figure 2.1 shows participants who are actively interacting with other human beings on cell phones, but with limited talk to people next to them. This study argues that these people are using translingual interactions, through various languages and semiotic symbols. Such translingual practices can be directly linked with the seven forms of translanguaging practices identified in the previous section, with crosslingual interactions, under themes reflecting either 'oneness or togetherness' spirit.

To analyse quantitatively the extent to which translingual interactions and translanguaging practices promote social versus unsocial dynamics among WhatsApp group users, a five Likert scale (5 = very high; 4 = high; 3 = average; 2 = low; and 1 = very low) attitudinal survey questionnaire was administered to 60 participants whose WhatsApp posts were selected for qualitative findings. WhatsApp users filled in the questionnaire, weighing the extent to which their translanguaging practices boost positive social dynamics like familiarity, friendship, social cohesion, freedom of expression per excellence and togetherness; or unsocial dynamics like unfamiliarity, unfriendliness, unclarity of message, social injustice based on limited language choice, inhibitor of freedom of expression per excellence and oneness or language isolation. Figures 2.2 and 2.3 present the summation of the five Likert scales on social versus unsocial dynamics:

Figure 2.2 reveals that all components of positive social dynamics (familiarity, friendship, social cohesion, free language choice, freedom of expression per excellence and togetherness) scored higher than components of unsocial dynamics. Hence, participants perceived that the use of forms of translanguaging practices on WhatsApp boosts more positive social dynamics than negative social dynamics. Figure 2.3 pairs them for clear comparison.

Figure 2.3 gives evidence that all aspects of positive social dynamics scored higher than all aspects of unsocial dynamics that were investigated. The summation scores for the five Likert scales for familiarity is 257 against 101 for unfamiliarity; friendship scored 245 against 105 for unfriendliness, and social cohesion scored 234 against 128 for unclarity that may hinder cohesiveness. In the same vein, free language choice scored 202 against 120 for limited language choice; freedom of expression per excellence scored 251 against 102 for inhibition of freedom of expression per excellence; while togetherness scored 249 against 106 for oneness or language isolation.

The study also explored the extent at which forms of translanguaging practices promote three types of literacy among WhatsApp group users, as summarized in Figure 2.4.

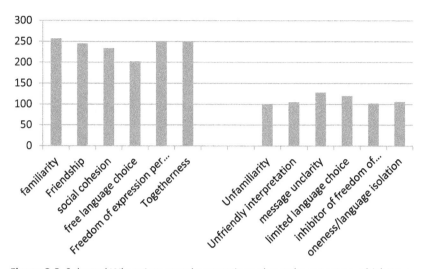

Figure 2.2 Selected WhatsApp users' perceptions about the extent to which translanguaging practices promote social versus unsocial dynamics

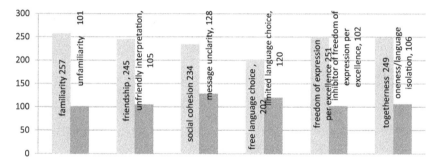

Figure 2.3 Comparison between paired social and unsocial dynamics on the extent to which translanguaging practices promote them

Figure 2.4 revealed that participants perceived that the identified forms of translanguaging practices boost multiliteracies at a higher level (281 total scores of Likert scale), followed by digital literacy (257) and then mere literacy (245). Seligmann (2012: 318) describes literacy as 'the ability to read and write' or 'the uses of reading and writing to achieve purposes in the context of use'. Multiliteracies among the participants was perceived from The New London Group (2000) perspective as the plurality of texts that are exchanged or a variety of text forms that are linked with new information and technologies, to address the need to communicate across languages and cultures. Mere literacy was also viewed from The New London Group (2000) perspective as focusing on letters. Digital literacy was viewed from the perspectives of Androutsopoulos and Juffermans (2014) and Gutiérrez (2008) as digitally mediated communication or digital

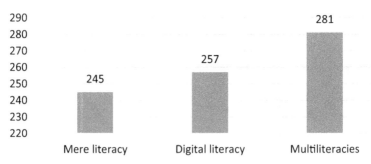

Figure 2.4 The extent to which forms of translanguaging practices promote literacy

manipulation aiming at dealing with communication and information. As all participants were adults communicating from Rwanda and other parts of the world, the three types of literacy could also be explored from adult literacy perspective but governed by digital literacy. From these findings, it is evident that the participating WhatsApp group users considered the selected forms of translanguaging practices as boosters of these three types of literacy.

Discussion

This study revealed that forms of translanguaging practices and translingual interactions boost positive social dynamics among communicators on WhatsApp groups. This finding supports Canagarajah's (2013) argument that languages are not necessarily in conflict but rather in mutual complementarity for communication. The qualitative findings identified seven forms of translanguaging practices that are practiced among the WhatsApp groups users investigated. The new insight is that those forms of translanguaging practices were found to be predominantly practiced on WhatsApp, within the themes or topics symbolizing positive social dynamics and togetherness spirit. These are (a) polylanguaging as a symbol of solidarity in difficult times like death and stressful situation; (b) vertical/horizontal languaging as a symbol for social support, sensitization and financial collaboration; (c) metro-languaging as a symbol for jokes with words for entertainment; (d) code-translation and code-switching as boosters of the spirit of togetherness, festive season wishes and distant greetings among international friends; (e) code-meshing as a symbol of togetherness and friendship from distant greetings; (f) transnational language practices as a provider of opportunity to learn and use languages across national borders; and (g) translocal language practices as a symbol of political rally, togetherness and confidence in leadership. They were identified within the examples of topics and themes posted on WhatsApp groups, based on their characteristics provided in literature.

Overall, the findings on the effect of the identified forms of translanguaging practices on social media in this study, tend to support the argument presented by Bamgbose (2000), Barnes (2003) and Alexander and Von Scheliha's (2014) that language is a powerful instrument in unifying a diverse population. The evidence is that WhatsApp group users were located in different parts of Rwanda, Africa and abroad, but they reported that mixing various languages or using forms of translanguaging practices in their digital communication amplified their positive social dynamics, especially their social cohesion and the spirit of togetherness. The implication for these findings is that various forms of translanguaging practices are found in different forums where languages come into contact. While various studies explored translanguaging practices in schools and in multilingual classrooms (García, 2009; Kagwesage, 2013; Makalela, 2013; Niyibizi, 2015; Van der Walt & Dornbrack, 2011; Williams, 2000), this study has added a new insight by demonstrating how different forms of translanguaging practices are practiced on social media, particularly on WhatsApp groups. Hence, we join other scholars who argue that monolingualism and monoglossic dominance is no longer the norm in the 21st century. Here, we agree with scholars who contend that 'monolingual ideology' (see Gafaranga, 2015) seems not to dominate in all social settings. Rather, the findings in this study are in congruence with Makalela's (2016) argument that 'confluence of languages' is vividly operational within individuals, among group interactions and community or nation interactions. It has entered the digital technology, in the Global South, as the findings in this study have shown. From African multilingual perspective, the findings from this chapter are also in congruence with several African scholars like Kwesi Phrah, Ali Mazrui, Sinfree Makoni, Salikoko Mufweni, Eyamba Bokamba, Ayo Bamgbose, Neville Alexander, Martha Qorro, Leketi Makalela, Ngugi wa Thiongo, and others, who unanimously support the view that languages, both African indigenous languages and foreign languages are mutually complementary as long as each language is given its due value, at all levels of communication. It is within this perspective that Makalela (2015), Makoni and Pennycook (2007), Mignolo (2000) and Mazrui (2002) contend that languages are no longer static, they are rather porous and complex systems of communication that overlap. Their arguments support Ngugi (1987), Bamgbose (2000), Alexander (1999), Prah (1998), Mwaniki (2016) and many African linguists who claim fluidity between African languages and other foreign languages, taking into consideration African culture and African multilingual setting.

Within this African perspective, the participating WhatsApp group users perceived the identified forms of translanguaging practices as supporting more social dynamics than the unsocial dynamics. Figures 2.2–2.4 revealed that all the scores for positive social dynamics (familiarity, friendship, social cohesion, free language choice, freedom of expression par excellence and togetherness) were almost double of the scores of unsocial dynamics (unfamiliarity, unfriendly interactions, unclarity of message, limited language choice, inhibition of freedom of expression par excellence and oneness or language isolation). Hence, this finding seems to support and expand Paxton's (2009) view on code-switching as a kind of form of translanguaging practice, contending that it enables interlocutors to explore ideas and concepts in a familiar environment, implying familiarity, friendship, closeness and cohesiveness. Such higher level of familiarity is expanded to other forms of translanguaging practices highlighted in this study. The findings also highly support Makalela's (2015) 'togetherness' as opposed to 'oneness' as a result of the use of translanguaging. In addition to Paxton's (2009) view of translanguaging as a booster of familiarity, friendship, closeness and cohesiveness, the finding in this study tend to be in line with Cioè-Peña and Snell's (2016) view on translanguaging as a promoter of social justice and interconnectedness, as well as Li Wei and Hua (2013) who view it as a signal of linguistic free movement in new social spaces. Beyond all these, the key impact of this study is that it has revealed that different forms of translanguaging practices and translingual interactions promote positive social dynamics, reinforce social cohesion, peace building and harmony in the multilingual society and in digital era of the 21st century, giving interlocutors freedom of expression par excellence. Hence, this chapter has qualified translanguaging practices and translingual interactions as a new symbol of social dynamics.

The Rwandan context where the investigation took place is a multilingual but endoglossic country, with apparent predominance of Kinyarwanda (Niyomugabo, 2012; Niyibizi, 2015). The post-genocide era in Rwanda has registered high level of reconciliation, positive vision, quest for sustainable peace and stability and languages have played a central role. The promotion of multilingualism based on four languages might have been one of the justifications for the predominance of positive social dynamics and social interactions among the WhatsApp group users who participated in this study, but there were participants from foreign countries as well. This tends to confirm that the spirit of togetherness among people and among languages tends to get momentum over the spirit of oneness in the 21st century. That is why there is possibility of applying the findings from this study in other parts of Africa and elsewhere, as suggested in conclusion.

Conclusion and Possible Application Elsewhere

This study revealed that a number of forms of translanguaging practices are practiced on digital platforms and social media. They mainly present positive effects since components of social dynamics scored higher than components of unsocial dynamics. Thus, while Gafaranga (2015) observed on Igihe online newspaper that translanguaging from Kinyarwanda to either French or English was far more common than the other way round due to language ideology, this study found that WhatsApp users intermingle Kinyarwanda, French, English, Kiswahili and other languages together with various semiotic codes. Such freedom in mingling and mixing languages on social media has given languages and their translingual interactions a new look or a new symbol in regards with their contributions in social interactions and social dynamics in the Rwandan context and beyond, supporting Makalela's (2015) argument of fluidity in diversity within the spirit of Ubuntu translanguaging.

Therefore, this new symbol is applicable not only in the Great Lakes region where Rwanda is located, but also in other African multilingual communities and beyond. From these findings and from the new literacies perspective and Ubuntu translanguaging among African communities, we argue for the use of translanguaging on social media in multilingual interactions for new meaning making, especially for unifying social dynamics. This study therefore recommends their strategic use on social media like WhatsApp group, Facebook and others, to promote digital literacy and multiliteracies. In other contexts like the classroom, we are cognizant that scholars like Creese and Blackledge (2010), Probyn (2015), Mkhize (2016) and others have recommended teachers and learners to use translanguaging strategically and purposefully so that it may not be detrimental to their learning. This study also recommends strategic use of translanguaging practices so that they may not lead to the dominance of unsocial dynamics, which were rejected by the findings in this chapter.

While the quantitative sample of this study was limited to 60 WhatsApp group users and may not constitute the representative sample to generalize the findings to other social media, the study might be extended to other digital platforms as well. Similarly, the selected WhatsApp groups were made of heterogeneous groups with some levels of friendship and familiarity, but there is need for further research with a bigger sample for generalization across language groups, across nations, across different age groups and across social media platforms like Facebook, YouTube, Twitter, Instagram, Skype, LinkedIn, Imo and Messenger, We Chat and others, particularly in the 'Global South' perspective.

All in all, this chapter has shed light on how digital communication in African multilingual countries is in contact with influences from the wider world. The chapter has provided clear evidence on the effects which digital communication demonstrates in the debate on translanguaging practices, within the 21st-century digital era. We can confirm that our chapter has fed the theme of the book on how digital communication among Africans supports the multilingual practices. The evidence is that the chapter highlighted seven forms of translanguaging practices and how they are used on social media, specifically among WhatsApp group users. The chapter brought on board the effects of translanguaging practices on social dynamics, by revealing that the 21st-century digital communication era prefers togetherness of languages over oneness, linguistic diversity over monolingual bias, and supplementarity of languages in communication over one language dominance. Hence, this chapter supplements other chapters and the overall focus of the book, which explore digital technology and African multilingualism. Findings and examples provided in this chapter on various forms of translanguaging practices among the investigated WhatsApp group users tend to concretize what Makalela describes as 'digital translanguaging' in his chapter of this volume.

Acknowledgements

We are very grateful to AEGIS TRUST, a non-government organisation operating in Rwanda, which provided financial assistance for this study. Their assistance enabled us to contact the informants in different parts of Rwanda and beyond to get the required material and collect data.

References

Alexander, N. (1999) An African Renaissance without African languages? *Social Dynamics* 25 (1), 1–12.
Alexander, N. and von Scheliha, A. (2014) *Language Policy and the Promotion of Peace: African and European Case Studies*. Pretoria: UNISA Press.
Androutsopoulos, J. and Juffermans, K. (2014) Digital language practices in superdiversity: Introduction. *Discourse, Context and Media* 4–5, 1–6.
Auer, P. (2005) A postscript: code-switching and social identity. *Journal of Pragmatics* 37 (3), 403–410.
Bamgbose, A. (2000) *Language and Exclusion: The Consequences of Language Policies in Africa*. Hamburg & London: Litverlag.
Barnes, L. (2003) Language, war and peace: An overview. *Language Matters* 34, 3–12.
Bock, Z. and Mheta, G. (2013) (ed.) *Language, Society and Communication: An Introduction*. Pretoria: Van Schaik Publishers.
Bo Sanchez (2011) How your words can change your world (use positive faith to create your desired future). See https://www.amazon.com/Bo Sanchez/e/B009NN4WN6/ref=la_B009NN4WN6_pg_2/164-4934798-5851007?rh=n%3A283 (accessed 5 November 2016).
Canagarajah, S. (2011a) Codemeshing in academic writing: Identifying teachable strategies of translanguaging. *The Modern Language Journal* 95, 401–417.
Canagarajah, A.S. (2011b) Translanguaging in the classroom: Emerging issues for research and pedagogy. *Applied Linguistics Review*, 1–28.
Canagarajah, A.S. (2013) *Translingual Practice: Global Englishes and Cosmopolitan Relations*. New York: Routledge.

Cioè-Peña, M. and Snell, T. (2016) Translanguaging for social justice. *Theory, Research and Action in Urban Education (TRAUE)* 4 (2), 11–26. The Graduate Center, City University of New York.

Creese, A. and Blackledge, A. (2010) Translanguaging in the bilingual classroom: A pedagogy for learning and teaching? *The Modern Language Journal* 10, 103–115.

Cresswell, J.W. (2012) *Educational Research: Planning, Conducting, and Evaluating Quantitative and Qualitative Research* (4th edn). Boston: Pearson Education, Inc.

Dovchin, S. (2015) Language, multiple authenticities and social media: The online language practices of university students in Mongolia. *Journal of Sociolinguistics* 19 (4), 437–459.

Dovchin, S., Sultana, S. and Pennycook, A. (2015) Relocalizing the translingual practices of young adults in Mongolia and Bangladesh. *Translation and Translanguaging in Multilingual Contexts* 1, 4–26.

Durlauf, S. and Young, P. (2001) *Social Dynamics*. Cambridge, MA: MIT Press.

Gafaranga, J. (2015) Translinguistic apposition in a multilingual media blog in Rwanda: Towards an interpretive perspective in language policy research. *Language in Society* 44, 87–112. See http://www.cambridge.org/core/terms. http://dx.doi.org/10.1017/S004740451400075X (accessed 2 December 2016).

García, O. (2009) Education, multilingualism and translanguaging in the 21st century. In A. Mohanty, M. Panda, R. Phillipson and T. Skutnabb-Kangas (eds) *Multilingual Education for Social Justice: Globalising the Local* (pp. 128–145). New Delhi: Orient Blackswan.

García, O. and Leiva, C. (2014) Theorizing and enacting translanguaging for social justice. In A. Blackledge and A. Creese (eds) *Heteroglossia as Practice and Pedagogy* (pp. 199–216). Dordrecht: Springer.

García O. and Li Wei (2014) *Translanguaging: Language, Bilingualism and Education*. London: Palgrave Pivot.

Georgalidou, M., Hasan, K. and Aytac, C. (2008) Code alternation patterns of the bilingual in Greek and Turkish Muslim Community of Rhodes. *Studies in Greek Language: Language and Society* (pp. 125–137). Thessaloniki: Modern Greek Language Institution.

Gutiérrez, K. (2008) Developing a sociocritical literacy in the third space. *Reading Research Quarterly* 43 (2), 148–164.

Guzula, X., McKinney, C. and Tyler, R. (2016) Languaging-for-learning: Legitimising translanguaging and enabling multimodal practices in third spaces. *Southern African Linguistics and Applied Language Studies* 34 (3), 211–226.

Habyarimana, H. (2014) Investigation of Attitudes and Classroom Practices of Educators and Learners in Relation to English as the Medium of Instruction at four Primary Schools in Rwanda. Unpublished PhD thesis. University of the Witwatersrand, Johannesburg.

Huaman, E.S. and Stokes, P. (2011) Indigenous language revitalization and new media: Postsecondary students as innovators. *Global Media Journal* 11 (18), 1–15.

Internet World Stats (2018) Usage and population statistics. See https://www.internetworldstats.com/stats1.htm (accessed 29 March 2018).

Ivanov, V. (2000) Heterglossia. *Journal of Linguistic Anthropology* 9 (1–2), 100–102.

Jacquemet, M. (2005) Transidiomatic practices: Language and power in the age of globalization. *Language & Communication* 25, 257–277.

Jørgensen, J.N. (2008) Polylingual languaging around and among children and adolescents. *International Journal of Multilingualism* 5 (3), 161–176.

Jørgensen, J.N, Karrebæk, M.S., Madsen, L.M. and Møller, J.S. (2011) Polylanguaging in superdiversity. *Diversities* 13 (2), 23–38.

Kagwesage, A.M. (2013) Coping with English as Language of Instruction in Higher Education in Rwanda. *International Journal of Higher Education* 2 (2), 1–12.

Kress, G. (2010) *Multimodality: A Social Semiotic Approach to Contemporary Communication*. London: Routledge.

Li Wei (2011) Moment analysis and translanguaging space: Discursive construction of identities by multilingual Chinese youth in Britain. *Journal of Pragmatics* 43, 1222–1235.

Li Wei and Hua, Z. (2013) Translanguaging identities and ideologies: Creating transnational space through flexible multilingual practices amongst Chinese university students in the UK. *Applied Linguistics* 34, 516–535.

Makalela, L. (2014) Teaching indigenous African languages to speakers of other African languages: The effects of translanguaging for multilingual development. In L. Hibbert and C. Van der Walt (eds) *Multilingual Universities in South Africa: Reflecting Society In Higher Education* (pp. 88–104). Bristol: Multilingual Matters.

Makalela, L. (ed.) (2015) *New Directions in Language and Literacy Education for Multilingual Classroom in Africa*. Cape Town: CASAS.

Makalela, L. (2016) Ubuntu translanguaging: An alternative framework for complex multilingual encounters. *Southern African Linguistics and Applied Language Studies* 34 (3), 187–198.

Makoni, S. and Pennycook, A. (eds) (2007) *Disinventing and Reconstituting Languages*. Clevedon: Multilingual Matters.

Mazrui, A.A. (2002) The English language in African Education. In J.W. Tollefson (ed.) *Language Policies in Education: Critical Issues*. New Jersey: Lawrence Erlbaum.

McMillan, J.H. and Schumacher, S. (2006) *Research in Education: Evidence-based Inquiry* (6th edn). New York: Pearson Education, Inc.

Mignolo, W. (2000) *Local Histories/Global Designs. Coloniality, Subaltern Knowledges, and Border Thinking*. Princeton: Princeton University Press.

Ministry of Information Technology and Communications – MITEC. (2016) *ICT Sector Profile 2016*. Kigali: Republic of Rwanda.

Mkhize, D. (2016) Mediating epistemic access through everyday language resources in an English language classroom. *Southern African Linguistics and Applied Language Studies* 34 (3), 227–240.

Moodley, V. (2013) *Introduction to Language Methodology*. Cape Town: Oxford University Press

Moodley, V. and Kamwangamalu, N.K. (2004) Code-switching as a technique in teaching literature in a secondary school ESL classroom. *Alternation* 11 (2), 186–202.

Motlhaka, H.A. and Makalela, L. (2016) Translanguaging in an academic writing class: Implications for a dialogic pedagogy. *Southern African Linguistics and Applied Language Studies* 34 (3), 251–260.

Mwaniki, M. (2016) Translanguaging as a class/lecture-room language management strategy in multilingual contexts: Insights from autoethnographic snapshots from Kenya and South Africa. *Southern African Linguistics and Applied Language Studies* 34 (3), 197–209.

Ngugi, W.T. (1987) *Decolonizing the Mind: The Politics of Language in African Literature*. London: James Currey.

Niyibizi, E. (2014) Foundation phase learners' and teachers' attitudes and experiences with the Rwandan language-in-education policy shifts. PhD thesis. The University of the Witwatersrand, Johannesburg.

Niyibizi, E. (2015) The Rwandan teachers' and learners' perceived speaking proficiency in both Kinyarwanda and English after 2008-2011 consecutive Language-in- Education policy shifts. *The Rwandan Journal of Education (RJE) 3* (1), 91–116.

Niyibizi, E., Makalela, L. and Mwepu, D. (2015) Language-in-education policy shifts in an African country: colonial confusion and prospects for the future. In L. Makalela (ed.) *New Directions in Language and Literacy Education for Multilingual Classrooms* (pp. 123–151). Cape Town: CASAS.

Niyomugabo, C. (2012) Kinyafranglais as a newly created 'language' in Rwanda: Will it hamper the promotion of the language of instruction at Kigali Institute of Education? *Rwandan Journal of Education* 1 (1), 20–30.

Nkadimeng, S. and Makalela, L. (2015) Identity negotiation in a super-diverse community: The fuzzy languaging logic of high school students in Soweto. *IJSL* 234, 7–26.

Otsuji, E. and Pennycook, A. (2010) Metrolingualism: Fixity, fluidity and language in flux. *International Journal of Multilingualism* 7 (3), 240–254.

Paxton, M.I.J. (2009) It's easy to learn when using your home language but with English you need to start learning language before you get to concept: Bilingual concept development in an English medium university in South Africa. *Journal of Multilingual and Multicultural Development* 30 (4), 354–359.

Pennycook, A. and Otsuji, E. (2014) Metrolingual multitasking and spatial repertoires: 'Pizza mo two minutes coming'. *Journal of Sociolinguistics* 18 (2), 161–184.

Prah, K. (1998) *Between Extinction and Distinction. Harmonization and Standardization of African languages.* Johannesburg: Witwatersrand University Press.

Probyn, M.J. (2006) *Language and Learning Science in South Africa. Language and Education* 20 (5), 391–414.

Seligmann, J. (2012) *Academic Literacy for Education Students.* Cape Town: Oxford University Press Southern Africa Ltd.

Stæhr, A. (2014) Social media and everyday language use among Copenhagen youth. PhD dissertation. University of Copenhagen.

The New London Group (2000) A pedagogy of multiliteracies: Designing social futures. In B. Cope and M. Kalantzis (eds) *Multiliteracies: Literacy Learning and the Design of Social Futures* (pp. 9–37). London and New York: Routledge.

The New Times Rwanda's Leading Daily (2017, September) Rwanda's mobile phone penetration rate rises marginally in June. See http://www.newtimes.co.rw/section/read/219255 (available 26 March 2018).

UNESCO (2010) *Why and how Africa should invest in African languages and multilingual education: An evidence- and practise-based policy advocacy brief.* Hamburg: UNESCO Institute for Lifelong Learning.

Van der Walt, C. and Dornbrack, J. (2011) Academic Biliteracy in South African Higher Education: Strategies and Practices of Successful Students. *Language, Culture and Curriculum,* 24 (1), 89–104. http://dx.doi.org/10.1080/07908318.2011.554985.

Williams, C. (2000) Welsh-medium and Bilingual Teaching in the Further Education Sector. *International Journal of Bilingual Education and Bilingualism* 3 (2), 129–148.

Wolff, H.E. (2014) Language and hegemonic power: How feasible is conflict management by means of language policy. In N. Alexander and A. von Scheliha (eds) *Language Policy and the Promotion of Peace: African and European Case Studies* (pp. 11–32). Pretoria: UNISA Press.

Zappavigna, M. (2012) *Discourse of Twitter and Social Media: How We Use Language to Create Affiliation on the Web.* New York: Continuum International Publishing Group.

Part 2

Linguistic and Cultural Maintenance

3 Creating Translated Interfaces: The Representations of African Languages and Cultures in Digital Media

Elvis ResCue and G. Edzordzi Agbozo

Approximately 30% of the world's languages are in Africa, but on Facebook – one of the biggest social media sites – only five African languages have their orthographies built into the site. The Ewe language of West Africa is one of the underrepresented languages on Facebook. Research suggests that about half of the world's languages may be endangered or may die by the end of this century. However, the prevalence of social media usage could help change this trend. Ewe users on Facebook improvise new lexis and orthography among others to communicate and represent their culture. This paper examines the nature of this communication and the rhetorical purposes that constrain these innovations. We analysed posts from five Facebook-focused groups with a total of 178,940 members who use any form of Ewe for interaction. In particular, we interrogate socio-cultural and linguistic features on the pages. Following Moring (2013), we adopt the 'COD-model' (Competence, Opportunity and Desire), originally attributed to Grin *et al.* (2003), in our analysis. The COD model provides a basis for exploring the impact of media on language use. We also invoked Fairclough (2000, 2003) in our analysis to explore the spaces between text and 'orders of discourse'. The findings suggest that social media sites such as Facebook have provided interfaces for users of minority languages to translate their daily multilingual repertoires and have created the opportunity for cultural maintenance. The study also reveals the intersections between digital technologies and multilingualism, and demonstrates that digital technologies thus far allow for continuation of language use in different forms, therefore, crumbling traditional boundaries and enabling language users' daily linguistic assemblages to manifest online. It is thus recommended that creators of technology should involve users in the heuristic process.

Introduction

In this chapter we discuss how social media sites such as Facebook, offer avenues for users to assert their linguistic and cultural presence through *linguistic assemblages* (Pennycook, 2017) – language users' transportation of daily offline language practices, which contrast normative notions of language as a monolingual signification, into digital spaces. We reveal how digital technologies intersect with multilingualism and vitality of African languages. Specifically, we discuss Ewe language users' digital writing practices on Facebook to show how digital technologies allow for the continuation of language use in a different form where traditional codes/boundaries become fluid if not irrelevant. This is important because Facebook does not support Ewe language orthography. Such a situation could have prevented Ewe users from participating in any digital writing in their language; rather, they created their own form of writing on Facebook, thus supporting the idea that language is not a static set of form and style (see Agbozo & ResCue, 2020; Makalela, 2015; Li Wei, 2011). Language contact scholars such as Salikoko Mufwene have pointed out how language gains and loses some features in multilingual spheres as a result of speakers' attempts to accommodate audiences (Mufwene, 2001). As we argue in this paper, in line with many works on translanguaging (García & Li Wei, 2014; Lewis *et al.*, 2012; Makalela, 2015; Pennycook, 2017), focus needs to shift from static notions of language as a system toward the idea of language as a linguistic repertoire where translanguaging is 'a functional process of multilinguals' utilisation of their repertoire as part of an integrated communication system' (Agbozo & ResCue, 2020: 16).

The use of online media shows a long history of creative modification of resources to enable communication in the face of technical and other restrictions. Digital technology provides avenues for witnessing the fluidity of language in practice. The lack of interfaces for some African languages such as Ewe on digital platforms means that Ewe users have no way of realising their presence in the world of cyberspace. We might be tempted to see this as a disadvantage but Ewe users demonstrate every day that such a situation is an opportunity to build linguistic assemblages and to show that digital spaces are not cut off from the daily offline language practices of multilinguals (cf. Yevudey, 2018). What Ewe users are doing on Facebook fits largely into what happens in many minority language contexts such as Welsh (Cunliffe *et al.*, 2013) and Kashubian (Dołowy-Rybińska, 2013).

The emergence of social media has been met with varied views regarding its effect on languages. For Krauss (1992), electronic media is a cultural nerve gas because of its adverse effects of language mortality. Crystal (2000) and Cunliffe (2009) suggest, however, that electronic media presents the chance for bringing threatened languages back to life through the production and reproduction of accessible versions of languages and connecting speakers of minority languages to a larger population that could learn these languages. Digital technologies, on their own, however, are incapable of enhancing the wider use or revitalisation of a language. Language users in digital spaces, as we argue in this work, engage linguistic assemblages that meet their needs based on their own language use in other spheres such as in offline domains. This proposition is emphasised in the chapter by Kirsty Rowan, in this volume, that any form of language revitalisation process, for instance language documentation, should be informed by the sociocultural evidence obtained from the community and through active engagement of the language users. Language practices by the users might not meet societally expected 'norms' so Krauss (1992) might describe these language practices as deficient; however, such practices are a reflection of the actual linguistic choices.

Welsh, for instance, is a minority language in the United Kingdom. A recent study found that although young people still use traditional face-to-face contact, modern technology and social networking sites are increasingly becoming the means of networking among these populations (Cunliffe *et al.*, 2013) and with these interactions come the use of the Welsh language in these cyberspaces. Wagner (2013) reports a similar situation where she suggests that many young people are increasingly using Luxembourgish on Facebook in Luxembourg within the sociolinguistic context where Luxemburgish competes with French and German in almost all public spheres. This has created a positive attitude to Luxemburgish as the users connect the use of the language to their identity, although the Luxemburgish that is practised on Facebook differs significantly from the normatively prescribed one.

Dołowy-Rybińska (2013) reports a similar case where young people who use Kashubian on the internet have to blend Polish and Kashubian languages since both belong to the same language group: Western Slavic. This happens because no internet site supports the orthography of Kashubian languages. Based on this observation, Dołowy-Rybińska posits that the status of minority languages on the internet is mostly in the hands of the users. It is left with them to use all forms of heuristic techniques to create their own version of the language on the internet. Such studies show that digital technological spaces themselves are possible interfaces to which users translate personal and societal multilingual practices rather than spaces that stifle such translations.

What Dołowy-Rybińska observed about Kashubian users on the internet is similar to what pertains to African language users online. Makalela (2016) argues, for instance, that there are 'infinite relations of dependency between languages and literacies' in the context of pre-colonial Bantu languages, thus reflecting 'a cultural competence' that signals the African value system of Ubuntu (Makalela, 2016: 187). Everyday languaging offline in African contexts exemplifies these connections between languages and cultural experiences in the classroom as well (Banda, 2017; Mwaniki, 2016). We focus our discussion here on only one language: Ewe. However, we are aware, from our experiences in using social media platforms, that other languages in West Africa are also used on digital platforms in a fluid performative manner. In focusing on Ewe, therefore, we intend to provide evidence of such a fluid language practices as well as a research praxis for other scholars to adapt in investigating other African language writing in digital spaces.

In the next section, we discuss Ewe, then we provide an explanation of the COD-model we used in our analysis. We continued our discussion with a textual analysis of our data and conclude with proposals about what our analysis means for the intersections between digital technologies and multilingualism.

Ewe on Social Media

Ewe belongs to the Gbe subgroup of Kwa languages of the Niger Congo language family. In Ghana, Ewe has about 3,820,000 total speakers with 3,320,00 L1 speakers (Ethnologue, 2018). There are also speakers in other parts of Africa including Togo, Benin and Nigeria. The total number of users in all these countries is 4,685,760 (Ethnologue, 2018). Ewe is used in schools (in Ghana and Togo), churches (in Ghana, Togo, Benin and parts of Nigeria as well as in Ewe immigrant communities in Europe and North America) and in traditional media like print newspapers in Togo and new media such as on Facebook and Twitter. It is also used in news broadcasts, for programmes on some television stations (such as Volta1 TV, TV Africa, Ghana Television (GTV) and Télévision Togolaise) and on some radio stations (such as Dela Radio in Adidome, Volta Star Radio in Ho, Unique FM in Accra and Radio Maria in Togo). In Ghana, there were attempts at producing newspapers in the language. For example, in the 1960s, there was a regional newspaper called *Mɔtabiala* and later *Kpodoga*. They became extinct after a short period of publication (Agbedor, 2009). In addition, there were translation of canonical pieces of European literature such as the works of William Shakespeare, Russian literature such as the works of Leo Tolstoy and Middle Eastern literature such as the Arabian Tales into Ewe. These translations, however, are now almost extinct (Agbozo, 2018; Anyidoho, 2003).

In Ghana, Ewe is a Low language in relation to English. Batibo (2005) recounts a triglossic relation among languages with multilingual African countries. In this relation there are High (H) and Low (L) languages. The H language functions as the official/national language and is used for

Table 3.1 Structure of language use in Ghana

H	*Ex-colonial language:* English	
L	*Dominant indigenous language/West African Lingua Francas*	H
	9 government-sponsored languages: Akan, Dagaare, Dangbe, Dagbane, Ewe, Ga, Gonja, Kasem, Nzema, (Hausa; a West African Lingua Franca)	
	Minority language	L
	Other Ghanaian indigenous languages	
	E.g. Likpakpalm, Tafi,/Tegbo Lelemi/Lefana, Likpe/Sɛkpɛle, Wali, Chakali, Sehwi, Krache	

Source: Yevudey and Agbozo (2019: 4).

high-level functions. Dominant indigenous language(s) like Ewe perform L functions in relation to the language above it (English) and H functions in relation to the languages below (like Ghana-Togo Mountain languages). Yevudey and Agbozo (2019) provide a specific case of Ghana in Table 3.1.

Mark Zuckerberg founded Facebook with Eduardo Saverin at Harvard University and launched it on 4 February 2004.[1] About 170 million people registered accounts on Facebook in Africa. This population is predicted to grow at 42% every month (Shapshak, 2017). Although the population of users may be large, the languages they use are mostly European languages on the continent: English, Spanish, French and Portuguese among others. It is difficult to know the exact number of Ewe speakers that are on Facebook. In the same way, it is challenging to make a similar categorical statement on the other African languages that Facebook supports. What we are certain about is that Ewe users exhibit certain digital writing practices. Some of these include a display of cultural competence (Makalela, 2016), linguistic assemblages (Pennycook, 2017) such as the font adaptation, and bilingualism and translanguaging. We analyse evidences of these practices with the COD-model (Grin *et al.*, 2003; Lindström, 2012; Yevudy, 2018).

The COD Model, Textual Analysis and Data

Language use among interlocutors in face-to-face and online communications plays an important part in sharing information and experiences. Communication being a process of transmitting and receiving information (Sekyi-Baidoo, 2003) creates the opportunity for speakers and writers to share their experiences, cultures, perspectives, among others. Speakers of majority languages have the privilege to use their languages in many domains, whereas speakers of minority languages may only use their languages among themselves or are challenged to create avenues through which they can use their languages. Creating communicative contexts for using minority languages is often in pursuit of language (re)vitalisation and maintenance. Successful language revitalisation requires efforts such as 'a sense of group solidarity, immersion language teaching environments, literacy, the use of mass media, and the development of a sufficiently large group of speakers' (Anonby, 1999: 36). In addition, speakers of minority languages who intend to use and to revitalise their languages ought to have competence in the languages and to create the opportunities to use the languages. These variables are captured comprehensively within the *competence*, *opportunity* and *desire* model, thus the COD model (Grin *et al.*, 2003; Lindström, 2012; Yevudey, 2018).

The COD model presents key elements that should be considered in addressing the impact of media on language use, which, as we have previously mentioned, includes *competence*, *opportunities* and the *desire*. The tenets of the model stipulate that speakers of a language must have the *competence* to use the language; this is achievable only when there are *opportunities* to do so; and the speakers should have the *desire* to use their language when they have the opportunity (Grin *et al.*, 2003). These elements ascertain the usability and vitality of a (minority) language in a community and can equally be applied to the use of language by an individual (Lindström, 2012). When people become physically disconnected from an offline social network (Honeycutt & Cunliffe, 2010), they can create an online community when they have the competence to do so; creating such online platforms will provide the opportunity for them to use their language and other linguistic practices; and more so demonstrate that they have the desire to use their language. In view of this, minority language users create the opportunity to transcend the challenges posed by technological interfaces and engage in languaging through assemblages on digital media sites such as Facebook, Twitter, WhatsApp, Instagram and so on.

The model is adopted in exploring how speakers of Ewe demonstrate their competence through their online communications; analysing how they create opportunities for their translanguaging practices; and their desire to enhance the possibilities of Ewe and other African languages in digital media spaces. Ewe focused groups on Facebook were selected for this purpose. The selection of the groups was done through the 'Related Groups' feature where the groups being selected have members in common (Honeycutt & Cunliffe, 2010). Thus, members of one group are also members of a related group. The COD model, therefore, is adopted to explore how members in these related groups have demonstrated their *competence* in Ewe through their posts, how they have created the *opportunity* to use their language through the creation of the groups, and how that also shows their *desire* to use and vitalise their language. The relatedness of the groups and their membership demonstrate that all the groups have a similar and, more so, a common purpose which is to promote the use of the Ewe language in its varied and fluid realisations, and the Ewe culture. As presented in Table 3.2, five selected Ewe focused groups were observed with a total membership of 178,940. Posts from the pages were extracted onto a separate document for the purposes of analysis.

Table 3.2 Facebook pages

Name	Population	Type: Open/Closed
ANLO EWE COMMUNITY FORUM	8588	Open
Ewe Culture	47,766	Open
Ewe Community Forum	100,928	Open
Ewe Literary Prize	89	Open
MINA MÍADO EƲEGBE (EWE LANGUAGE ONLY)	21,569	Closed
Total	**178,940**	

The *ANLO EWE COMMUNITY FORUM* is a group made up of over 8588 members and the purpose of the group is to promote the use of Ewe. This group was created on 14 March 2013 with the aforementioned name, however, the name of the group was changed to Ɛʋè-Nyigba Community Forum on 4 December 2018. No specific message was posted on the page to explain the motivation behind the name. The inferences that can be drawn from the change of name is that the initial name ANLO EWE COMMUNITY FORUM seemed to be specific to a particular sub-ethnic group of Ewe speakers, Anlo. The change of name to Ɛʋè-Nyigba Community Forum makes that name more general and inclusive of all Ewe sub-ethnic groups. The study maintains the initial name of the group because that was the name during the data collection.

As the name depicts, *Ewe Culture* is a group that aim to promote Ewe culture and the group was created on 7 May 2014. The *Ewe Community Forum* is a group created to promote Ewe heritage. As the description of the page states: 'The Ewe forum was created for anyone who identifies with the Ewe heritage including, the Language, People and Culture to come together in harmony and to promote a common interest through the exchange of information and experience by talking about our Geography, History, Education, Development, Health and Social Welfare issues in our communities….' The group was created on 13 October 2010.

The *Ewe Literary Prize* is a page created to promote the Ewe language particularly through '[a] creative writing prize in the Ewe language', as stated in the group's description. The group was created on 8 January 2016. The group, *MINA MÍADO EUEGBE (EWE LANGUAGE ONLY)*, is created mainly to promote the use of monolingual Ewe on the page. This is evident in their group description, which was written exclusively in Ewe, and equally all the posts on the page were written in Ewe. The group was created on 15 September 2011. The commonality among the groups is the promotion of the Ewe language, culture and heritage.

The study explores the sociocultural and linguistic choices and assemblages on recent posts on the various pages. The aim is to present the recent conversation exchanges on the pages and how they reflect the sociolinguistic realities among members of Ewe groups. The textual analysis technique, which is an essential part of discourse analysis, is adopted to explore the sociocultural and linguistic choices in the posts. Adopting textual analysis helps to oscillate between the texts and the 'order of discourse' in unravelling the social structuring of language and networking of social practices (Fairclough, 2003: 3). The textual analysis explores not only the linguistic choices on the pages, but also looks at the interdiscursive analysis by discussing how the posts on the pages reflect communication strategies outside the online communication domain (Fairclough, 2000). This approach to analysing the posts offers the description and interpretation of the texts (Frey *et al.*, 1999).

Data Analysis

Linguistic choices and assemblages

In a recent interview with the *Diggit Magazine* (2018, n.p.), Jan Blommaert asserted that,

> The digital layer of social conduct is still often treated as superficial, an add on of relatively restricted relevance to offline 'real' social behavior. Hence the frequently used dichotomy between the 'real' offline world and the 'virtual' online one. It takes a while before scholars take online phenomena for what they are: *social facts as 'real' as any other social facts*, and in need of a well-founded description and interpretation (our emphasis).

Blommaert's observation underscores the similarity of linguistic choices on social media platforms and offline linguistic behaviours such as bilingual practices and translanguaging. Members of an online platform adopt bilingual practices and translanguaging in their communication exchanges that exhibits their linguistic backgrounds (Reershemius, 2017; Yevudey, 2018). Exploring bilingual practices and translanguaging reveal the fluidity and flexibility of how the repertoire of interlocutors are maximally used in order to achieve a communicative purpose. Bilingual practices refer to how speakers shuttle between two or more languages within a given interactive event (Reershemius, 2017; Yevudey, 2017). Translanguaging refers to how speakers adopt multilingual discursive practices in their pursuit to making meaning, shaping experiences, and gaining and understanding and knowledge through the use of two or more languages (Baker, 2011; Creese & Blackledge, 2010; García, 2009; García & Li Wei, 2014, Otheguy *et al.*, 2018). This conceptualisation of bilingual and multilingual code choices underpins the *unitary view* (Otheguy *et al.*, 2018) where, despite the sociocultural concepts of languages as an individual linguistic system, speakers use their linguistic repertoires in a flexible manner when communicating with others with whom they share the same repertoires.

In online communications among members of a particular group, there is the assumption that other members in the group will comprehend any form of code choices. In the Ewe focused groups observed, members adopt code choices that elucidate their linguistic repertoires. Speakers of Ewe stretch across different geographical contexts and countries. Ewe is spoken in Ghana, Togo, Benin, some parts of Nigeria and other immigrant communities in Africa, Europe and North America. This geographical diversity is represented in the linguistic choices on some of the pages, as reflected in, on one hand, the dialects of Ewe that manifest in our data, and, on the other hand, the number of languages that are mixed in varying texts.

The use of codes at the macro and micro levels present bilingualism and multilingualism on the pages. At the macro level, as presented in Except 1, for instance, members of the groups post information and comments on the pages in various languages including Ewe, English, French, and combination of these languages. Though the pages are often meant to promote the Ewe language and cultures, there is evidence of the deployment of full linguistic repertoires of members on the pages (Otheguy *et al.*, 2015). Members freely post on the pages in the language they felt suitable and may assume that members of the group will comprehend their linguistic choices. In post A in Table 3.3, for instance, is a comment on an online article titled *Napoléon et la Suisse* 'Napoleon and Switzerland', which was written in French.

In post B, the member commented on a scene from a movie in Ewe and English. The scene was about a pastor who was riding a motorcycle and who offered to give a lift to a gentleman standing by the side of the road. The gentleman had some luggage which contained electric cables referred to in Ewe as *dzoka* dzo – 'fire' and ka – 'thread/cable'. In Ewe, however, *dzoka* can also mean 'magic'. The pastor then started praying over the *electric cable* assuming that it was a *magic*. After a while nothing miraculous was happening and when the pastor opened the bag he realised that it was an electric cable. He then said to the gentleman that the cables are called *kuraaka*, thus kuraa – 'electric' and ka – 'thread/cable'. The interesting linguistic point to note is that in some dialects of Ewe, electric cable is called *dzoka* while other dialects refer to the same thing as *kuraaka*. There was, therefore, a misunderstanding in that communication exchange in terms of what *dzoka* means, whether *an electric cable* or *magic*. Equally, what is linguistically interesting in the post by member B is the switching between Ewe and English in the same post. The comment shows the flexibility and fluidity that characterised code choices on the pages, therefore representing the bilingual and multilingual repertoires of the members.

The post by member C, was presented in monolingual English. Member D was commenting on a demonstration video in which there was a switch between Ewe and English, and member E commented in monolingual English. As presented in post E, members F, G, H, I, J, K and L

Table 3.3 Posts and comments on Ewe Focus Group Pages

	Posts and comments	Translations
Post A	**(Part of a comment on a post on Napoléon et la Suisse)** *Member A:* Même Napoléon Bonaparte, le grand centralisateur, oppresseur, nivellateur, uniformisateur, fondateur de l'État unitaire français sur les ruines de la république fragmentée, anarchiste, éclatée, des révolutionnaires de 1789, reconnait l'impossibilité d'une formule d'État unitaire lorsqu'il y a hétérogénéité sociologique. C'est d'une vérité élémentaire qui échappe curieusement aux technocrottes et politichiens tarés Françafricains. Pour ce qui seraient tentés d'opposer la taille (superficie ou population) comme argument, nous leur disons que c'est tout le contraire(les petites entités sont plus facilement fédéralisables que les grandes: le Togo, le Bénin, le Burkina, la Guinée, etc. sont largement plus facilement fédéralisables que l'Afrique: qui peut le plus peut le moins.) que avec cette image : la fourmis a 2 yeux, l'éléphant aussi. Le plus petit état du monde mais l'un des plus puissant est le Vatican : 0,439 km² pour moins de 1000 habitants. Combien d'États de cette dimension on peut avoir dans chaque État unitaire africain. Enfin les mensurations d'une fédération célèbre et très ancienne, la Suisse et celle d'une très jeune fédération auparavant état unitaire qui n'a réussi son unité que par la formule fédérale, la Belgique.	*Member A:* Even Napoleon Bonaparte, the great centraliser, oppressor, leveler, standardiser, founder of the French unitary state on the ruins of the fragmented Republic, an anarchist, exploded, the revolutionaries of 1789, recognized the impossibility of a unitary state when he formulated a sociological heterogeneity. It is a basic truth that escapes curiously from technocrats and politicians. For what would be tempted to oppose the size (area or population) as an argument, we say that it is the opposite (small entities are more easily federalisable than large ones: Togo, Benin, Burkina Faso, Guinea, etc. are more easily federalisable than Africa: who can do it the least.) that with this image: the ants have 2 eyes, the elephant too. The lowest state in the world but one of the most powerful is the Vatican: 0,439 km² for less than 1000 inhabitants. How many states of this dimension can be in each African unitary state? Finally, the measurements of a famous and very old Federation, Switzerland and a very young federation formerly unitary state which succeeded only in the Federal Formula, Belgium.
Post B	**(A comment on a video from a movie scene)** *Member B:* Dzoka alo Kuraaka Wokata ka wonye 😄😁 Pastor mistook electric cable to be a charm and had casted the devil out of it 😄	*Member B:* Electric cable or electric cable. They are all cables 😄😁 Pastor mistook electric cable to be a charm and had casted the devil out of it 😄
Post C	(A post from a member of the group) *Member C:* But without faith it is impossible to please Him, for he who comes to God must believe that He is and that He is a rewarder of those who diligently seek Him. (Heb 11:6) Blessings!	

(Continued)

Table 3.3 Posts and comments on Ewe Focus Group Pages (*Continued*)

Posts and comments	Translations
Post D **(Comments on a demonstration video)** Member D: me nyii ba na mi kaaaataaaa great demo out there xedzra kataka be ye de azi de wotete gbe ayekooooo!!!! Inong live one volta region long live Anloland Anlo my pride my heritage nyatefe amenorvio woe nya awu u have really demonstrated it	*Member D:* I acknowledge all of you. Great demonstration out there. You have prepared for a day like this. Well done!!!! Long live one Volta region, long live Anlo land. Anlo, my pride my heritage. It is the truth; we are one people. You have really demonstrated it
Member E: I love that	*Member E:* I love that
Post E **(Comments on a video of a traditional dance)** *Member F*: The Gadzo Togo, Ghana and Benin. Gadzo is a war dance drama of the Southeastern Anlo-Ewe of Ghana, which came from Notsìe in the Republic of Togo. Originally, this dance-drumming was performed after wars so that the warriors could re-enact battle scenes for those at home. Gadzo is performed presently during ancestral stool festivals, Anlo state festival, Hogbetsotso, funerals of important chiefs and members of the group and by professional and amateur groups for entertainment. For more Infos visit my blog site at [url] *Member G*: But this is not gadzo rather adogbo or adzogbo *Member H*: Thanks for the correction. *Member I:* Continue to educate Anlo our our heritage *Member J*: Proud of my Ancestor beautiful culture *Member K:* This is not a Gadzo dance …..I know that dance well 😊….please come again so others doesn't mistake this for Gadzo Thanks *Member L*: Plz,don't u have a WhatsApp group so that we can also join ?? *Member K*: Dozens of them *Member L*: [number] Hook me up to it	

(*Continued*)

Table 3.3 Posts and comments on Ewe Focus Group Pages (*Continued*)

Posts and comments	Translations
Post F **(A post and comments on a demonstration)** **(Post)** *Member M:* 🔥 🔥 *DEMOSTRATION ! DEMOSTRATION!!!* 🔥 🔥 🔥 *CONCERNED CITIZENS OF VOLTA REGION* *The leadership of Concerned Citizens of Volta Region wish to invite all citizens to a demonstration against the division of Volta Region on Wednesday, 4th April ,2018.* *This peaceful march starts from Vume, R.C school park through Sokpoe to Sogakope* *For further information, kindly call the following numbers* *[name] : [number]* *[name] : [number]* *[name] : [number]* *GREAT VOLTA!! WE STAND FOR UNITY* 💚 *GREAT VOLTA!! WE SAY NO TO THE DIVISION OF OUR LAND* ✖ 😡 ✖	
(Comments) *Member N:* waow kaleo on the move *Member O:* Aborkatrika Abormekua kaletor O!. *Member P:* Mia nor deka deworwor me nusele *Member Q:* Mi dzo kpla!	**(Comments)** *Member N:* waow the warriors on the move *Member O:* More strength. Do not give up, you warriors! *Member P:* You should be as one. There is strength in unity. *Member Q:* Let us go immediately!

were commenting on a video of a traditional dance. Apart from their suggested names for the dance *gadzo*, *adogbo* or *adzogbo*, (in Ewe) the comments were in English. In post F, member M posted a notice on a demonstration that was organised in response to the division of Volta Region, one of the regions of Ghana. The post was in English. The comments, however, were in bilingual Ewe-English codes.

At the micro level, language choices on the pages demonstrate certain linguistic forms such as the adaptation of Ewe characters, the use of truncated forms, and non-use of diacritics. Adaptations of characters in online communication has become significant feature of languaging practices, thus, digital technology enables going beyond traditional codes.

As presented in Table 3.4, the sound /ɖ/ was adapted as [d] (as in posts by Members D & P), the sound /ɔ/ was constantly adapted as [-or] (as in posts by Members O and P), and the sound /ŋ/ was adapted as /n/ (as in

Table 3.4 Linguistic forms: The adaptation of Ewe fonts, the use of truncated forms and non-use of diacritics

Member	Adapted form	Original form	Translation
B	Wokata	'wokată'	'all of them'
D	de azi	'ɖe'	'on...'
	u have	'you'	'you'
L	u have	'you'	'you'
O	Aborkatrika	'abɔkadrika'	'more strength'
	Abormekua	'abɔmekua'	'not to give up'
	kaletor.	'kalɛ̃tɔ'	'warrior'
P	nor	'nɔ'	'be in...'
	deka	'ɖeka'	'one'
	deworwor	'dewɔwɔ'	'unity'
	(for:dekaworwor)	(for: ɖekawɔwɔ)	'strength'
	nuse le	'ŋusɛ̃'	
Q	Mi dzo	Mìdzo	'2PL-go'
		Mídzo	'1PL-go'

post by Member P). There were also instances of the use of truncated forms such as [u] to represent 'you' (as in the posts by Members D and L). Such truncations are features of mobile phone texting that are being transferred to digital writing practices here. Certain cultural competences enable interlocutors to understand these truncations, thus making them integral parts of their linguistic repertoire.

Diacritics in Ewe are morphologically and phonologically marked, therefore, contribute to meaning variations in words or clauses. In the posts, however, most diacritics were not used. For instance, the Front – Half – Open – Unrounded vowel /e/ in the words **kaletor** and **nuse** is to be nasalised as /ẽ/, as in words such as kalẽtɔ 'warrior' and ŋusẽ 'strength'. Equally, the low and high tones in Ewe were sometimes not marked as in the post by Member Q in Mì (low tone: 'you' 2PL) and Mí (high tone: 'we' 1PL).

The linguistic features adopted on the pages present the fluidity and flexibility that characterised linguistic assemblages. Members of the group use languages that they think best expressed their comments whether it is a monolingual choice or bilingual/multilingual choices. Similarly, the adaptation of Ewe characters, the use of truncated forms and non-use of diacritics in the posts present the innovative ways through which the members use their linguistic repertoire in their online communications. The presence of Ewe focused groups on Facebook shows that the Ewes have created the *opportunity* to use their language and to promote their culture. These groups also demonstrate their *desire* to use their languages, and their *competence* is exhibited through the use of the language, especially through the adaptations of Ewe characters. All these realisations of translanguaging are made possible by digital technologies. We argue therefore that instead of seeing digital technologies as anathema to languages, they thus far allow for continuation of language use in different forms; crumbling traditional boundaries and enabling language users' daily linguistic assemblages to manifest online.

Sociocultural features

Sociocultural features are the combination of established social and cultural factors that are cross-generationally transmitted and which shape people's identities and affiliations (McCarty, 2009), where cultural identity is generally 'those aspects of our identities which arise out of our "belonging" to distinctive ethnic, racial, linguistic, religious, and above all national cultures' (Hall *et al.*, 2000: 598).

There are varied sociocultural features examined on the various platforms. These are quintessential discourse elements that reflect the social and cultural aspects of Ewe life. Prominent among these are educational discourses about Ewe dance ensembles, historical narratives, dressing, food, maps and festival celebrations. While some of the narratives are composed with only characters, others employ varied forms and other elements in multimodal forms. Multimodality is basically the combination of textual, aural, linguistic, spatial, and visual resources in the creation of a message (Lunsford *et al.*, 2017). These sociocultural features further demonstrate the fluid nature of Ewe in digital spaces since digital technology allows for discussion of diverse topics through diverse linguistic assemblages. Digital technology thus allows this African language to thrive in the digital space as fluid systems serving the communication needs of its users. The following examples show some sociocultural elements in our data:

Excerpt 1: Reflections of collective identity

Member R:	Gadzo is a war dance drama of the Southeastern Anlo-Ewe of Ghana, which came from Notsìe in the Republic of Togo. Originally, this dance-drumming was performed after wars so that the warriors could re-enact battle scenes for those at home. Gadzo is performed presently during ancestral stool festivals, Anlo state festival, Hogbetsotso, funerals of important chiefs and members of the group and by professional and amateur groups for entertainment.
Member S:	But this is not gadzo rather adogbo or adzogbo
Member R:	thanks for the correction
Member T:	continue to educate Anlo our our heritage
Member U:	Proud of my Ancestor beautiful culture
Member V:	This is not a Gadzo dance .....I know that dance well 🥲 ....please come again so others doesn't mistake this for Gadzo
Thanks	

Member R attempts to educate other members of the *ANLO EWE COMMUNITY FORUM* platform about Gadzo dance. His post, however, generated a conversation about the accuracy of the information. Some of the comments suggested a correction to the post of Member R and s/he accepted the correction. Member T sees this exercise as appropriate and encourages it. Through this interaction, members are constructing a collective identity for themselves as people who belong to and understand a particular culture. They engage in this identity creation not by adhering to the forms of a singular linguistic system but by oscillating between forms of Ewe and forms of English.

In social movement theory, collective identity is the common definition that a group assigns to itself or one that emerges from the group members' shared interests, experiences, and solidarities (Melucci, 1995). For the proponent of this concept, Alberto Melucci, 'collective identity is an interactive and shared definition produced by several individuals (or groups at a more complex level) and concerned with the orientation of action and the field of opportunities and constraints in which the action takes place' (1995: 59). Since collective identity is not fixed, it changes based on the varied struggles that the group engages in at particular points in time. In our data, we see the fluid nature of identity emanating from the linguistic assemblages of users.

The posts that we found on these Facebook pages illustrate this fluidity of collective identity through shifts in discourse prosody. Excerpt 2 below illustrates this politics of identity. In this post, the author admonishes members and tells them to shift their identity from being Ghanaian to that of Western Togo. This post is promoting the agenda of a secessionist group called Homeland Study Group Foundation (HSGF) that has been advocating for independence of Western Togoland for the past ten years. To concretise his point, the author adds the map of Western Togoland and its flag to this post.

Note that the dominant singular language in Excerpts 1 above and 2 below is English. While English is not usually considered as an African language (Ngũgĩ, 1986), authors on Ewe pages use it as the readily available means of expressing aspects of their sociocultural life. The discourse prosody of the English in use here is peculiar to the social media pages. By that, we mean sentences such as 'Proud of my Ancestor beautiful culture' might not be grammatical in English but it served the purposes for which such a construction is being used – education on Ewe culture. In light of such fluid uses, we may perhaps question the assumption that English is not an African language. This echoes the old debate of the language question, especially in African literature, where Achebe and his followers think that the use of English in Africa is distinct enough for it to be considered a language of the continent; a language capable of carrying Africa's literary burden (cf. Jeyifo, 2017; Mugane, 2017).

Excerpt 2: Reflections of collective national identity

Member W: Let all **torgos** RISE UP, FOR THE TRUTH , IS ONLY
THE TRUTH THAT CAN SET YOUR GENERATIONS
TO COME
FREE, YOU ARE NOT GHANAIANS, LOOK
YOUR sovereignty state of WESTERN TOGOLAND
___??????????

The word 'torgos', in this multimodal text calls for special historical attention. 'Torgo' (Ewe: tɔ 'river', go 'side') refers to the land between the two great rivers called Mono (to the east) and Amu or Volta (to the west). This is regarded as the homeland of the Ewe people until Germany lost the Second World War. After the Second World War, this space was divided between France and Britain. The French territory is the Republic of Togo today and British Togoland become the Volta region of Ghana in 1956 (Beigbeder, 1994; Spieth, 2011). The author of the post uses the historical name as an invocation of collective identity, but this time, it is an invitation towards a national identity for a people divided among four countries. Again, we see a movement between Ewe and English in this post.

Some of the posts were written in Ewe. Three forms of Ewe were written: Ewe alphabet without the diacritics, Ewe alphabets with diacritics and flexible keyboard adaptations, as we discussed earlier under linguistic assemblages. We identify some posts related to sociocultural aspects that are written in any of the aforementioned styles. Table 3.5 exemplifies this.

Member X posted the picture of a fruit and asks for its name. They start the sentence with *today's lesson,* implying that other lessons about Ewe culture have been going on. This also shows that this digital platform is a classroom as well, a place for cultural education. There were other lessons on personal names, animal and fish names, beads and their uses, traditional prayer formulas, among others. In addition to Member AB's answer, there is an invitation of ideas for promoting Ewe identity. They

Table 3.5 African velvet tamarind

Member X: Egba nusɔsrɔ atikutsetse sia fe ŋukɔɖɛ	Member X: Today's lesson, what is the name of this fruit
Member Y: Atitoe	Member Y: Atitɔe (velvet tamarind)
Member Z: Ablayiboi	Member Z: Ablayibɔe (velvet tamarind)
Member AA: Atit)e....lol	Member AA: Atitɔe....lol (velvet tamarind)
Member AB: Atike (amatsi) veviwoe bye esiawo hee. Metsi megbe vie gake maga donku edzi be efe English nkor enye Velvet tamarind (Google) Mede kuku. Medi be made asixoxor blibo miafe Ewenuwo nu be gbegbogblor bubuwo ha woabu mi Mina miadze adanu mehia susu vovovowo tso miagbor yom le (*phone number*) akpe	Member AB: These are important medicines. I am a little late but I remember that its English name is Velvet tamarind (Google). I want to give a lot of respect to our Ewe things so that speakers of other languages will respect us. Let us plan. I need different thoughts from you call me on (phone number) thanks

Table 3.6 Ewe Movie: Gbana va glo (Debt is too much)

Member M: We should support our people those millionaires in Volta region wake up and build Volta.	
Member N: Avuawoe nye nugbanã fle la, srɔ a kple via. wónye avuwo elabena, wó fle nu le afenɔa si wógbe fea xexe nɛ.	Member N: The fools are the ones who bought on credit: the spouse and the child. They are fools because they bought from the lady and refused to pay. (This is a commentary explaining why a character insulted another character.)
Member O: Agbana doa' me nkpe loooo!	Member O: Poverty brings so much shame to a person
Member P: (mentions a name) pls come for your chillingmama	Member P: ... chillingmama (a comic character in the movie)
(Named person): laugh enter Akatsi market	(Named person): I laughed and entered Akatsi market (This is an exaggerated way of saying I laughed so much, probably rolled on the ground until I reached Akatsi market. Akatsi is a popular Ewe city that arguably has the largest market in the Volta region of Ghana.)
Member Q: this woman go mafia you straight	Member Q: this woman will cause you trouble

take the *opportunity* that this post provides to make their own plea, which feeds into the goals of members of this platform.

There are also reflections of Ewe culture in the literary works that are circulated on these platforms. These include poetry, movies and songs. Table 3.6, for instance, shows some reactions to a seven-minute movie clip that someone uploaded on one of the pages. The owner of this text did not solicit for any comments, but commentators volunteered reactions. Member N even attempted an explanation of a rude character's behaviour. Member P associates a character with another member asking that member to take away the rude character from the scene. In reacting to Member P, the invited member simply said they laughed so hard.

Two issues emerge here. Firstly, some members identify with certain characters because the characters speak their language in particularly comic ways that, though insulting, causes laughter. A non-Ewe may find the rude character's insult awful; but not the Ewe speaker who laughs so hard at these insults. Secondly, some members (like Member M) felt that movies like these are important for the promotion of Ewe cultural identity and invites wealthy folks to invest in the Ewe movie industry. By these two behaviours towards the excerpts of the movie *Gbana va glo*, we see an affiliation not only between the characters and authors of these comments, but also a strong link between the discourses of the movie and comments, to a larger Ewe identity and desire for sustenance of that cultural identity through movies.

Like the movies, poetry receives positive reception on these pages. One particular poet's work keeps circulating on all five Facebook pages that we examined. The poet's stage name is Torgbui Olokodzoko. He is a performance poet who plies his trade on Ewe radio and TV stations in Ghana and Togo, at individual and corporate events, and stages his own concert in Ghana and Togo. On one occasion in 2018, he performed at the birthday celebration of a former first lady of Ghana, Nana Konadu Agyemang-Rawlings. According to his Facebook update, he was invited to this event by Ghana's former president Flt. Lt. J.J. Rawlings, an Ewe.

Among Torgbui Olokodzoko's recorded poetry videos, the most popular by shares and views is 'Xegbe ye xe dona' (A bird speaks bird-language). This poem questions the Ewe people's lack of enthusiasm in using their own language. Some lines from the poem are presented in Table 3.7.

As can be seen in the comments in Table 3.8, this poem receives positive commentary. While some members of the groups thank the poet for the appropriateness of the poem's theme, others praise the 'wisdom' embodied in the poem itself. Indeed, there are many popular sayings, traditional songs, and aphorisms that carry the sense of 'a bird speaks bird-language'. One of the most popular Ewe poets, ranked among the cannon of Ewe literature, Heno Akpalu (Anyidoho, 2003), has a poem with the same title 'Xegbe xe dona'. Olokodzoko echoes this recurring theme that is at the core of Ewe identity. It is no surprise that this particular work is widely circulated. Member T even extends the conversation to 'our African languages'. 'Our' is a pronoun of possession and inclusion. As such, this member overtly declares their belonging to a particular group that is even larger than their immediate Ewe identity.

In this section, we attempt to understand how sociocultural elements of these pages are assembled and their importance. Our discussion here emphasises the fluid use of Ewe in digital writing on these Facebook pages. We show that digital technology enables the possibility of engaging diverse topics using linguistic and cultural assemblages. We found in this discussion some more evidence of how digital technology intersects with multilingualism and multiculturalism by serving as a space for sociocultural identity construction and an environment for cultural education. In the next section, we conclude our discussion with what all these mean for African languages in digital spaces.

Table 3.7 'Xegbe xe dona'

Ʋevi le gbe dzi, ese Ʋegbea? Ʋevi le gbe dzi, edoa EƲegbea?	Ewe child abroad, do you know Ewe language? Ewe child abroad, do you speak Ewe language?
…	…
Ke Ʋevi yi doa EƲegbe, sea EƲegbe eye wozaa EƲegbe hedaa ɖe Eɓegbe dzi le gbedzi fe yayrawo dzea abe anya ene	But the blessings of the Ewe child who speaks, knows and uses Ewe language and takes pride in the language grows like *anya*. (Anya is a particularly beautiful tree that even blossoms in dry seasons.)

Source: Torgbui Olokodzoko (2018).

Table 3.8 Comments on 'Xegbe xe dona'

Member R: Very very good point Great God bless you	
Member S: Wise and sensible poem	
Member T: Akpé na wo han looo. Mawu névé nouwo	(Togo dialect of Ewe: Mina) Thanks to you too. God's mercy on you.
Member T: Well done. I share. We must value our African languages.	

Conclusion

We set out to identify how African languages and cultures such as those of the Ewe people of Ghana manifest in digital technology through *linguistic assemblages*. Our findings show that users device varied heuristic techniques in their digital languaging practices. Linguistically, Ewe users on Facebook adapt keyboard letters and also alternate between different linguistic systems through strategies such as bilingual practices and translanguaging in their discourses. In addition to their digital writing strategies, digital technology also provides the space for Ewe cultural education and sociocultural identity construction. The activities of Ewe users on this platform show that they indeed desire to use this space that digital technology provides to show their linguistic and cultural competence, and to educate themselves about their language and culture.

Our discussion establishes how users of African languages such as Ewe in digital spaces are exploring ways of creating presence. Digital technology is thus providing new communication spaces for demonstrating multilingual repertoires. We emphasise that digital technologies intersect with multilingualism and assist in the vitality of African languages. Our chapter has evidenced this intersection. The findings suggest that social media sites such as Facebook have provided interfaces for users of minority languages to translate their daily multilingual repertoires onto their online communication, and have created the opportunity for cultural maintenance. Creators of technology should therefore involve users in the heuristic process in order to make social media platform more user friendly and as a platform for language maintenance and culture preservation.

Note

(1) For the full account of Facebook's founding, see: Carlson, Nicholas (2010). 'At Last — The Full Story of How Facebook Was Founded.' *Business Insider* (online, 5 March). See http://www.businessinsider.com/how-facebook-was-founded-2010-3#we-can-talk-about-that-after-i-get-all-the-basic-functionality-up-tomorrow-night-1 (accessed 21 February 2018).

References

Agbedor, K.P. (2009) *LING 333: Phonetics and Phonology of Ewe*. Centre of Distance Education, Institute of Adult Education: University of Ghana, Legon.

Agbozo, G.E. and ResCue, E. (2020) Educational language policy in an African country: Making a place for code-switching/translanguaging. *Applied Linguistics Review* 11 (3), 1–21.

Agbozo, G.E. (2018) Translation as rewriting: Cultural theoretical appraisal of Shakespeare's *Macbeth* in the Ewe language of West Africa. *Multilingual Shakespeare: Translation, Appropriation and Performance* 18, 44–56.

Anonby, S.J. (1999) Reversing language shift: Can Kwak'wala be revived? In J. Reyhner, G. Cantoni, R.N. St. Clair and E. Parsons Yazzie (eds) *Revitalizing Indigenous Languages* (pp. 33–52). Flagstaff, AZ: Northern Arizona University.

Anyidoho, K. (2003) The back without which there is no front. *Africa Today* 50 (2), 3–18.

Batibo, H. (2005) *Language Decline and Death in Africa: Causes, Consequences, and Challenges*. Clevedon: Multilingual Matters.

Baker, C. (2011) *Foundations of Bilingual Education and Bilingualism* (5th edn). Bristol: Multilingual Matters.

Banda, F. (2017) Translanguaging and English-African language mother tongues as linguistic dispensation in teaching and learning in a black township school in Cape Town. *Current Issues in Language Planning* 19 (2), 198–217.

Beigbeder, Y. (1994) *International Monitoring of Plebiscites, Referenda and National Elections: Self-determination and Transition to Democracy*. Cham: Springer.

Creese, A. and Blackledge, A. (2010) Translanguaging in the bilingual classroom: A pedagogy for learning and teaching? *The Modern Language Journal* 94 (1), 103–115.

Crystal, D. (2000) *Language Death*. Cambridge: Cambridge University Press.

Cunliffe, D. (2009) The Welsh language on the Internet: Linguistic resistance in the age of network society. In G. Goggin and M. McLelland (eds) *Internationalizing Internet Studies: Beyond Anglophone Paradigms* (pp. 96–111). New York: Routledge.

Cunliffe D., Morris, D. and Prys, C. (2013) Investigating the differential use of Welsh in young speakers' social networks: A comparison of communication in face-to-face settings, in electronic texts and on social networking sites. In E.H. Gruffydd Jones and E. Uribe-Jongbloed (eds) *Social Media and Minority Languages: Convergence and the Creative Industries* (pp. 75–86). Bristol: Multilingual Matters.

Diggit Magazine (2018) Jan Blommaert on digital culture in 2018 and 2019. See https://www.diggitmagazine.com/interviews/jan-blommaert-digital-culture?fbclid= IwAR0Dr7TT9uRwJondBf2EYmcSb6hG7wXwz16h4ArIySUdQGBpMlSzYyZqqU0 (accessed 30 January 2019).

Dołowy-Rybińska, N. (2013) Kashubian and modern media: The influence of new technologies on endangered languages. In E.H. Gruffydd Jones and E. Uribe-Jongbloed (eds) *Social Media and Minority Languages: Convergence and the Creative Industries* (pp. 119–129). Bristol: Multilingual Matters.

Ethnologue (2018) Ethnologue: Languages of the World (21st edn). Dallas, Texas: SIL International. Online version: http://www.ethnologue.com/.

Fairclough, N. (2003) *Discourse Analysis: Textual Analysis For Social Research*. London: Routledge.

Fairclough, N. (2000) Discourse, social theory and social research: the case of welfare reform. *Journal of Sociolinguistics* 4, 163–195.

Frey, L., Botan, C. and Kreps, G. (1999) *Investigating Communication: An Introduction to Research Methods* (2nd edn). Boston: Allyn & Bacon.

García, O. and Li Wei (2014) *Translanguaging: Language, Bilingualism and Education*. London: Palgrave Macmillan.

García, O. (2009) *Bilingual Education in the 21st Century*. Oxford: Wiley-Blackwell.

Grin, F., Moring, T., Gorter, D., Häggman, J., Riagáin, D.Ó and Strubell, M. (2003) *Support for Minority Languages in Europe. Final Report on a Project Financed by the European Commission*, Directorate Education and Culture. See http://europa. eu.int/comm/education/policies/lang/langmin/support.pdf. (accessed on 1 February 2016).

Hall, S., Held, D., Hubert, D. and Thompson, K. (2000) *Modernity: An Introduction To Modern Society*. Oxford: Blackwell Publishers.

Honeycutt, C. and Cunliffe, D. (2010) The use of the Welsh language on Facebook. *Information, Communication & Society* 13 (2), 226–248.

Jeyifo, B. (2017) English is an African language–Ka Dupe! [For and against Ngũgĩ]. *Journal of African Cultural Studies* 30 (2), 133–147.

Krauss, M. (1992) The world's languages in crisis. *Language* 68 (1), 4–10.

Lewis, G., Jones, B. and Baker, C. (2012) Translanguaging: Origins and development from school to street and beyond. *Educational Research and Evaluation: An International Journal on Theory and Practice* 18 (7), 641–654.

Li Wei (2011) Moment analysis and translanguaging space: Discursive construction of identities by multilingual Chinese youth in Britain. *Journal of Pragmatics* 43, 1222–1235.

Lindström, J. (2012) Different languages, one mission? Outcomes of language policies in a multilingual university context. *International Journal of Sociology of Language* 216, 33–54.

Lunsford, A., Body, M., Ede, L., Moss, B.J., Papper, C.C. and Walters, K. (2017) *Everyone's an Author*. New York/London: W.W. Norton and Company.

Makalela, L. (2015) Translanguaging as a vehicle for epistemic access: Cases for reading comprehension and multilingual interactions. *Per Linguam* 31 (1), 15–29.

Makalela, L. (2016) Ubuntu translanguaging: An alternative framework for complex multilingual encounters. *Southern African Linguistics and Applied Language Studies* 34 (3), 187–196.

McCarty, S. (2009) Social networking behind student lines in Japan. In M. Thomas (ed.) *Handbook of Research on Web 2.0 and Second Language Learning*. Hershy/London: IGI Global.

Melucci, A. (1995) *The Process of Collective Identity*. Temple University Press.

Moring, T. (2013) Media markets and minority languages in the digital age. *Journal of Ethnopolitics and Minority Issues in* Europe 12 (4), 34–55.

Mugane, J. (2017) Contemporary conversations: Is English an African language? *Journal of African Cultural Studies* 30 (2), 1–3.

Mufwene, S.S. (2001) *The Ecology of Language Evolution*. Cambridge: Cambridge University Press.

Mwaniki, M. (2016) Translanguaging as a class/lecture-room language management strategy in multilingual contexts: Insights from autoethnographic snapshots from Kenya and South Africa. *Southern African Linguistics and Applied Language Studies* 34 (3), 197–209, doi: 10.2989/16073614.2016.1250357.

Ngũgĩ wa, T. (1986) *Decolonising the Mind. The Politics of Language in African Literature*. Nairobi: Heinemann.

Otheguy, R., García, O. and Reid, W. (2018) A translanguaging view of the linguistics system of bilinguals. *Applied Linguistics Review* 10 (4), 1–27.

Otheguy, R., García, O. and Reid, W. (2015) Clarifying translanguaging and deconstructing named languages: A perspective from linguistics. *Applied Linguistics Review* 6, 281–307.

Pennycook, A. (2017) Translanguaging and semiotic assemblages. *International Journal of Multilingualism* 14 (3), 269–282.

Reershemius, G. (2017) Autochthonous heritage languages and social media: Writing and bilingual practices in Low German on Facebook. *Journal of Multilingual and Multicultural Development* 38 (1), 35–49, doi: 10.1080/01434632.2016.1151434.

Sekyi-Baidoo, Y. (2003) *Learning and Communicating* (2nd edn). Accra: Infinity Graphics Ltd.
Shapshak T. (2017) Facebook has 170 million African users, mostly on mobile. *Fobes* (online, April 2017). See https://www.forbes.com/sites/tobyshapshak/2017/04/05/facebook-has-170m-african-users-mostly-on-mobile/#7bd6d9ef53dc (accessed 21 February 2017).
Spieth, J. (2011) *The Ewe People, a Study of the Ewe People in German Togo*. Accra: Sub-Saharan Publishers.
Wagner, M. (2013) Luxemburgish on Facebook: Language ideologies and writing strategies. In E.H. Gruffydd Jones and E. Uribe-Jongbloed (eds) *Social Media and Minority Languages: Convergence and the Creative Industries* (pp. 87–98). Bristol: Multilingual Matters.
Yevudey, E. and Agbozo, G.E. (2019) Teacher trainee sociolinguistic backgrounds and attitudes to language-in-education policy in Ghana: A preliminary survey. *Current Issues in Language Planning* 20 (4), 338–364. doi: 10.1080/14664208.2019.1585158.
Yevudey, E. (2018) The representation of African languages and cultures on social media: A case of Ewe in Ghana. In A. Agwuele and A. Bodomo (eds) *The Routledge Handbook of African* (pp. 343–358). London: Routledge.
Yevudey, E. (2017) Bilingual practices in Ghanaian primary schools: Implications for curriculum design and educational practice. PhD Dissertation in Applied Linguistics. Submitted to School of Languages and Social Sciences, Aston University.

4 Mdocumentation: Combining New Technologies and Language Documentation to Promote Multilingualism in Nubian Heritage Language Learners of the Diaspora

Kirsty Rowan

The first decades of the 21st century have generally seen a repositioning of linguists' focus from the explanation of language towards documentation of languages instead. Language endangerment has become a major concern for linguists and has given rise to the crucial and imperative linguistic endeavour of language documentation as a core practice. Documentary linguistic practices were predominantly initiated by North American and Australian scholars mainly working on individual endangered languages in these geographical areas. Conventionally, documentary linguists compile grammars and dictionaries of single endangered languages with the documentation products being published into print formats as a record of the formal properties of the language. However, along with quantifying reductions in vulnerable languages' speaker numbers, this traditional methodology of documentation also ignores the fact that 'languages are constantly being reshaped by their speakers and are not static' (Mufwene, 2006: 130). It is no wonder then that language documentation methodologies and activities are currently being revised by scholars working on African languages (Ameka, 2015; Batibo, 2005, 2009; Essegbey *et al.*, 2015; Mufwene, 2004). Many of the traditional documentation practices do not apply because of the dynamic nature of language and because these practices ignore the multilingual language ecologies as predominantly found in Africa. Therefore, a focus is needed on the fluid nature of language use and its sociocultural context in language documentation (Seyfeddinipur, 2016), whereby '[A] broader understanding of a larger set of language use patterns, linguistic contexts and ecologies can in turn feed into our understanding of how languages evolve, shift and change, and how multilingual patterns arise and how they either persevere or decline' (Seyfeddinipur & Chambers, 2016: 1).

In order for documentation to be holistic and capture the interactional and context-based and mediated nature of multilingual speakers, it needs to be performed from a bottom-up approach which foregrounds the social dimension (Migge & Léglise, 2012). Advances in accessible digital technologies to conduct, share and archive the documentation assist with this focus on more ethnographic and sociocultural documentation practices. Furthermore, this documentation practice can be accomplished by utilising technology that is already in the hands of a community of speakers and by situating the community not only as the subjects of documentation but as the documenters themselves. Advances in these technologies does not only complement conventional language maintenance activities but can also revise them to include engagement with endangered languages' heritage speakers in the diaspora.

This chapter demonstrates how training in new technologies delivered to the Nubian diaspora by the SOAS (School of Oriental and African Studies, University of London) World Languages Institute and the Nubian Languages and Culture Project can promote multilingualism through heritage language learning. It also discusses how the creation of a new social space permits the language learning to be put to practical use. Using new technology which is financially viable is discussed in relation to language learning through exposure and guided description in language documentation. New social spaces are created which also connect heritage language learners in the diaspora with the communities of speakers in Nubia (Sudan and Egypt). These initiatives can be a model for promoting the vitality of heritage languages for other communities of speakers in situ and in the diaspora, while at the same time contributing to the maintenance and promotion of multilingualism. This chapter shows how digital communication in the form of mobile language documentation can contribute to the use and vitality of African languages.

Mobile Technology and Mlearning

Devices such as mobile smartphones and tablets are enabling users in the Global South access to technology-enhanced education which desktop computers in various ways were unable to (UNESCO, 2013). The use of these devices as learner-centred has given rise to the term 'mlearning'.

This is where learning takes place 'across multiple contexts, through social and content interactions, using personal electronic devices' (Crompton, 2013: 4). Theories of mlearning discuss how the spatial and temporal dynamic nature of mlearning means that it is the learners who are mobile rather than the technology, which promotes a learning environment which is anytime, anywhere (Shuler, 2009). A tentative definition of mlearning is given by Sharples *et al.* (2010: 91) as 'the processes of coming to know through conversations across multiple contexts among people and personal interactive technologies.' It is this 'coming to know through conversations' which is at the heart of mlearning, thereby, learning becomes implicit. Conversation and collaborative knowledge building are some of the fundamental processes by which we all come to understand the world (Sharples, 2009).

While some scholars see mlearning as an extension of elearning (Kadirire, 2009), mlearning is differentiated from elearning by various criteria such as in mlearning the content is user-generated and there are learning schedule differences. Furthermore, elearners have set schedules when learning takes place whereas mlearners can determine their own learning schedules; it is learning on the go. The interactive nature of mlearning is the major factor which makes mlearning distinct from elearning practices which are mostly unidirectional and where there is a minimal social learning dimension.

It is not just interactivity that makes mlearning distinct from elearning, but also the technology in which it is delivered. In developing countries such as many on the African continent, access to mobile devices has meant that there are multiple benefits of this technology over more standard desktop computers or 'fixed' technologies. Internet access is one of the major benefits of mobile devices as 'fixed-line connectivity failed indigenous peoples, mobile technologies are appropriate to their geographic locations, their socioeconomic circumstances and their cultures' (Dyson, 2016: 2). In many areas across the globe, the physical infrastructure for fixed-line connectivity and landlines, including electricity, is poor or non-existent. This created a situation where many indigenous peoples were left without internet connectivity even if computer hardware was available. As internet connectivity of mobile devices is not dependent upon the physical infrastructure of a country or region, it means that this technology is crucial in allowing internet access for communities who were left behind by fixed-line technologies.

Even if certain people or communities were able to have fixed-line connectivity, the affordability of using this connectivity was in the main cost-prohibitive. Fixed-line connectivity resulted in unpredictable bills, where users had no ability to quantify their usage and therefore to restrict associated costs (Castells *et al.*, 2007), whereas mobile technologies' connectivity can be pre-paid, and does not put users into unexpected financial difficulty. Affordability of the actual devices is another benefit to many who are economically marginalised. Smartphones are more affordable than desktop computers and are becoming increasingly cheaper. In Africa, for example, technology companies are now developing their own smartphone devices which will retail for $30 and which are to be made in Africa (CNN, 2017), making these devices not only more affordable but also more easily repaired.

The rapid advancement and accessibility of these communication technologies has led to them being identified and used as powerful tools for education and in particular language learning and teaching (Chinnery, 2006; Walker & White, 2013), along with transforming teaching and knowledge construction (Ofemile this volume), these technologies can extend language use beyond the traditional boundaries of discrete languages (Leketi, this volume). However, access to mobile technologies does not only mean that these technologies can be utilised for mlearning but also for documentation practices, particularly in the case of endangered language documentation. Aside from affordability and portability, the advantages of using mobile technology in language documentation are manifold. The most obvious advantage is that affordable mobile technology puts the communities of speakers at the centre of documentation. Instead of the documentary linguist(s) being the sole proprietor of the recording technology, the community are now all able to own the documentation technology, such as by owning a smartphone with inbuilt video technology. Every owner of a smartphone is now in a position to be a documentary linguist (which essentially decolonialises the documentation). Ownership of this technology permits a change or combination of roles which were traditionally one where a respondent would only appear in the documentation, now the respondents can also direct the documentation by being the documenter or owner of the video technology. Engagement with mobile technology in this way creates a shared community of documentation practitioners. As computer-based technologies which are used in certain documentation activities (transcription, translation, annotation) often only engaged or included younger members of the community, a move towards using mobiles in documentation ensures that technology is accessible for all members of a community and subsequently increases the demographics of community members who are able to participate in documentation. Many community elders who were not engaged with computer-based technology are now the owners and users of smartphones and are no longer on the edge of engaging with technology or participating in documentation activities.

Mobile technology also enhances a community's ability to share the recordings whether for promoting social interactivity or for archiving and development of these materials. With this technology users do not need sophisticated equipment or skills in which to share or transfer their recordings, whether they are uploading them to Web 2.0 platforms like YouTube, Facebook or sharing them within their own networks such as

WhatsApp. Mobile technology makes flash-drives, memory cards, disks etc. redundant to transfer data as platforms or apps can and are being developed to do this. This also increases the affordability of language documentation for the community as documenters. As mobile phones are no longer devices used to just communicate, but have in-built functionalities such as audio and video recorders, their use in documentation permits communities which are predominantly oral and those which lack an orthography, or an accepted standardised orthography such as Nubian, a huge advantage in accessible recording equipment. GPS is also enabled on most smartphones, which means that the place where the documentation is recorded can be specified more accurately. This is particularly helpful for documentation projects which take place in remote regions, as is usual in endangered language documentation work. Perhaps most importantly, access to these technologies allows small linguistic communities 'to take their virtual places alongside all the peoples of the world and to preserve their languages as expressions of modernity' (Alexander, 2006: 8).

Engagement with and research into the use of mobile technology for language documentation is still in a nascent stage, although certain projects across the globe have been quick to utilise this technology. Indigenous-led innovations in using mobile technologies have been pioneered by the First Peoples Cultural Council in Canada for documenting, learning and teaching heritage languages (Brand et al., 2016). This project has developed mobile dictionaries, phrase books and language learning lessons, along with a texting app for typing in over 100 indigenous languages of Canada, USA, Australia and New Zealand. Connecting elders with the younger community members in a project on the transmission of sacred botanical knowledge is active in the Penan community in Malaysia by using tablet PCs (Zaman et al., 2016).

Documentary linguistics is also engaging with these advances in access to mobile technology by research and development into mobile apps that support a range of documentation activities (Bettinson & Bird, 2017). While these apps are mostly still in the development stages, it is notable that these will permit more usability by the communities of speakers than previous digital tools which often required specialist training, and access to fixed-line or unaffordable computers. Documentation projects which feature mobile recording show that indigenous communities can progressively rely less on the documentary linguist to conduct the documentation as the linguist is no longer the sole proprietor of the technology for recording the language (Bird et al., 2014). While mobile phone technology is sometimes evidenced as being directly responsible for an accelerated decline in an endangered language's use, this technology can at the same time permit a community to be more connected through accessing a common language of communication (Temple, 2016).

In the main, projects which are currently fully utilising mobile technology in language documentation show that this mdocumentation can be used to inform mlearning development into language learning and teaching and language maintenance activities. Mdocumentation practices appear to be suitable to fulfil reusability, as previously pointed out by Bird and Simons (2003: 558) '[i]f digital language documentation and description should transcend time, they should also be reusable in other respects: across different software and hardware platforms, across different scholarly communities (e.g. field linguistics, language pedagogy, language technology), and across different purposes (e.g. research, teaching, development).'

Importantly, utilising mdocumentation connects indigenous speakers with heritage language learners in the diaspora. In the case of communities where many have been forced to migrate, whether internally and/or externally, and have left many family members, more often the elderly members of the community, residing in their ancestral lands, mobile technology has permitted long-distance and affordable communication and connectivity with those in the diaspora. Research is currently needed on the extent to which mobile technology helps maintain ancestral languages spoken in the diaspora, as certainly this is the creation of a new domain. Domains are understood as the context in which languages are spoken; these can be the home, work, school, market-places, etc., or domains can indicate different situations or content, such as one language is spoken when talking about sport whereas another when talking about community issues. Therefore, sport and community issues are both domains. For example, by using apps and platforms (Whatsapp, Facetime, Lime etc.) whereby users can make audio or video calls for free, we find that this increases connectivity between separated communities of speakers. This surely leads to more usage of any specific endangered language, if the language is used in this domain (audio/video calls). Documentation which utilises mobile technology can also be appropriate if it increases an endangered language's use, albeit in a different or novel domain.

Mobile technology creates a 'levelling' of access and ownership of technology between those in the Global South and those outside. Communities of speakers wherever they reside, be it in ancestral lands or in the diaspora, all now possess the same technology. This means that documentation activities which are conducted with mobile technology easily permit a lateral sharing of materials between separated and scattered communities of speakers. This is something that was not possible with previous documentation technologies and is a further benefit of recent innovations in technology and connectivity.

This levelling of access and lateral sharing permitted by mobile technology is discussed in this chapter in relation to how documentation practices engages heritage language learners. This practice at the same time promotes multilingualism. The following sections detail an mdocumentation project working with the Nubian community who are speakers of an endangered language and their heritage language learners in the UK diaspora. It is proposed here that mdocumentation should be considered as a form of mlearning whereby the 'anytime, anywhere' principle also applies, and most importantly, it is this core principle which promotes multilingualism and/or the vitality of African languages.

Nubia and Nubian

Nubia is an ancient civilisation which is situated between the first cataract of the river Nile in Egypt to a less defined boundary in the north of the Republic of Sudan, typically considered as the fourth cataract. Nubia has a rich and extensive archaeological heritage and possesses one of the oldest writing systems in Africa. Nubian is a collective term for speakers of a group of related languages (East Sudanic, Nilo-Saharan) that are spoken in the predominantly Arabic-speaking countries of Egypt and the Republic of Sudan. Nubian languages can be classified into two broad categories of Nile Nubian (Nobiin, Andaandi and Kenuz) or non-Nile Nubian (Haraza, Birgid, Hill Nubian and Meidob). While the non-Nile Nubian languages are encountering severe endangerment (Bell, 1975; Simons & Fennig, 2017), the Nile Nubian languages are also under immediate threat, as both groups of languages are experiencing a shift towards Arabic. Traditionally, approximations of speaker numbers are used as one of the major criteria for assessing the extent of a language's endangerment.

However, estimating speaker numbers is challenged and complicated by the multilingual environment. Older Nobiin Nubian speakers in Nubia and those that are internally displaced or have migrated to other areas and countries for socioeconomic reasons, and in the diaspora are predominantly bi- and multilingual. Different Nubian languages (Kenuz, Andaandi and Nobiin), Arabic, English, French, etc. can all belong to the linguistic repertoire of Nubian speakers. The context of what language is spoken when is integral to understanding the Nubian language ecology and informing the extent of Nubian language shift. The personal communications of multilinguals utilise alternate languages whether they are spoken or written, used in the home or socialising, at work or in business, education, commerce, or administration. The language ecology of Nubia obscures quantifying definitive speaker numbers. The criterion of absolute speaker numbers and their proportion in the local population are proposed as 'irrelevant or inapplicable' for assessing an African language's vitality (Lüpke, 2015: 76). However, anecdotal evidence indicates a shift towards monolingualism is taking place among the younger generation of Nubians in Nubia (Arabic) and amongst Nubian heritage speakers in the diaspora (English in the UK and US, Dutch in Holland etc.).

Many Nubians have migrated to other countries for economic reasons as their agricultural practices can no longer be sustained with so much disruption and destruction of their lands due to dam construction. This migration has created large communities of Nubians in the diaspora, not only in the Middle East, but also in Europe and the US. This migration pattern is set to increase with more projected dam building programmes and the Nubian community are highly aware of the detrimental impact this has had on the vitality of their languages and culture (Bonta, 2018). The dam building has prompted the Nubian community in Sudan and Egypt and in the diaspora to actively initiate safeguarding practices towards the continuity of their intangible heritage and languages through setting up Nubian cultural centres, social clubs and associations. These are spaces created to support the continuity of the Nubian languages and culture and to maintain community connections with those outside of Nubia and those within. As more sites within Nubia are being confirmed as areas for future dam construction, the Nubian community are increasingly seeking more ways in which to protect their languages and culture. One such community initiative has been the organisation of a Nubian cultural festival which runs in Khartoum and in Nubia. This is a showcasing event of Nubian crafts, music, literature, dance, discussions and workshops which helps to 'strengthen the social bonds between Nubians throughout Sudan and Egypt [and to] reinforce and develop cultural ties' (The First Nubian Culture and Tourism Festival 2012 brochure).

Community-driven Initiatives

One of the major ways that the Nubian community are actively initiating safeguarding measures is through the use of technology, in particular mobile technologies. Through online platforms, Nubians are sharing images of their architecture, lifestyle, foods, craft-practices and anything else which typifies their culture. For their language, Nubians are recording and uploading language instruction classes, songs, music, poetry and proverbs onto various web-based platforms. Recently, a successful language learning app has been developed (The Nubia Initiative) for Nubian which has been downloaded thousands of times.

These community-driven initiatives are also taking place in the Nubian diaspora. Many of the younger generation of Nubian community members are also actively utilising this same technology and methods which assists them with acquiring proficiency in Nubian along with gaining familiarity of their cultural practices. These second and third generations of Nubian community members can be defined as heritage language learners.

Technology and Heritage Language Learning

A heritage language can be defined as an ancestral language which individual(s) feel a cultural connection with (Van Deusen-Scholl, 2003) and which can refer to the languages other than the dominant language(s) in a given social context. For example, English is the dominant language in the UK, therefore any other language aside from English can be defined as a heritage language for speakers or community members of that other language. Identity, language and family background are proposed as being integral in assessments of defining who constitutes as a heritage language learner (Carreira, 2004), although a heritage language is not a 'foreign language'; as Kelleher (2010: 1) points out, as a heritage language learner has distinct needs from a second language learner (Montrul, 2015), which are shaped by their linguistic experience. It should be borne in mind that heritage languages should not be assumed to be tied to some defined geographical place (Canagarajah, 2013; Tan, 2017), but can have multiple points of origin (Tan, 2017).

In formal teaching practices of heritage languages, the use of technology is now a familiar and beneficial tool (Henshaw, 2016). The advantages of incorporating technology in heritage language learning and teaching range from an expanded access to resources to learners' being self-directed and self-selecting of these resources. The utilised technology encompasses various forms. Online publishing such as blogging creates a strengthened connection to the cultural heritage of learners (Lee, 2011), and social media allows learners to connect with other learners or speakers, and create their own interest pages. Social media can also promote electronic literacy in the heritage language. Synchronous communication is also another form in which technology assists with heritage language learning. Conversation practice can be performed in real-time with native speakers over various targeted platforms, or through affordable, usually free apps such as WhatsApp or Skype. Online technologies are highly constructive for heritage language learning as they support the fostering of collaborations with learners across the diaspora. Ranging from pure online learning to more blended learning environments, which combine these technologies with perhaps more traditional pedagogic techniques, technology has permitted heritage learners more autonomy and access than prior to their availability. Evidence shows that heritage language learners' skills and intrinsic motivation are enhanced through the use of online technologies (Szecsi & Szilagyi, 2012).

Through the utilisation of these technologies, heritage language learners can now experience a transformation in the transmission of knowledge. The previously unidirectional approach to the transmission of knowledge has now had a paradigm shift to a more collaborative, independent and constructive approach. However, presently in the UK, there is no formal provision for teaching or learning Nubian nor for the many other heritage languages, whether purely online, blended or traditionally taught. Given that London in particular is identified as one of the major multilingual cities in the world, it appears that educational maintenance of multilingualism in heritage speakers is somewhat neglected. This situation has necessitated the Nubian community in the diaspora to investigate and implement their own suitable ways of promoting their heritage language in their heritage speakers, and as a way of ensuring the vitality of their heritage language in the diaspora. Recognising this need in discussions with the Sudanese Nubian Association UK, the author, who is engaged in Nubian language documentation, considered this documentation which utilises technology could be enhanced by directly involving the Nubian diaspora community in its collection, which at the same time would develop a new social space in which the language could be used by the heritage speakers. Furthermore, this practice would allow an increased opportunity for the heritage learner's exposure to the language and the development of more technological skills.

In particular, it was identified that this type of documentation needs to be driven not by the elders through their concerns of safeguarding their rapidly disappearing languages and culture, but by the younger and young members of the Nubian community. As the vitality of Nubian is in their hands, they need to take ownership of this safeguarding. The importance of centring younger members in language vitality activities is that '[y]oung people play pivotal roles in shaping the most dramatic sociolinguistic phenomena of our times, including the global consumption and employment of new technologies, the negotiation of language practices in immigration and the spread of new cultural forms' (Wyman, 2012: 1). As the heritage language learners are the younger generation, positioning them as integral in any activity which seeks to support language vitality and promote multilingualism is critical and necessary. This was the impetus for supporting the UK Nubian community's call for assistance through training them in mdocumentation activities. This support also built upon the observed practice within the Nubian diasporic community of using technology to maintain their culture. Nubians actively share, upload and discuss aspects of their threatened culture and practices in online forums and social media platforms. Their self-directed initiative and familiarisation with these forms of technology could be adapted to support the maintenance of their languages also. The theory underpinning this training is from mlearning whereby the learners 'come to know through conversations'.

The Study

Members of the Sudanese Nubian Association UK (SNAUK) and their youth members were invited to SOAS, University of London by the Nubian Languages and Culture Project (www.nubianlanguagesandculture.org) and SOAS World Languages Institute for a weekend of training in endangered language documentation in April 2016. The training was made financially accessible particularly for the Nubian youth members as it was delivered without any charge, with the instructors volunteering their time for free in order to prepare and deliver this training. In preparation for delivering the training, the instructors met with members of the SNAUK to find out what their expectations were for the training, and to discuss how they had an integral role in the successful delivery and continuity of the documentation training with their youth members. Suitable dates were agreed between all parties to ensure the maximum number of community members could attend. This was important because the Nubian diaspora in the UK are not particularly concentrated in London but reside in other towns such as Manchester and Reading, and in other counties. The SNAUK are in touch with approximately 600 Nubian families residing in the UK. The attendance for the training numbered 20 members with half of these being the youth members (or heritage language learners). The training was specifically tailored to suit the needs of this cohort whereby the heritage language learners who are mainly monolingual in English were paired with older Nubian community members who are mostly multilingual (English, Arabic and Nubian).

The training started with an introduction to the importance of documenting endangered languages and how this can support heritage language learning in the diaspora and in the ancestral lands. Moving on from this short introduction, training in effective and essential record-keeping of the documentation through metadata was also delivered to the participants. They were shown what types of data (metadata) about the recordings are needed to record structured information that describes each piece of documentation. The importance of metadata is that it enables the documentation to be found and used (Bird & Simons, 2003). Participants were given examples of a metadata sheet that they can fill in or record that details information about the speakers. This metadata can be divided into three broad categories: (1) cataloguing – such as name, age, place of birth, gender, languages/dialects spoken (level of fluency), length of residence in non-birth country, attitudes to the heritage language, identity of the documenter etc. Participants were also shown how to record metadata about the documentation itself (2) which describes the documentation such as the interview session, date and place of recording, description about the topic documented or content genre (discourse, elicitation, explanation, folktale, narrative, interview, religious/ritual, song, speech, wordlist etc.). An important factor in the metadata is also recording which languages are used in the documentation. This permits a contribution to discovering more about the multilingualism of the Nubian speakers, and (3) administration metadata is recorded such as agreements for archiving, distribution and sharing.

Participants also explored the fundamental ethical principles that should be followed in language documentation (Dwyer, 2006) and considered how these relate to Nubian in particular. The Nubian community in the diaspora and in Nubia are all too aware of how their actions towards safeguarding their heritage can compromise their personal safety. Nubian protests about further dam building programmes and the right to return to ancestral lands have resulted in arrests and detentions in Egypt

(Middle East Monitor, 2017), and in Sudan, protests about the dams and the torching and destruction of Nubian palm groves (their main cash crop) have not only led to detentions but also to the deaths of activists (The Guardian, 2014). Documentation which makes public any recordings which may relate to the political situation of Nubians and Nubia could result in endangering the participants' personal safety. This is a very serious situation and one which was explored thoroughly in the training session on ethics. As the Nubian language community are in a politically volatile position, if documentation is recorded which is politically sensitive and could cause them to be identified and thus targeted in some way, then an informed decision has to be taken on anonymising the data and recording or restricting the sharing of this documentation. This means that an agreement needs to be sought on what type of documentation is conducted (photographic/audio/video/notes) and on what access restrictions should be applied. These agreements should not just be sought through political sensitivity of the documentation but also based upon the participants own attitudes towards being recorded in any way, such as shyness. Therefore, the participants of the training understood the importance of obtaining informed consent, whether this is through a verbal agreement, which could be recorded, or through written agreements.

The participants were given suggestions for eliciting different types of genres and how to structure their documentation sessions. We then came to the major part of the training which was using mobile technology for language documentation. All participants had their own personal smartphone, and other equipment was provided for them to use such as tablets and iPads, along with conventional video camera recording equipment. Affordable additional technology and equipment was discussed such as the app 'Filmic Pro' which is available for under £10. This app allows smartphones to be used as a professional video camera. This app also has an upload button whereby the recordings can be directly sent to an email account. This means that the memory on the smartphone does not get overloaded as documenters can email the video as soon as it is recorded and then delete the video from their phone. Necessary affordable equipment to stabilise any camera-shake and movement such as tripods and 'gorilla-pod' stands were shown as being paramount for enhancing any video recordings from hand-held devices. The importance of audio clarity was stressed, and it was explained how there are effective strategies and equipment that can ensure that recorded sound is clear. Many cheap and affordable microphones can be bought to enhance the sound quality of documentation and differences in these microphones was also discussed (omnidirectional etc.). Participants were reminded of other issues which may affect sound quality such as the wind, and extraneous noise (traffic, animals etc.), and strategies were presented which would help to reduce their affects (windshields on microphones, remembering to eliminate these at source or using free online noise removal tools).

Issues such as ensuring that all video documentation is recorded in the landscape feature were discussed, as all screens (monitors, computers, TVs) are viewed in widescreen, video should not be recorded vertically (even though most smartphones can record using both features). Positioning of the smartphone for effective recording in relation to the sun or light sources was also overviewed. Additionally, image quality of videos was discussed in relation to clip-on lenses for mobiles, which were shown only to be relevant if more wide-angle recording is needed. Finally, participants were reminded that having a back-up power source such as power-banks are always important.

The goals of the recordings were discussed as a group. The community led these discussions and agreed that the elder members should give reflections on various ways of life in Nubia. These would not only be informative for the younger members but would bring out the rich descriptions in the language and terms which were barely used anymore. For instance, one theme on life in Nubia that was selected was on the traditional waterwheel. These wooden, oxen-driven wheels have all but now disappeared on the Nile, but the older community members still remembered the terminology connected to them, how and who constructed them, why they were crucial to the community, along with their associated songs and proverbs. These themes were also opportunities for oral history to be recorded. One participant declared: 'I want my children to know about Nubia, and to speak Nubian. It makes me sad to talk about all the great things we had and now they are disappearing. If I talk about these things, they stay alive.'

Youth members were then paired with the elder community members and spaces were allocated to each group where they could conduct their recordings. These teams of documenters each mutually decided themes that they wanted to record, and over the next few hours, recording sessions took place. The coordinators were on-hand to deliver advice and suggestions and to note how the sessions were progressing. Some teams needed reminders about issues that affect the video image quality such as lighting, as they had the sun directly in front of the mobile camera. Other teams needed advice on capturing the full interactive environment. For instance, some teams focused on videoing the speakers with just their head and shoulders in view. They were advised that they needed to also capture the gestures used by the speakers as these carry metalinguistic information, and so this is to be kept in mind when positioning the mobile camera. Video documentation allows a record of the language as it is actually spoken which means that the accompanying unique gestures and actions, which are missing from dictionaries and grammars, need to also be captured.

Once these sessions were finished, we all convened to discuss any issues that arose and feedback the experience including problems and successes in the documentation. We also viewed a sample of the recordings to comment on what worked well or not so well, although overall this initial videoing session was a great success. For instance, some of the native Nubian speakers commented that they had learnt specific Nubian vocabulary from the videoing sessions and others had encountered vocabulary that they had forgotten.

Participants were then shown how to use freely available software, such as WeTransfer, which would allow their recordings to be shared with one of the project team members who would collate and coordinate the documentation. Their video, audio or photographic files could be easily copied and transferred which meant that they could free up their mobile phone memory if necessary. The participants were also the proprietors of this documentation and respecting any access restrictions, they are able to also use the documentation for their own projects, learning, sharing or adaptation. For example, one member is a student at university and wanted to document proverbs as a way of investigating how Nubians conceptualise their worldview through the use of proverbs or wisdom sayings for a university project.

The project coordinator ensures that there is a central repository and sustainability of the documentation which is a crucial factor. Documentation from the project is being deposited in the Endangered Languages Archive (ELAR) at SOAS. This archive is a searchable digital repository of multimedia collections which are free to access. This archive can be accessed by all after registering, although certain materials can be restricted according to the wishes of the documenters and/or the originating speakers and communities. The materials collected have sustainability as they are bound to the lifetime of the institution (SOAS) and so the archive provides a secure and long-term repository for documentation collections. Deposits can be accessed from anywhere which enables communities, speakers and researchers to view the collections without any associated costs. Housing the Nubian documentation in the Endangered Languages Archive means that the materials are easily deposited, accessible and usable not only for scholars but importantly for the community in Nubia and the diaspora. This enables access to the language and the culture of the Nubians, and so can be used for teaching and learning of Nubian heritage.

The participants agreed that they would apply this documentation outside of the training by setting up documentation sessions with the elder members in other spaces such as Association events, meetings and scheduled home sessions. These youth members could also take this training and inform other members such as friends and family on the requirements for effective documentation.

Results

The success of the training was measured in various ways. A primary measure was the feedback received by the attendees, captured by the

Chairman of the Sudanese Association UK 'May I take this opportunity to appreciate the effort you both made to enhance our role to preserve our heritage and language'. All participants recognised the value in performing and conducting the documentation, not only as support towards the maintenance of Nubian but also for the collection of materials that can be utilised for teaching and learning their heritage language. This was captured in the feedback from the head of the Nubian Youth members who stated 'thanks so much for the event today – it was really informative and inspirational, and I'm so excited to see where the project will go from here!'. This documentation was seen as especially relevant for them in the continuation of the Nubian languages, as they are creating a source of authentic and culturally relevant materials which Nubian teachers can utilise in their classes on Nubian language learning while at the same time showcasing aspects of the intangible heritage. They recognised that in order to safeguard their languages and intangible heritage it needs to be continuously performed which in turn facilitates intergenerational transmission, which documentation is able to contribute towards. Subsequently, not only the collection but the distribution prompts the community to recognise and continue their linguistic, cultural and social practices.

Accessible technology

The training was noted as effective in delivering the skills and knowledge needed by the community in using affordable and usable technology. One member who spoke for the group, told us 'this is really great. We know we can do this now. We do not have to rely on anyone else. Now, my children will learn my language.' Before attending the training, participants believed that to do effective recording, they needed particular and costly equipment, however, after completing the training they are now aware that smartphones and tablets are accessible, suitable and economically viable technologies in which to do documentation. Building a central repository for the compilation of these recordings was another concern that the participants had prior to the training. Even though they know how to record and share Nubian materials online through their social networks, they were concerned that there was no effective way of bringing these resources together. The participants agreed that it was important that the process of selection and collection of the documentation was in the hands of the community. Feedback was also received on how video recordings can increase the valorisation that Nubians (and other communities) attach to their languages and culture, particularly aspects which are taken for granted or considered mundane. This was captured in the following feedback: 'I thought everybody knows the kissar [Nubian traditional instrument], now they will see what wonderful musicians we are'; Not only is visible access to aspects of their culture and heritage as it is performed available, but documentation ensures it has a central role in assisting with its continuation as it requires the performance of the cultural and linguistic expressions to be enacted.

Dr Geili of the SNUK on the left preparing to be interviewed

Determining the documentation

Other successes of the training were measured by how the participants were able to initiate their own topic areas for documentation, such as how some of the youth members are now running a documentation project collecting Nubian proverbs and wisdom sayings and how these reflect the peaceable society of the Nubians (Encyclopedia of Peaceful Societies, 2018). Other topic areas that are currently being documented are human rights in relation to the Nubians experience of forced displacement and the Egyptian and Sudanese subsequent allocation of substandard housing for these communities. Another success of this training is that the documentation is being shared and used on social networks. The recordings from the day and our instructions were distributed on platforms such as Facebook and Whatsapp, thereby reaching a bigger audience. This widens the accessibility of documentation which can be adapted, used and developed for Nubian language teaching and learning materials which highlight the sociocultural context.

A new social space

Fundamentally, the training enabled the creation of a new social space (an 'affinity space' following Ogbay and White this volume) in which Nubian heritage language learners could have exposure to the language of their elders. Further, traditional discourse contexts are adapted to create new social relationships and interactional spaces among community members with the heritage language learners. As the recorded Nubian genres were also described in Arabic and English, this permits the youth documenters as heritage language learners to develop real-time engagement with the content of the documentation and familiarity with the sounds and structure of the Nubian language. This was evidenced in the feedback from one younger attendee 'I can hear the rhythm of my parents' language [Nubian] now.' At the same time, this mdocumentation permits the sharing of indigenous cultural knowledge, where the context of words is retained including any gestural information. Foregrounding genres in mdocumenation situates the exposure to the language in its sociocultural context, rather than through formal methods which follow a grammar and dictionary-based approach. Genres link languages and culture.

Contribution to other documentation practices

The materials gathered can also contribute to other new technologies that are also being used to develop additional packages that can promote multilingualism and assist with endangered language maintenance such as mobile apps. For the Nubian language, the newly developed 'Nubi' app was developed by a young Nubian who wanted to preserve and help maintain the ancestral language. Lessons in Nubian are offered along with historical facts, stories and photos from old Nubia. The app also includes links to Nubian songs and proverbs, and books written by Nubian authors. Within the first few months of the app's launch, it was downloaded over 13,000 times by users in Sudan, Egypt and the diaspora (Egypt Independent, 2017). The development of these additional technologies which run on smartphones or mobiles complements the implementation of documentation practices which focus on mdocumentation activities. Now, any community member with a smartphone can become a potential creator of content that can be used to support multilingualism.

Connecting the diaspora

As there are new social spaces being created by the Nubian community in Nubia, where there are now available and prepared arenas in which the documentation can also be distributed, such as language learning classes, Nubian cultural festivals, and Nubian cultural centres, along with smartphone owners in Nubia itself. I was able to take recordings of this documentation out to Nubia in February 2018 to show them during a formal class in Nubian language learning. These recordings helped these students connect with the stories of Nubians in the diaspora. This documentation has the possibility to increase valorisation of the languages and culture by more members of the community who may not in themselves be participating in the mdocumentation but are instead audience to the materials in some of these various new social spaces.

Intergenerational interaction

The participation in the training event and its subsequent mdocumentation by Nubian youth members has also shown to be similar to other youth movements who are reversing language shift by moving into positions of agency (Wyman *et al.*, 2014). There is increasing evidence which shows that many younger generations of heritage learners want to speak their heritage languages (Lee, 2014). New language learning opportunities are now available to the Nubian heritage learners who are able to interact with elder speakers. The documentation promotes intergenerational interaction by members of the community in the language learning. The setting in which the documentation takes place can also assist with raising levels of confidence for language learners with the creation of a safe space, i.e. outside of a traditional educational classroom language learners' confidence can be improved.

An important factor in engaging heritage language learners with mdocumentation of their heritage language is that it promotes multilingualism. In the diaspora, where many heritage language learners may only be monolingual in the dominant languages of other countries, documentation permits an engagement with the language ecology of the ancestral lands of Nubia, which is itself multilingual, while at the same time contributing to activities which seek to safeguard the language and intangible heritage of a community under threat.

Mdocumentation as mlearning

Fundamentally, the mdocumentation practices should mirror the theoretical approach of mlearning whereby it is the documenter which becomes mobile through the use of mobile technology, and as such the documenter is also the learner. A focus on the mobility of the documenter/learner permits the beyond boundaries approach of anytime, anywhere capturing and accessible to the diasporic and in situ communities of speakers. In this way, mdocumentation, just like mlearning, should be seen in a sociocultural perspective with the documentation being a contextually situated social endeavour, directed and developed through social interaction and conversation by a community of speakers. The importance of digital mobile technologies is outlined by Sharples *et al.* (2005: 1) who state that '[t]here is a need to re-conceptualise learning for the mobile age, to recognise the essential role of mobility and communication in the process of learning, and also to indicate the importance of context in establishing meaning, and the transformative effect of digital networks in supporting virtual communities that transcend barriers of age and culture.' If there is a drawing together of mdocumentation practices, as described herein, with mlearning, then the transformative effects of new technologies can be shown to be hugely positive for not only language maintenance but also language learning and therefore multilingualism too.

Concluding Remarks

This chapter has presented a project which engaged community members in the Nubian diaspora by using technology to support their heritage language learning. Previous to the development of smartphones and Web 2.0 technology, engaging community members in documentation was highly problematic. Not only was access to technology, and the necessary training, prohibitive to a community's inclusion in documentation practices, but typically the infrastructure to support these activities was another huge obstacle. However, since this type of technology for recording, whether audio or video, and archiving and distribution (social media) has become highly accessible, documentation can now be placed in the hands of the community. This chapter has outlined how direct and concise training can enable a community to become self-directed and self-selecting in documentation practices. This has a dual benefit for a community. For one, it supports and widens the collection of authentic materials for languages which are currently threatened or endangered, and secondly, it permits heritage language learners in the diaspora to connect with their cultural and linguistic heritage, which can motivate their desire for learning their heritage languages.

These practices also permit a connection between the diaspora community and the heritage community in situ. The importance of technology in this new area of access, endangered language documentation and heritage language learning cannot be overstressed. Linguists can support empowering a community in their own documentation and language learning practices through initiating short, direct and intensive training events, like the one discussed in this chapter. New digital capacities, such as the Endangered Languages Archive at SOAS, also complement the distribution of this documentation through the usual social media platforms by being sustainable and as an open access repository.

This chapter has shown that new technologies are actually empowering communities, wherever they reside, to have locus of control in their own (heritage) language learning and maintenance through mdocumentation as a form of mlearning. Within an African context, digital technologies are not actually accelerating the decline of the multilingual ecology, but in fact, not only do they enhance this ecology but they extend it also - beyond national and continental boundaries with the documenters as learners coming to know through conversations.

There are many areas of further research which are necessary to assess the effectiveness of these practices, although they would need a longitudinal investigation. One of these research areas is the types of documentation being recorded. This would reveal an understanding of what genres are important to a community through an assessment of what is being recorded. This could also uncover an understanding of how a community inventories their cultural and linguistic heritage. For the heritage language learners, an evidence-base needs to be built as to how their multilinguistic skills are being developed through their exposure to the language as they perform the documentation. There are many questions to be asked if linguists and teachers facilitate a sea-change in documentation and learning practices, in which a community has the authority and autonomy in maintaining their language and culture. Conclusively this chapter has shown that new technologies can assign authority and autonomy to communities of speakers in language learning and maintenance. Furthermore, in the capacity of 'anytime, anywhere', these technologies can contribute to promoting the vitality of African languages.

Acknowledgements

I would like to thank Dr Mandana Seyfeddinipur (Director of the Endangered Languages Documentation Programme, and SOAS World Languages Institute, SOAS) for her help and support in preparing and teaching on this documentation training, and Dr Fawzi Saleh of the Sudanese Nubian Association UK, and Basma Osman SNAUK Youth programme for their assistance in organising and contributing to this training event. I would also like to dedicate this paper to the memory of Dr Geili who sadly passed away in 2017 who helped to support the success of this documentation project.

References

Alexander, N. (2006) Communicating in local languages: a prerequisite for community access. Input prepared for the thematic debate 'Giving Voice to Local Communities: From Community Radio to Blogs' in the framework of the fourth session of the Intergovernmental Council for UNESCO's Information for All Programme (IFAP), Paris 22 March 2006.

Ameka, F. (2015) Unintended consequences of methodological and practical responses to language endangerment in Africa. In J. Essegbey, B. Henderson and F. Mc Laughlin (eds) *Language Documentation and Endangerment in Africa* (pp. 1–15). Amsterdam: John Benjamins.

Batibo, H.M. (2005) *Language Decline and Death in Africa: Causes, Consequences and Challenges*. Clevedon: Multilingual Matters.

Batibo, H.M. (2009) Language documentation as a strategy for the empowerment of the minority languages of Africa. In M. Matondo, F. Mc Laughlin and E. Potsdam (eds) *Selected Proceedings of the 38th Annual Conference on African Linguistics: Linguistic Theory and African Language Documentation* (pp. 193–203). Somerville, MA: Cascadilla Proceedings Project.

Bell, H. (1975) Documentary evidence on the Haraza Nubian language. *Sudan Notes and Records*, 1–35.

Bettinson, M. and Bird, S. (2017) Developing a suite of mobile applications for collaborative language documentation. In *Proceedings of the 2nd Workshop on the Use of Computational Methods in the Study of Endangered Languages* (pp. 156–164). Honolulu, Hawai'i, USA, 6–7 March 2017.

Bird, S. and Simons, G. (2003) Seven dimensions of portability for language documentation. *Language* 79 (3), 557–582.

Bird, S., Florian R. H., Oliver A. and Haejoong L.(2014) Aikuma: A Mobile App for Collaborative Language Documentation. Workshop on the Use of Computational Methods in the Study of Endangered Languages, Baltimore, USA, 1–5.

Bonta, B. (2018) Nubians protest big dams in Sudan. Peaceful societies: alternatives to violence and war. See https://cas.uab.edu/peacefulsocieties/2018/06/28/nubians-protest-big-dams-in-sudan/. (accessed on 19 January 2019).

Brand, P., Herbert, T. and Boechler, S. (2016) Language vitalization through mobile and online technologies in British Columbia. In L.H. Dyson, S. Grant and M. Hendriks (eds) *Indigenous People and Mobile Technologies* (pp. 265–273). New York and Abingdon, Oxon: Routledge.

Canagarajah, S. (2013) *Translingual Practice: Global Englishes and Cosmopolitan Relations*. New York and Abingdon, Oxon: Routledge.

Carreira, M. (2004) Seeking explanatory adequacy: A dual approach to understanding the term 'heritage language learner'. *Heritage Language Journal* 2 (1), 1–25.

Castells, M., Fernandez-Ardievol, M., Qiu, J.L. and Sey, A. (2007) *Mobile Communication and Society: A Global Perspective*. Cambridge, MA: MIT Press.

Chinnery, G.M. (2006) Emerging technologies, going to the MALL: Mobile Assisted Language Learning. *Language Learning and Technology* 10, 9–16.

CNN (2017) Is Africa's $30 smartphone a game changer? [Online]. See: https://edition. cnn.com/2017/05/05/tech/africa-30-smartphone/index.html

Crompton, H. (2013) A historical overview of mobile learning: Toward learner-centered education. In Z.L. Berge and L.Y. Muilenburg (eds) *Handbook of Mobile Learning* (pp. 3–14). Abingdon: Routledge.

Dwyer, A.M. (2006) Ethics and practicalities of cooperative fieldwork and analysis. In J. Gippert, N.P. Himmelman and U. Mosel (eds) *Essentials of Language Documentation* (pp. 67–86). Berlin/New York: Mouton de Gruyter.

Dyson, L.E. (2016) Framing the indigenous mobile revolution. In L.E. Dyson, S. Grant and M. Hendriks (eds) *Indigenous People and Mobile Technologies* (pp. 1–21). New York and Abingdon, Oxon: Routledge.

Egypt Independent (2017) Nubi app aims to protect heritage, preserve traditional languages [Online]. See http://www.egyptindependent.com/nubi-app-aims-protect-heritage-preserve-traditional-language/

Encyclopedia of Peaceful Societies (2018) [Accessed online] See https://cas.uab.edu/ peacefulsocieties/societies/ Department of Anthropology, College of Arts and Sciences, University of Alabama at Birmingham.

Essegbey, J., Henderson, B. and Mc Laughlin, F. (eds) (2015) *Language Documentation and Endangerment in Africa*. Amsterdam: John Benjamins.

Henshaw, F. (2016) Technology-enhanced heritage language instruction: Best tools and best practices. In M. Fairclough and S.M. Beaudrie (eds) *Innovative Strategies for Heritage Language Teaching* (pp. 237–254). Washington, DC: Georgetown University Press.

Kadirire, J. (2009) Mobile learning demystified. In R. Guy (ed.) *The Evolution of Mobile Teaching and Learning*. Santa Rosa, CA: Informing Science Press.

Kelleher, A. (2010) 'What is a heritage language? *Heritage Briefs*. Center for Applied Linguistics. See http://www.cal.org/heritage/pdfs/briefs/What-is-a-Heritage-Language.pdf

Lee, L. (2011) Blogging: Promoting learner autonomy and intercultural competence through study abroad. *Language Learning and Technology* 15 (3), 87–109. See http:// llt.msu.edu/ issues/october2011/lee.pdf

Lee, T.S. (2014) Critical language awareness among native youth in New Mexico. In L.T. Wyman, T.L. McCarty and S.E. Nicholas (eds) *Indigenous Youth and Multilingualism: Language, Identity, Ideology, and Practice in Dynamic Cultural Worlds* (pp. 130–148). New York: Routledge.

Lüpke, F. (2015) Ideologies and typologies of language endangerment in Africa. In J. Essegbey, B. Henderson and F. Mc Laughlin (eds) *Language Documentation and Endangerment in Africa* (pp. 59–105). Amsterdam/Philadelphia: John Benjamins.

Middle East Monitor (2017) 24 Nubian activists arrested during protest in Egypt. [Online]. See https://www.middleeastmonitor.com/20170906-24-nubian-activists-arrested-during-protest-in-egypt/ [accessed 7 March 2018]

Migge, B. and Léglise, I. (2012) *Exploring Language in a Multilingual Context: Variation, Interaction and Ideology in Language Documentation*. Cambridge: Cambridge University Press.

Montrul, S. (2015) *The Acquisition of Heritage Languages*. Cambridge: Cambridge University Press.

Mufwene, S.S. (2004) Language birth and death. *Annual Review of Anthropology* 33, 201–222. doi: 10.1146/annurev.anthro.33.070203.143852.

Mufwene, S.S. (2006) Language endangerment: An embarrassment for linguistics. In J. Bunting, S. Desai, R. Peachey, C. Straughn and Z. Tomková (eds) *CLFS 42: The Panels, 2006* (pp. 111–140). Proceedings from the Parasessions of the Forty-second Meeting of the Chicago Linguistic Society: Volume 42-2. Chicago Linguistic Society.

Seyfeddinipur, M. (ed.) (2016) *African Language Documentation: New Data, Methods and Approaches*, Special Publication No. 10 of Language Documentation & Conservation. University of Hawai'i Press. http://hdl.handle.net/10125/24648.

Seyfeddinipur, M. and Chambers, M. (2016) Language documentation in Africa: turning tables. In M. Seyfeddinipur (ed.) *African Language Documentation: New Data, Methods and Approaches* (pp. 1–7). Special Publication No. 10 of Language Documentation & Conservation. University of Hawai'i Press. See http://hdl.handle.net/10125/24648

Sharples, M., Arnedillo-Sanchez, I., Milrad, M. and Vavoula, G. (2009) Mobile learning: Small devices, big issues. In N. Balacheff, S. Ludvigsen, T. Jong, A. Lazonder and S. Barnes (eds) *Technology-Enhanced Learning* (pp. 233–249). Dordrecht: Springer Netherlands. doi:10.1007/978-1-4020-9827-7.

Sharples, M., Taylor, J. and Vavoula, G. (2005) Towards a theory of mobile learning. University of Birmingham, UK.

Sharples, M., Taylor, J. and Vavoula, G. (2010) A theory of learning for the mobile age. In B. Bachmair (ed.) *Medienbildung in Neuen Kulturräumen*. VS Verlag für Sozialwissenschaften.

Shuler, C. (2009) Pockets of potential: Using mobile technologies to promote children's learning. New York: The Joan Ganz Cooney Center at Sesame Workshop.

Simons, G.F. and Fennig, C.D. (eds) (2017) *Ethnologue: Languages of the World, Twentieth Edition*. Dallas, TX: SIL International. Online version: http://www.eth-nologue.com.

Szecsi, T. and Szilagyi, J. (2012) Immigrant Hungarian families' perceptions of new media technologies in the transmission of heritage language and culture. *Language, Culture and Curriculum* 25 (3), 265–281. doi: 10.1080/07908318.2012.722105.

Tan, E.K. (2017) A Rhizomatic account of heritage language: The case of Chinese in Singapore. In S. Canagarajah (ed.) *The Routledge Handbook of Migration and Language* (pp. 468–485). New York: Routledge.

Temple, O. (2016) The influence of mobile phones on the languages and cultures of Papua New Guinea. In L.H. Dyson, S. Grant and M. Hendriks (eds) *Indigenous People and Mobile Technologies* (pp. 274–292). New York and Abingdon, Oxon: Routledge.

The Guardian (2014) 'Sudan's anti-dam movement fights the flooding of Nubian culture' [Online]. See https://www.theguardian.com/world/2014/dec/12/sudans-anti-dam-movement-fights-the-flooding-of-nubian-culture (see 7 March 2018).

UNESCO (2013) *The Future of Mobile Learning: Implications for Policy Makers and Planners.* United Nations Educational, Scientific and Cultural Organization, Paris, France. See http://unesdoc.unesco.org/images/0021/002196/219637E.pdf

Van Deusen-Scholl, N. (2003) Toward a definition of heritage language: Sociopolitical and pedagogical considerations. *Journal of Language, Identity and Education* 2–3, 211–230.

Walker, A. and White, G. (2013) *Technology Enhanced Language Learning: Connecting Theory and Practice.* Oxford: Oxford University Press.

Wyman, L. (2012) *Youth Culture, Language Endangerment and Linguistic Survivance.* Bristol: Multilingual Matters.

Wyman, L.T., McCarty, T.L. and Nicholas, S.E. (eds) (2014) *Indigenous Youth and Multilingualism: Language, Identity, Ideology, and Practice in Dynamic Cultural Worlds.* New York: Routledge.

Zaman, T., Kulathuramaiyer, N. and Yeo, A.W. (2016) eToro: Appropriating ICTs for the management of Penans' indigenous botanical knowledge. In L.H. Dyson, S. Grant and M. Hendriks (eds) *Indigenous People and Mobile Technologies* (pp. 253–264). New York and Abingdon, Oxon: Routledge.

Part 3

The Effects of Communication Outside Africa

5 A Network of Anger and Hope: An Investigation of Communication on a Feminist Activist Facebook Website, the Network of Eritrean Women (RENEW)

Sarah Ogbay and Goodith White

Digital social networking tools allow individuals who are geographically dispersed and socially disparate to communicate with each other easily and rapidly. In the case of nationals who have left their homeland for economic or political reasons, tools such as Facebook and Paltalk link them to others in the diaspora for purposes of solidarity, comfort and advice as well as social and political action. Such 'digital diasporas' have become a common global phenomenon (Brinkerhoff, 2009; Oiarzabal & Alonso, 2010) and they display complex relationships both with the homeland and the places where migrants have settled, and between recent and earlier migrants (Bernal, 2005; Safran, 1991). In fact, such digital social networks problematise notions of a division between diaspora and homeland, creating shifting and complicated networks of connection which are neither dependent or separate from the geographical territories where members are currently located or those they discuss, including the homeland.

This chapter examines communication between female members of the Eritrean diaspora, on the Facebook site Network of Eritrean Women (NEW), together with an associated Messenger stream called RENEW. The Facebook site itself is reserved for postings by the administrators of a more formal, public nature such as dates for important events and news about Eritrea. The Messenger stream is where dialogue between all members takes place and this will be our main research focus. The chapter discusses how the linguistic affordances and possibilities of the Messenger thread are used by members to promote political and social change for women outside and inside Eritrea, as well as some of the communication difficulties associated with such transglobal, multilingual and frequently unregulated spaces. It draws on theories of communication power proposed by Castells (2015), as well as analysing the ways in which different semiotic resources such as video, emoticons, symbols, images and dialogue both spoken and written are integrated to make meaning, express identity, create solidarity among members, spur them into action and resolve conflicts.

Historical Background

Communications in social media are produced within a particular historical, social and political context and this context is important in research design as it influences what is studied and how findings are interpreted (Quan-Haase & Sloan, 2017). It is therefore useful at this point to outline the context which led to the formation of the NEW Facebook Group and to describe its aims and output. The reasons for its formation relate both to the situation for women in the historic homeland of Eritrea which has been left behind, as well as the migrant context in which the members of this network now find themselves. Eritrea is a small country situated in the Horn of Africa with a population of roughly five million according to a number of recent sources such as the British Broadcasting Corporation (BBC) at https://www.bbc.co.uk/news/world-africa-13349078, the Canadian Broadcasting Corporation (CBC) at https://www.cbc.ca/news/world/eritrea-diaspora-ethiopia-hope-mistrust-return-1.4756704, as well as in Wikipedia's description of Eritrea. It experienced a thirty-year armed struggle from 1961 and finally achieved independence from Ethiopia in 1991, becoming a sovereign state in 1993. It is fair to say that during this long period of war women experienced improvements in their legal and social status, and a National Union of Eritrean Women was established by the Eritrean People's Liberation Front (EPLF). Women were fighting at the front on the same terms as men, and the EPLF made efforts to change land owning and voting rights and to provide education for women. However, after Eritrea became independent, the increasingly authoritarian government failed to support women. As one of the authors of this chapter has experienced, even during the fight for independence, efforts to improve the status of women were made so that they could serve the country better rather than develop themselves as individuals. This view is substantiated by research carried out at the University of Asmara among women undergraduates (Müller, 2004) in which she found that after independence an instrumentalist view of education as producing human capital for the advancement of the nation ignored the need to develop personal identity and agency.

Over the last 10 years the situation for women in Eritrea has worsened. The University of Asmara was closed by the government in 2002 and indefinite National Service was instituted for both young men and women aged eighteen. Many families in Eritrea now prefer to marry off girls early rather than send them to face possible rape and violence in a military camp far from home. Women in general do not hold positions with any meaningful power in the government or business so young women lack role models. There are also very few jobs for educated women outside the capital, Asmara, and many women who fought during the war are now living in poverty. Female genital mutilation is forbidden by law but goes on undercover.

Given the scenario of a repressive government and poor economic conditions over a considerable period, it is not surprising that many women have left the country to join a diaspora which began during the war years and is now said to be proportionally to the internal population one of the largest in the world. The United Nations reported that Eritreans comprised the ninth largest refugee group in the world in 2017, with 486,200 forcibly displaced. Their main host countries were Ethiopia (164,600), Sudan (108,200), Germany (49,300), Switzerland (30,900), Sweden (27,200) and Israel (22,000). During their perilous refugee journeys, these women have frequently encountered financial extortion, sexual violence and torture, as described, for example, in Hailemariam *et al.*, 2015. If they do get to a third country, they are often placed in the position of having to portray themselves as victims to courts and government authorities in order not to be deported (Ghebrezghiaber & Motzafi-Haller, 2015), whereas in fact the women have shown considerable agency and resourcefulness to order to escape and survive. Mental illness, poverty, racial discrimination, family break-up and intergenerational cultural differences are common (Goitom, 2017). As refugees, these women were likely to experience isolation and loneliness without the support of family back home. Matsuoka and Sorenson (2001) reported how those who fled to Canada from Eritrea during the war years of the 1980s did not really feel that they had made true friends among other members of the diaspora; they perceived that these relationships were superficial. Part of the reason for this may be due to political, educational and religious differences; diasporic communities tend to be heterogeneous and to throw together individuals and groups who may not have had much to do with each other in their home country. It is also the case that the Eritrean diaspora are beset by government spies, creating a climate of fear and division:

> A network of spies and informers has been carefully nurtured by the Eritrean regime to monitor and control its citizens abroad. (Plaut, 2016: 187)

All these factors explain why women in the Eritrean diaspora feel the need to connect online with like-minded individuals in other parts of the world, and also why there is the potential for misunderstanding and disagreement among disparate contributors to these social networks, as became the case on (RE)NEW later on. However, as we will demonstrate, these networks also have the possibility for positive effects on the lives of their members. They can expose them to new perspectives and ideas from the varied people and places represented in the network, raise their consciousness of issues, and provide information and knowledge from all the global spaces in which members operate.

The Network of Eritrean Women Online

As with many other online diaspora communities, the membership and languages used in the network have changed over time, although the aims remained constant until very recently. The network was founded by four professional Eritrean women in June 2013, who knew of each other outside the digital sphere, following a three-way skype conversation. Two of the women were resident in the UK, and one was in Germany. They were all professional women: a university lecturer, a nurse and a doctor. They were soon joined by eight others who were linked to each other in real life, all well-educated, confident and proficient in English. It is not surprising, therefore, that all the early communication on the website was in English, with a few Tigrinya words to express particular concepts (Tigrinya is one of the semi-official languages of Eritrea, spoken by many in the Christian uplands around the capital, Asmara, as well as in northern Ethiopia).

The aims of the network stated on their Facebook page are: 'This is a Network of Eritrean Women (NEW) that mainly campaigns to address issues related to women's rights, to empower each other and share experiences'. NEW has been active in organising protests in the Hague and other parts of Europe, raising awareness of conditions inside Eritrea including the activities of the governing party, and discussing issues for Eritrean women which inevitably, given the members are living in the diaspora, include mention of the position of women in other African countries such as the Sudan, and even further afield such as Saudi Arabia. As this activism became more geographically spread out, there was a perceived need to widen communication on the website and to include members of other women's groups in Europe in discussions. The decision was taken in early 2018 to invite these groups to join the network. Facebook membership now stands at 453 (as of February 2019). However, the founders feel that the original, serious aims are being undermined; frivolous music videos, pictures of flowers and so forth are posted, which is not the type of communication which the founders of the group had originally envisioned. There is now greater political and religious divergence on the site and therefore more potential for conflict. Because communication is now in a number of languages (predominantly Tigrinya, but also Arabic and other European languages as well as English) there is often a need for translation, which hinders immediate communication. The core members/

Figure 5.1

administrators attempted very courteously and gently to remind members of the original aims, but to no avail. Is this the inevitable fate of websites ironically constructed to provide a platform for free speech, when widening membership produces dissent and multiplies aims, as the Facebook site increasingly represents different world views and life experiences? Some other online Eritrean discussion groups which started at roughly the same time as (RE)NEW, such as ESMNS UK (a network mainly consisting of younger men) have disintegrated after descending into open conflict and name calling. Are the founders of the website correct in discouraging postings such as Figure 5.1 above because they are seen as serving no useful function in the communication on the website?

- HAPPY LOVE MONTH!!! Forward this beautiful flowers to your best friends and love one you can forward it also to me if i'm one of your friends.

How are conflicting views aired? Can they be successfully managed or will this adversely affect the fate of NEW? This chapter attempts to address some of these questions for the light it might shed on communication in other online activist communities, while bearing in mind the limitations of drawing data from one single such website.

Research Focus

Given the aims of the site and the types of communication we have outlined above, the chapter will examine the ways in which communication in the RENEW network attempts to positively impact women's lives, by (1) raising awareness of damaging practices or inspiring examples of activities and individuals, (2) by creating opportunities for joint dialogue and action, and making connections with other global digital networks and (3) by resolving differences and conflicts between members. We will examine how modes such as text, image, video and emoticons interact to produce messages (Unsworth & Cleirigh, 2009), and how emotions

(Castells, 2015; Chouliaraki, 2006) play a role in influencing debate and action. We will also discuss some of the ways in which individual members have influenced the discourse of the network over time, and how power resides in some of these individuals. (Who owns the space in the network? Who introduces topics and has more airtime? Why do these particular individuals hold power and how do they exert control over the space?) We also consider issues of identity and how the borders between public and private identities typically merge in such networks (Chouliaraki, 2012) reflecting a change in the ways in which participants understand and practice citizenship. For instance, such sites give participants the opportunity to suggest new and previously unimagined solutions which may be drawn from their experience as citizens of the country to which they have migrated, such as vocal public demonstrations and meetings with UN representatives. The formation of the network itself also provides members with a collective social agency they may not have experienced before ('strength in numbers'). Finally, we will consider the link between discussion on the network and action in the 'real world'; how do 'watching' and 'posting' get converted into 'doing'? Chouliaraki's theories concerning the ways in which messages are mediated across the space between seeing and acting will be drawn on to explain how viewers of the website come to 'recognise non-local realties as a potential domain for [their] own effective action' (2006: 156–157).

Researching Social Media Communication

The study of social media has presented new methodological issues for researchers, and in this section we will discuss some of the challenges for collecting and analysing the data for our research, and the decisions we made. Williams *et al.* (2016) have famously categorised the issues as the '6Vs'; *volume, velocity, variety, veracity, virtue* and *value*. Social media produce an enormous amount of postings (volume), with very rapid responses by other participants (velocity). This vast amount of data can present a problem. Researchers can either choose to collect and compare 'big data' quantitatively from a number of platforms and forums, using computational tools and applications such as Application Program Interfaces (APIs). This is the approach adopted by Niyibizi *et al.* (this volume) and also to a certain extent by Yevudey *et al.* (this volume). The other choice is to focus on and analyse postings which form a 'small narrative' as we have done in this case. We have undertaken 'participant observation' of a number of postings on the site in question, plus drawing on personal reflections on the postings from one of the administrators. From these observations, we identified a number of features which seemed important for achieving the group's aims and objectives and formulated our research questions, which focused on these objectives. Small data produces further challenges such as sampling and the relationship of the researchers with the social media site. In this study, we focused on points in the interaction which were of interest for our research questions. As far as positioning is concerned, one of the authors of this chapter is Eritrean and a founding member of NEW and the other is British, so we were able to take both an 'emic' and an 'etic' stance, and verify our perceptions of the data with each other. 'Variety' refers to the fact that the data consists of images, videos and audio as well as words. All these semiotic resources not only convey meaning in themselves, but they gather meaning from the way in which they interact with other elements in a text (Kress & van Leeuwen, 1996). Visual elements operate differently to create meaning; for instance Callow (2005) argues that images are not just another kind of word, and they operate in ways which words cannot, with a sensual immediacy, and an appeal to desire and fantasy. We would argue that video clips, audio files and emoticons also have this immediacy, and this explains why they occur more frequently than written texts in our data, and are often unaccompanied by any written comment. Goldstein (2016) describes how visuals operate on the viewer on a number of levels to produce meaning: *affective* (what emotions are evoked?) *compositional* (how do the other media present interact with images to produce meaning?) and *ideological* (who is the audience, why were these images selected?). A knowledge of the audience is vital for understanding how the connotative meaning of an image might be understood in a particular context. One example which illustrates how connotation differs culturally are the stills shown in Figures 5.2, 5.3 and 5.4 below. They have been extracted from a video posted on the site. The video is part of a long running discussion of the peace agreement signed between Eritrea and Ethiopia in July 2018. Many in the diaspora disapproved of this move, pointing out that it had not resulted in any improvement in human rights for Eritreans, or any release of the thousands of prisoners of conscience. The video juxtaposes

Figure 5.2

Figure 5.3

actual photos of the peace signing event with photoshopped images of the Ethiopian prime minister Abiy Ahmed, who in Figures 5.2 and 5.3 is portrayed as a bride in a subservient bodily position to the bridegroom, Eritrean president Isias Afwerki, and being given a female hair style, again in a subservient position, in Figure 5.4. All three images denote the prime minister but their connotational meaning seemed to the British author to associate weakness with being female. She was somewhat surprised to find such images on this site, which promotes women's strength and ability, but for the Eritrean participants (using the emic standpoint of the Eritrean author of this chapter) there was a different cultural interpretation. The images were not about femaleness but about the traditional Eritrean notion that brides are somehow courted and tricked into

Figure 5.4

marriage. The Ethiopian prime minister was being portrayed as a dupe, being tricked by the Eritrean president.

Social media groups such as (RE)NEW make the most of the opportunities the space offers to be totally free to say what they wish, to be transgressive at will, and to play with desire and fantasy, as examples such as this video demonstrate. However, this brings us to the issues of virtue and veracity. Virtue involves being ethical, and protecting participants from harm. It is especially important for a site of this nature which consists of political dissidents for researchers to preserve the anonymity of contributors at all times. Veracity has to do with the accuracy, reliability and quality of data, the genuineness of those who provide it and how they present themselves, leading into the area of personal identity. NEW is a closed network, and you need to be approved by one of the administrators to join. All new members are personally known to one of the administrators or existing members, so they are who they say they are. Possible inaccuracies in information are swiftly pointed out, because truth is important to the members, who feel they have experienced censorship and distortion of the facts concerning their homeland. It is obviously important to the participants that information posted in the Messenger thread conforms to a commonly understood notion of veracity, and factual corrections are often made by the original founders and administrators of the group:

> 'While her success is inspiring for many. There is a lot of lies in this interview'.

> 'The above video regardless of very few facts, it is a vicious propaganda of the Amhara intended to create hatred among Eritrean and Tigray people. So while we fight each other they take control of our country. We should distinguish facts from hate filled propaganda of Ginbot 7'.

By making such comments, the administrators are exercising what Castells terms 'counterpower', challenging the government controlled narrative of events. A last point on veracity concerns the researchers' need to triangulate their online data if possible with interviews with those who have produced it; in our case we have discussed many of the posts and our interpretations of events with one of the administrators of the Facebook site.

Finally, value refers to the fact that social media data should increase our understanding of the social world by providing insights into communication of a scale, geographical reach and variety not previously available to us.

Raising Awareness of Women's Issues; The Roles of Emotion and Memory

Having established some of the constraints and challenges for researching communication on our social media site, we now turn to examining the first research question mentioned earlier in this chapter:

'how is the site used to raise awareness of damaging practices or provide inspiring examples of activities and individuals?' In essence, this refers to the site's core purposes of campaigning for women's rights and empowering its members and women internationally.

Emotion

It is useful to understand the role of emotion in the formation and momentum of such sites, because emotion plays a large part in determining what gets posted and how messages are framed. Castells (2015: 13) argues:

> social movements are emotional movements...the big bang of a social movement starts with the transformation of emotion into action...

Researching the new role of social media in the political movements of the Arab Spring and the Occupy movement in Europe and the US, Castells notes how social movements have always needed to occupy spaces, whether those are physical spaces controlled by dominant elites, or, more recently, digital spaces which give them the freedom to deliberate, discuss and plan actions. He calls these:

> spaces of autonomy, largely beyond the controls of governments and corporations that had monopolised the channels of communication as the foundation of their power throughout history. (2015: 2)

He points to the importance of anger, enthusiasm and hope in bringing like-minded individuals together and describes the importance of communication mechanisms such as social networks which propagate political action and the emotions attached to it:

> The faster and more interactive the process of communication is, the more likely the formation of a process of collective action becomes, rooted in outrage, propelled by enthusiasm and motivated by hope. (2015: 15)

We can therefore imagine that the motivation for posting on NEW/ RENEW, whether it is to arrange a meeting on Paltalk, publicise an event, provide news, or simply to encourage and exhort is highly likely to be driven by emotion, and the need to communicate those emotions to others with a view to encouraging concrete action. In order to explore the possible effects of some of the posts on the website on receivers, it is useful to refer to the work of Chouliaraki (2006). She discusses various ways in which news items on television depicting suffering can be mediated to have an effect on viewers and lead to action. These observations are relevant to what happens on the RENEW site on which video clips, either filmed on phones, or downloaded from television news broadcasts, as well as webcam interviews and solo pieces to camera featuring members of the group are by far the most popular mode of communicating information. Chouliaraki argues that video clips convince the viewer in three ways.

Firstly, they can persuade us of the tangible reality of what we see (so, for example, a video showing demonstration of Eritreans outside the Houses of Parliament in the UK or the Hague would be convincing because it features well-known landmarks, and we know it must have happened). Secondly they can evoke strong emotions such as pity, empathy, and outrage (such as displaying a photo of a woman imprisoned in Eritrea for her political or religious beliefs). Chouliaraki terms this 'reality of the heart'. Finally images can stir us to action if they confirm or align with 'our deeply rooted beliefs about what the world is like or should be like. This is what we call "ideological" realism' (2006: 160–161). So there are three ways – factual, emotional and moral – in which viewers can be influenced by what they see on the website. Chouliaraki mentions the importance of camera angles and body alignment for decreasing the distance between the spectator/viewer and an event ; for instance, if a video is shot in the middle of a crowd by a shaky handheld mobile phone, it places the viewer in the heart of the action. Faces directly turned towards viewers speak to them directly. Of course, there are risks in these efforts to 'make it real' for the spectator, affect them and stir them to action. It is common on this website for members of the diaspora to talk directly to camera but one of the founders of the site made the following comment after a video clip actually filmed in Eritrea was posted:

'Very sad but I am surprised that the person who filmed this decided to show peoples' faces. This is problematic for two reasons: one we should preserve someone's dignity especially when people have not given their consents, secondly, we have the responsibility to not expose our people's security'.

There is a narrow line between showing members of the site the reality of what is happening and endangering those present at an event.

Images are of course not the only story, and the words that surround them have the power to foreground certain parts of the image, and to embed it in a meaningful narrative. Words may describe the facts behind an event (description), or tell it as a story, or include value judgements (exposition). These three genres relate to the factual, emotional and ideological categories of realism we mentioned earlier.

Let's consider some posts made in the lead up to International Womens' Day on 8 March 2019 to see how words and images combine to form a meaning which transcends the affordances of one mode alone.

In Figure 5.5, the image denotes a raised fist encircled by the sign for female. The raised fist is a universal symbol suggesting solidarity, struggle and freedom, but it is especially associated with countries across Africa and their fight for liberation from colonialism and independence. It is also associated with the Black Power movement in the US. The choice of the symbol has therefore particular connotations for this group of African women because it also evokes the servitude of slavery and colonial domination, and it therefore packs a powerful emotional punch. The

Figure 5.5

accompanying text is expository and ideological, appealing to the moral beliefs of the members of the group; if you are strong you will empower not only yourself but other women. The key words are highlighted through the use of colour.

Memory

We have seen in Figure 5.5 how memories of a colonial past can be used, whether consciously or unconsciously, to influence participants emotionally. Memories are a risky thing on a diaspora website. Shared memories of the past in the homeland are often problematic in that they can unite but also divide members of the diaspora, who have left Eritrea at different times and for different reasons, and may have undergone very different experiences. Another thread associated with International Women's day illustrates this problem (see Figure 5.6).

Let's show our support to our mothers for peace 🧡

ኣጆኽን ክቡራት ኣደታት

ዓወትክን ዓወትናን ዓወት ህዝብናን እዩ ✊

https://youtu.be/i_hc6fHn1W0

The video clip is framed by the instruction which precedes it: ''Let's show our support to our mothers for peace 🧡.' This framing is problematic for some of the members of RENEW, as we will demonstrate. The first image in the video, shown in Figure 5.6, advertises a meeting to be held in Germany to facilitate reconciliation between various political factions. The organisers are mainly, but not exclusively, women in their sixties and seventies who are former fighters in the struggle for independence. The top banner reads, in both Tigrinya and Arabic. ''Information to all justice- seeking Eritreans in Europe' (notice how men are included in this appeal). This image and the video connect homeland and diaspora in interesting ways, link past and present, and present Eritrea in a particular way. Flags are potent symbols and carry many established connotations (Machin, 2007: 26). The two flags in the image are from different historical eras and show conflicting views of how Eritrea should be represented.

Figure 5.6

The map of Eritrea in the middle of the screen has been turned into a woman with a long scarf. The words in Tigrinya on the scarf mean 'mum is ill' so Eritrea is portrayed as a grieving, sick older woman. This metaphor is repeated elsewhere in the video (Figure 5.7) when a photo of a fighter from years ago is superimposed on a picture of four mourning elderly women, with the inscription: 'our children have been betrayed' and the word 'Enough!' in Tigrinya, Arabic and English. The soundtrack for this video is stirring Eritrean music, as it is for most of the domestically produced video clips which are posted on the site, and this also adds to the emotional impact of the video.

The rest of the video goes on to show current photos of Eritrean women from the European diaspora with their faces turned towards the viewer, together with texts of inspiring words in Tigrinya as if spoken by them directly to the viewer: 'We have to materialise the objectives of our martyrs. Every woman who believes in justice should set out with courage'; 'Say no to oppression. I will hold my head up. I do not want to be oppressed. I have chosen the table of peace and I stand for my people and my country'. One woman holds up a photo of a woman who has been imprisoned in Eritrea in the past for her political beliefs and is still being held prisoner. The reference to martyrs recalls the armed struggle. The

Figure 5.7

images in the video therefore simultaneously recall Eritrea as it was, as well as referring to the current situation, and to European contexts. Another woman is depicted as saying 'we have to tighten our belts for our unity' where belt tightening refers not to austerity measures but to tightening the traditional Eritrean female costume ready for work. The older women are in traditional dress, as in the white cheesecloth head coverings of the women in Figure 5.7, while the younger women pictured in Europe are in western clothes. In terms of the three kinds of reality described previously, this video contains very little factual information and depends pretty much on emotional and ideological reality, as well as an appeal to past memories of Eritrea. The concerns of the diaspora and those still in Eritrea become blurred and it becomes unclear whether we are talking about the position of women in Eritrea or outside it, or whether this is any longer about women's rights at all. This is a potential source of conflict and at several points in the ongoing discourse over five years on the site, some have called for more focus on the feminist aims of REN(EW) rather than getting deflected into general political issues such as peace talks between Eritrea and Ethiopia: 'I think we need to regroup, rethink, reflect and focus on what is it that we want to do and what is it that we can do.'

It is interesting to note that some of the women on the website (personal contacts, comments and discussion) objected to the association between political activism and motherhood, saying that women without children were equally entitled to take part in political comment and protest, and that the term 'mother' excluded young girls who were the most important part of the future. They felt that many of the images reflected past history and that it was time to look to the future. They also felt that this particular meeting needed to be better organised as reconciliation was a complex issue. A gap between the attitudes and experiences of the older and younger generation of women became evident in the discussions on the website.

Opportunities for Joint Dialogue and Action – and New Roles as (Global) Citizens

It is a paradox that the women who belong to the Facebook group have simultaneously experienced both an elevation and weakening of their status. Many of the women in the diaspora have found themselves taking part for the first time, as a result of their activism, in international conferences and dialogue with European government representatives and United Nations commissions. Their awareness of the Eritrean government's activities is more extensive than it would have been if they had remained in Eritrea. Inevitably they have been drawn into wider debates about politics and discussion about women's rights in a global sense, so there are posts on the website, for instance, about the lifting of the driving ban for Saudi women, Sudanese women's groups and clips about Trump and Brexit. Not surprisingly because RE(NEW) is challenging the status quo and existing institutionalised attitudes and policies, the participants tend to favour anti-establishment, left wing and socialist views. So there are anti-Trump posts and the UK Labour Party leader Jeremy Corbyn found some favour for a time. There are posts which are obviously circulating a number of sites as individuals repost them, for example a video purporting to show a 'Hindu woman burnt alive in Madha Pradesh because she attended a Prayer meeting in a Christian Church, please share this video as much as you can'. The connections with other groups of women works like a Russian doll or an onion; peel off or remove one layer and further and further layers and interconnections are revealed, facilitated both by digital and real-world communication. Figure 5.8 shows a poster for a conference which will take place in physical space at the School of Oriental and African Studies, University of London, who are hosting the event. It brings together a number of different groups under the umbrella of the UK branch of the Women's International League for Peace and Freedom (UK WILPF). The description of the event demonstrates how a number of women's organisations will be represented at the event in London, including (RE)NEW [authors' bold font]:

> 'UK WILPF invite you to celebrate the 10th anniversary of our incredible Voices of African Women campaign.
>
> Voices of African Women was set up by diaspora women living in the United Kingdom in 2009, and was initially founded to listen to the issues facing diaspora, refugee and immigrant African women. It has since become one of UK WILPF's leading campaigns, and has included impactful projects such as human rights training and Voices of Refugee women.

Figure 5.8

Members working within the project are very active in other communities too, such as Sudanese Mothers for Peace, Voice of Somali Women's Movement, **Network of Eritrean Women,** *and Voice of Dafur Women and Common Cause UK (a platform of D.R. Congolese Women). In bringing these groups together, the campaign amplifies the voices of women in the African UK diaspora.*

Please join us on Saturday 23rd of February, where we will give platform to and learn from an incredible range of speakers and campaigners representing over seven African nations. Consisting of various panel discussions and keynote speeches, sessions will include topics such as African women's participation in politics and African diaspora and the Law.'

WILPF is a non-governmental organisation with branches in 37 countries, a head office in Geneva and close ties with the United Nations. (RE) NEW's involvement with the UK branch links it globally with many other organisations. This is only one example of the way in which a network like (RE)NEW is able to communicate over ever extending physical as well as digital spaces.

Citizenship

After being granted the right to remain, members of the diaspora frequently become citizens of the country where they have settled. This process often involves citizenship tests, which means they have learnt in depth about other systems of government as well as different concepts of the rights and duties of citizens. One should also not forget that in many cases they have had to endure humiliation and financial hardship in the country in which they resettled, as well as a diminution of their status. Those who were teachers, businesswomen, doctors and scientists may have had a long struggle to get their qualifications recognised or to find steady work. The website is a place in which power and status could potentially still be asserted, because many of the participants know each other directly, or know of each other or of each other's families back in Eritrea. They will know who came from a rich or influential family, or who is highly educated. Yet they are very careful and conscious of not wanting to repeat the same power structures and control of communication which they have experience in the homeland or to impose the values and interests of the few on the rest of the participants. Nor do they wish to humiliate or disrespect any member. However, some mechanism for holding together the group, and not letting it disintegrate into vituperation and inaction (as the Viber group did) is required. The final section of this chapter considers the solutions which this group have found to the exercise of power and authority, which are largely linguistic.

Resolving Conflict – The Role of Power and Mediation

It's important to realise, as Gee (2005: 229) points out, that social media spaces are affinity spaces rather than close knit communities of practice:

> In such spaces, people who may share little, and even differ dramatically on other issues, affiliate around their common cause and the practices associated with espousing it

Gee goes on to describe affinity spaces as not being amenable to rigid hierarchies of power although we would note the key presence of administrators on the (RE)NEW site who wield some kind of authority. The participants on the (RE)NEW website are very disparate and brought together by one common interest, advancing the position of women in Eritrean society, whether that society is considered to be in the diaspora or the homeland. But this interest is only one aspect of their private and public identities. They are a disparate group in other ways, as far as age, religion, education, political views and life experiences are concerned. We have previously noted areas of conflict such as generational differences and a perceived lack of focus on group aims. How are such conflicts resolved successfully over the five year existence of the group?

It is useful to consider one incident as an example of how this site is regulated. One member posted a song from many years ago, featuring a fighter from one political group encouraging his comrades to kill those from an opposing group. Members of both these historic factions are participants on the website, and one of the administrators very quickly responded:

'Haftey please remove the above post. We need something that can unite us now. With all due respect my sister'. What immediately strikes the reader is the extremely polite language this request is couched in, and the use of the words 'my sister' both in English and Tigrinya ('haftey'). The post is written in English so that most participants will understand it, and perhaps because it seems more formal and serious. The original poster replies in Tigrinya with profuse apologies: 'Greetings my sister. I want to apologise to you all. I am trying to remove the post. Sorry sorry habiba (*darling* in Arabic).' The administrator then replies in a mixture of Tigrinya and English 'Thank you for understanding haftey 😸' ☺' A number of participants then wave and one participant cracks a joke in Tigrinya : 'What's this? Is it a revolution of the hand?' The potential conflict has been averted by politeness, an appeal to sisterhood, the use of emoticons and the support of other participants, who also use humour to lighten the mood.

A lot of work goes into averting conflict (personal communication) and when there are difficult people or inappropriate posts, two of the administrators often phone each other to discuss how to handle matters. They feel that often they are educating participants about how to have positive communication and dialogue online. They feel that sometimes members post without thinking and the comments of the administrators may help them to reflect. Their exercise of power, such as it is, is done in order to preserve harmony and so that members stay on the Facebook page. In this light, the posting of bunches of flowers and loving messages directly addressing the other members which we mentioned at the beginning of this chapter (Figure 5.1 is an example) appears in a non-frivolous light, as a way of preserving emotional closeness.

Conclusion

This small-scale study has demonstrated some of the ways (emotion, memory, attention to the diffusion of correct information) in which the participants in this Facebook group attempt to achieve their goals of campaigning to address issues related to women's rights, empowering each other and sharing experiences. We have illustrated some of the skilful verbal and non-verbal strategies which contributors have developed in order to avoid or resolve conflict. This is a disparate group whose participation in a social network has shown them how to talk to each other about political matters in a mature and considerate manner, and how to inhabit new roles and identities as global citizens.

References

Bernal, V. (2005) Eritrea on-line: Diaspora, cyberspace, and the public sphere. *American Ethnologist* 32 (4), 660–675.
British Broadcasting Corporation (BBC). See https://www.bbc.co.uk/news/world-africa-13349078.

Brinkerhoff, J. (2009) *Digital Diasporas: Identity and Transnational Engagement*. Cambridge: Cambridge University Press.

Callow, J. (2005) Literacy and the visual: broadening our vision. *English Teaching: Practice and Critique* 4 (1), 6–19.

Castells, M. (2015). *Networks of Outrage and Hope: Social Movements in the Internet Age* (2nd edn). Cambridge: Polity Press.

Canadian Broadcasting Corporation. See https://www.cbc.ca/news/world/eritrea-diaspora-ethiopia-hope-mistrust-return-1.4756704

Chouliaraki, L. (2006) Towards an analytics of mediation. *Critical Discourse Studies* 3 (2), 153–178, doi: 10.1080/17405900600908095

Chouliaraki, L. (ed.) (2012) *Self-ediation: New Media, Citizenship and Civil Selves*. Abingdon: Routledge.

Gee, J.P. (2005) Semiotic social spaces and affinity spaces: from *The Age of Mythology* to today's schools. In D. Barton and K. Tusting (eds) *Beyond Communities of Practice* (pp. 214–232). Cambridge: Cambridge University Press.

Ghebrezghiaber, H.M. and Motzafi-Haller, P. (2015) Eritrean women asylum seekers in Israel: From a politics of rescue to feminist accountability. *Journal of Refugee Studies* 28 (4), 570–594.

Goitom, M. (2017) 'Bridging several worlds': The process of identity development of second generation Ethiopian and Eritrean young women in Canada. *Journal of Clinical Social Work* 46, 236–248.

Goldstein, B. (2016) *Visual literacy in English language teaching: Part of the Cambridge Papers in ELT series*. [pdf] Cambridge: Cambridge University Press. See cambridge.org/betterlearning

Hailemariam, C., Ogbay, S. and White, G. (2015) Mediating between human traffickers and their victims: Mobility, discourse and identity. In C. Diskin, J. Martyn and V. Regan (eds) *New Approaches to Identity and Multilingualism in Transnational Contexts*. Frankfurt: Peter Lang.

Kress, G. and van Leeuwen, T. (1996) *Reading Images: The Grammar of Visual Design*. London: Routledge.

Machin, D. (2007) *Introduction to Multimodal Analysis*. London: Bloomsbury.

Matsuoka, A. and Sorenson, J. (2001) *Ghosts and Shadows: Construction of Identity and Community in an African Diaspora*. Toronto, ON: University of Toronto Press.

Muller, T.R. (2004) 'Now I am Free' – Education and human resource development in Eritrea: Contradictions in the lives of Eritrean women in higher education. *Compare: A Journal of Comparative and International Education* 34 (2), 215–229.

Oiarzabal, P. and Alonso, A. (eds) (2010) *Diasporas in the New Media Age: Identity, Politics, and Community*. Reno: University of Nevada Press.

Plaut, M. (2016) *Understanding Eritrea*. London: Hurst.

Quan-Haase, A. and Sloan, L. (2017) Introduction. *The Handbook of Social Media Research Methods*. London: Sage.

Safran, W. (1991) Diaspora in modern societies: Myths and homeland and return. *Diasporal* 1, 83–99.

Unsworth, L. and Cleirigh, C. (2009) Multimodality and reading: The construction of meaning through image-text interaction. In C. Jewitt (ed.) *Handbook of Multimodal Analysis* (pp. 151–164). London: Routledge.

Williams, M., Burnap, P. and Sloan, L. (2016) Crime sensing with Big Data: The affordances and limitations of using open source communications to estimate crime patterns. *British Journal of Criminology - Special Issue*. doi: 10.1093/bjc/azw031.

6 Identity, Language and Literacy in an African Digital Landscape

Bonny Norton

Introduction

Responding to an invitation by African scholars in 2003, I have since that time been interested in the potential of digital technology to transform educational practice in African communities, particularly with respect to multilingual literacy education. The invitation arose in the context of the Third Pan African Conference on Reading for All, which took place in Kampala, Uganda. This conference gave me the opportunity to share insights from my research across global sites, as well as forge an exciting collaborative research agenda with emerging and established African scholars, which remains vibrant to this day. The current chapter, which is based on a keynote address given at the BAAL Africa SIG conference in London, UK, in May 2016, enables me to reflect on my trajectory of research since the conference in Uganda, focusing on the changing digital landscape in African communities since that time, and the increasing recognition and promotion of African languages. This journey has been enriched by the opportunity to work with outstanding emerging scholars from the African, Canadian and global context, as demonstrated in our collaborative research and publications described in this chapter.

Drawing on research conducted in poorly resourced communities internationally (see Snyder & Prinsloo, 2007), Harriet Mutonyi and I identified five 'lessons' that are relevant to digital research in Uganda, and African communities more broadly (Mutonyi & Norton, 2007). These are: (1) to collect empirical data that can be used by policymakers and curriculum planners; (2) to recognize local differences between rural and urban areas; (3) to promote professional development of teachers and teacher educators; (4) to integrate in-school and out-of-school digital literacy practices; and (5) to provide opportunities to both access and contribute to global knowledge production. We concluded that research arising from such lessons needs to be conducted in the spirit of capacity-building advocated by such Indigenous scholars as Linda Tuhiwai Smith (1999). Tuhiwai Smith argues that research should be of benefit to all stakeholders in the research process, enhancing future possibilities for research participants and their communities.

In a prescient observation, Warschauer (2010) has argued that as efforts to expand educational technology into the developing world increase, a host of new research questions related to digital literacy become salient. The following question has remained relevant to my research agenda over time: *To what extent do identities shift as language learners and teachers engage with digital technology in diverse African communities?* To address this question, this chapter will focus on two digital research projects undertaken consecutively in Uganda over the past decade: the eGranary research project (2008–2012) and the African Storybook initiative (2013–present). The chapter begins with a description of the two projects, and locates them within wider global debates on the UN Millennium Development Goals (2000–2015), and the current UN Sustainable Development Goals (2015–2030). I then address the conceptual framework for research on these projects, focusing on theories of identity and investment that have been central to my work for many years. Following this, I turn to a discussion on the findings of our research on eGranary and the African Storybook initiative, addressing both the strengths and challenges associated with these digital innovations. My central finding is that digital technology increases the range of students' and teachers' imagined identities and that their investment in digital technology should be harnessed by supportive policies and practices. I conclude with reflections on future research.

Research Projects

The Dakar 2000 demand for *Education for All* by 2015 was based on the premise that education is a human right that enables people to improve their lives and transform their societies (UNESCO, 2000: 8), a process that is enhanced by engagement with technology and the internet (Burbules & Torres, 2000; Stromquist, 2002). The United Nations' Millennium Development Goals (MDGs) of 2000, and now the Sustainable Development Goals (SDG) of 2030, have thus called for global partnerships that make available the benefits of new digital technologies. Notwithstanding the excitement about the potential of digital technology to transform learning and teaching in Uganda, our team has learnt that conventional uses of digital technology, apart from mobile phones, are beyond the reach of most African students and teachers, particularly in rural areas (Mutonyi & Norton, 2007). In our search for more creative approaches to digital technology, we have participated in two exciting initiatives: the earlier 'internet in a box' eGranary portable digital library and the more recent African Storybook initiative, both of which are powerful resources for educational change.

Research Project 1: eGranary – 'Internet in a box'

The eGranary system, which is continually updated, has been developed by the Widernet Project at the University of Iowa in the United States of America (www.egranary.org). It is an intranet that comprises a hard drive with specialized browsing software, which can be attached to a PC or a local area network. It contains over 10 million educational documents, including Wikipedia, which can be searched like the internet. While electric or solar power is needed to run the system, there is no need for connection to the wider internet, and costs are kept relatively low. Not only does eGranary provide a wealth of information for users, but users can also develop digital skills like browsing and searching, without connectivity. Further, the system can be updated, and includes software that enables users to upload local content and distribute it to other users. While the development of eGranary remains in progress, the ones used in our 2008–2012 research program were the first generation made available by the Widernet Project. In June 2008, we invited Cliff Missen, the Director of the eGranary project, to meet our research team at UBC, and learnt that if eGranary is to achieve its potential in Ugandan education, both students and teachers needed to be able to adapt the system to local needs.

Our research program with eGranary was conducted at four separate sites in widely dispersed regions of Uganda. Research on eGranary was not the only focus of research at each site, but was incorporated into each respective case study. The four regions were in both rural and urban areas, including: the Masaka area in the southwestern part of Uganda, where we worked with Kyato youth in a community library (Norton & Williams, 2012); the Mbale area in the east, which focused on Sibatya Secondary School teachers and students (Early & Norton, 2014; Norton & Early, 2011); the Gulu area in the north, where Lauryn Oates worked with teachers from four primary schools (Oates, 2012); and the city of Kampala in central Uganda, which addressed teacher education (Andema *et al.*, 2013). Since an eGranary was already installed at the Kyato site when our research began, we donated an eGranary and laptop computer to each of the other three sites in our research program. Insights from research participants have been shared in diverse data forms, including face-to-face interviews (conducted in English), questionnaires, email exchanges, professional conversations, photographs, video-footage, and written and audio-taped reflections. The names of people and schools are pseudonyms.

Research Project 2: The African Storybook Initiative and Derivatives (See Appendix)

The African Storybook initiative (www.africanstorybook.org/) was launched in 2013 by the South African non-government organization Saide. It is a ground-breaking digital innovation that is addressing the lack of mother tongue reading materials for African children through the development of a powerful interactive website. The struggle for children's literacy represents a huge social and economic challenge to individuals and communities, particularly in sub-Saharan Africa, where more than 2000 languages are spoken (UNESCO Global Education Monitoring Report, 2016; Welch & Glennie, 2016) and only 40% of children in Grade 4 achieve minimum reading standards (UNESCO EFA Global Monitoring Report, 2013/2014). The inadequate provision of mother tongue materials exacerbates this reading challenge, since research has found that the best way for children to learn to read is in the mother tongue (Cummins, 2000; Trudell, 2013).

The African Storybook provides over 1300 beautifully illustrated open access digital children's stories with over 6000 translations, in over 190 African languages, as well as the official languages of English, French and Portuguese. On the African Storybook website, users can read, download, translate, adapt and create stories for local use, using a range of mobile devices. Teachers can project stories on classroom walls with battery-operated projectors and they can print out multiple copies without need for copyright permission. There is also a free App for both Android and iPhone – the African Storybook Reader – that makes it possible for users to access stories on smartphones and create a personal offline library. The focus of the African Storybook is thus to develop mother tongue literacy in African languages, which helps children, in due course, to transition to the country's official language.

I have served as the project's research advisor since its inception, and now also serve as a member of its steering committee. The invitation to join the African Storybook team arose because of my role in training leading members of the African Storybook team at UBC, including the late Juliet Tembe, the Uganda coordinator, and Sam Andema, the policy advisor. In my role as research advisor, I co-organized with Tessa Welch, the project lead, a 2013 colloquium in Stellenbosch, South Africa, and a second one at UBC in 2014, harnessing both local and global support for the initiative. I have conducted collaborative research on the African Storybook (Norton & Tembe, in press; Stranger-Johannessen & Norton, 2017; Stranger-Johannessen et al., 2018) and co-published on the project in the open access online newspaper, The Conversation (Norton & Welch, 2015; Norton et al., 2020). A number of public talks and presentations are available on YouTube.

My work on the African Storybook has also laid the groundwork for a range of exciting open access derivative digital projects, from Storybooks Canada to Global Storybooks, including Storybooks African Languages, which our UBC team has recently developed (see http://www.storybooks-canada.ca/ and http://globalstorybooks.net/) (see Appendix).The tools developed by our team , have enabled us to translate 40 African stories into more than 50 non-African languages, making these stories available in both print and audio, and customizing them into the dominant languages of diverse countries on the African continent and in the global community (Stranger-Johannessen *et al.*, 2018). The relationship between the African Storybook and Global Storybooks deliberately breaks with traditional flows of global knowledge, which have often tended to be from the Global North to the Global South. By bringing African stories into classrooms across the globe, and by drawing on the digital expertise of an African organization, we demonstrate that greater democratization of international knowledge flows is both possible and desirable.

Conceptual Framework: *Identity and Digital Literacy*

Having described the digital projects that have been central to my research for many years, I can now focus on the key research question: *to what extent do identities shift as language learners and teachers engage with digital technology in diverse African communities?* Brian Street (2001) argues persuasively that if literacy projects and programs are to be effective in diverse regions of the world, researchers need to understand the uses and meanings of literacy practices to local people themselves. He and scholars such as Jan Blommaert (2010) take the position that literacy practices cannot be isolated from other social practices, and that literacy must be understood with reference to larger historical, social and economic processes. However, as Prinsloo (2005) notes, much of the research on digital innovations has focused on research in wealthier regions of the world, and there is a great need for research in poorly-resourced communities to contribute to global debates on new literacies.

While some literacy scholars like Jan Blommaert express interest in the relationship between language, literacy and identity, this relationship is of central interest to my own work on identity and investment in the field of language education (Norton, 2013). Drawing on poststructuralist theory, particularly associated with the work of Christine Weedon (1997), I take the position that 'identity' is not a fixed character trait, but must be understood with reference to a learner's relationship to the wider social world, changing across time and space, and reproduced in social interaction. In this view, I argue, identity cannot be essentialized; it has multiple dimensions and is often a site of struggle. Further, the construct of investment, which I developed to complement notions of motivation in the field of language education, has broader application to other areas of language, literacy and learning (Norton, 2013). Inspired by the work of Bourdieu (1977, 1991), and drawing on a wide range of research, I make the case that learners invest in the target language because they believe they will acquire a wider range of symbolic and material resources, which will increase the value of their cultural capital and social power. As the value of learners' cultural capital increases, so learners reassess their sense of themselves and their desires for the future. Hence, I argue, there is an integral relationship between learner investment and learner identity.

Given our increasingly digital and mobile world, I have more recently collaborated with Ron Darvin to develop an expanded model of investment (Figure 6.1), locating it at the intersection of identity, capital and ideology (Darvin & Norton, 2015). We draw on Norton (2013) to conceptualize identity as multiple, changing, and a site of struggle; capital as associated with economic, social and cultural resources; and ideology as 'dominant ways of thinking that organize and stabilize societies while simultaneously determining modes of inclusion and exclusion' (Darvin & Norton, 2015: 72). With reference to research in both Uganda and Canada, we illustrate the ways in which the model might prove analytically useful as students and teachers negotiate increasingly invisible relations of power in the 21st century. In this spirit, the 2015 model seeks 'to go beyond the microstructures of power in specific communicative events and to investigate the systemic patterns of control that communicative events are indexical of' (Darvin & Norton, 2015: 42).

Related to the construct of investment is that of imagined communities and imagined identities (Anderson, 1991; Kanno & Norton, 2003; Norton, 2013). Developing this construct with reference to language education, I have argued that in many language classrooms, learners may have the opportunity to invest not only in the classroom community, but in communities of the imagination – communities that offer possibilities for an enhanced range of identity options in the future. Imagined identities can be highly varied, from the imagined identity of the more public professional, such as doctors, lawyers and teachers, to that of the more local homemaker or farm worker. I argue that an imagined community assumes an imagined identity, and that investment in language or literacy practices must be understood within this context.

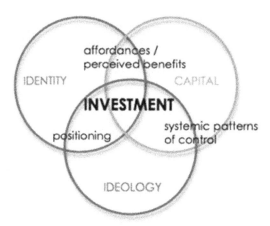

Figure 6.1 Darvin and Norton's (2015) Model of investment.
Source: *Annual Review of Applied Linguistics* 35: 42.

Findings and Analysis

In response to the question, *To what extent do identities shift as language learners and teachers engage with digital technology in diverse African communities?* I begin with findings from the earlier eGranary research project and then address our research on the African Storybook initiative.

EGranary and digital identities

As digital innovations 'travel' from highly industrialized sites in the Global North to poorly resourced sites in African communities, what value is ascribed to these innovations, what functions do they serve and what identities are renegotiated? In seeking to understand the relationship between identity and digital technology in Ugandan education, I begin with an extract of a conversation I had with a number of teachers at Sibatya Secondary School in August 2009 (Norton, 2014: 118). The teachers were commenting on the limited resources available at this rural school, where classes sometimes reach 200, and the teacher may be the only person with a textbook:

Teacher 1:   In fact the teacher is just the (whole) Bible-
Teacher 2:   The teacher is just the Bible in the school. [laughs]
Teacher 1:   There is no other [laughs]
Norton: Is that right, the teacher is the person who has the knowledge.
Teacher 2:   Yes.
Teacher 1:   Yeah
Norton: There is nobody else.
Teacher 1:   Yeah.
Teacher 2:   Because the students-
Early: The 'eGranary.'
Norton: You're the eGranary.
Teacher 1:   [laughs]

In local contexts where resources may be minimal, this conversation suggests that the teacher is often the sole source of information for students, constituting 'the whole Bible' or the metaphorical 'eGranary'. Teachers from Sibatya Secondary School noted that the eGranary has a wealth of information, and that in the absence of textbooks, is an extremely helpful resource. Teachers noted other advantages, including the fact that it is 'easy to store and access information', 'easily portable and usable where there is no internet service', 'cheaper' and 'more reliable' than the internet. Lauryn Oates, working with teachers in the Gulu area, noted to me in an email of 25 February 2010, that teachers particularly liked the Tools for Teachers resources, while Sam Andema, who participated in an eGranary workshop at Bondo Primary Teachers'

College in Kampala, on 18 June 2010, had similar findings (Norton, 2014: 118):

> At the end of the session I asked participants to share with me their experiences with the use of ICT broadly and the eGranary more specifically and the possibility of integrating it in their professional practice. Interestingly, participants were all positive about the possibility of integrating ICT in their professional practice. It was exciting to hear participants explaining how they could use ICT to improve their teaching in their respective subjects.

Both students and teachers saw in eGranary an opportunity to access a wide range of information, and to better understand their own location – geographical, political and personal. They eagerly sought information about their President Museveni, about the history of Uganda and its people, and about Africa more broadly, but they also used eGranary to make sense of more personal histories and experiences.

In our eGranary research at Kyato community library (Norton & Williams, 2012), the students who were part of the study were initially learners and trainees. By the end of the research, the students had transitioned from being learners and trainees to teachers and trainers, sharing digital skills, knowledge and information with fellow students, teachers and other members of the wider community. They took their identities as trainers very seriously, considering it their responsibility to make the eGranary accessible to the community, residents of other villages and even 'the world in general.'

Because our research study was not longitudinal, we were not able to follow up with the students over the years, to determine the social consequences of the project for them. However, we think it is significant that the project appeared to expand the range of imagined identities available to the students, as well as their hopes and desires for the future. As one student, Zuena said,

> I want help my generation also, our young sisters and brothers to have computers and to be allowed to come here in the community library and use computers because it is more important in the future to be knowing the computers. (Interview, November 24, 2008)

Zuena hoped to become a social worker in the future so that she could help her community learn and advance, and help local residents who were suffering from various health and social problems. She emphasized the importance of computers in the future education and progress of her generation, and was eager to play a part in this transformation. Similarly, Theo noted,

> I want to spread technology about, over the village and then, if time goes on, even the world in general, because there are many people in our villages that don't know about using the computer, and they cannot read. But if I train them how to use the computer, you never know, they can use it. (Interview, November 24, 2008)

As the students in the Kyato study developed their skills and it became known at the school that this particular group of students had access to information and technology, they were perceived as increasingly valuable members of the school community. As the student Mohammed said,

> The library scholars, the eGranary has helped us to be famous, known, because many students have come to know that we are (?) whereby we use the eGranary to teach them how to find information on the eGranary and also the outside people have tried to come across us so that we can teach them. (Interview, November 24, 2008)

Over time, the eGranary and the laptop computer were no longer seen as mere physical tools and material resources – they became meaningful symbolic resources as well. The eGranary was associated with improved academic performance, enhanced possibilities of employment, increased financial resources and greater access to social networking. Students were highly invested in the new technology, as they saw great benefits accruing from the knowledge gained and the digital skills acquired; indeed, a range of imagined identities emerged. The data suggest that practices associated with eGranary, including social networking, enhanced what was socially imaginable for these students. For example, Mohammed took the opportunity to learn the eGranary and the computer in order to develop a provisional plan for his future. In the event that he could no longer attend school due to financial constraints, he could take advantage of his computer skills to seek related employment until he was able to return to school. As he noted,

> For me, it will help me because I may, I may, I may leave the KCSS. I could, I should, I could finish my 'O' level when I have no further assistance for further education, so I may use that knowledge that I acquired from the eGranary to get jobs like secretariat and also some simple jobs like playing discos, playing music on discos, and also other jobs in the category of computers. So I'm gaining future knowledge on the eGranary. (Interview, November 24, 2008)

Further, it was interesting to note that eGranary also increased the social value of the educational site in which it was placed, at both local and translocal levels. As the student Joseph said,

> It is helpful that it can attract people to come and use it, eh? So that the eGranary can be known by many people, the library can be known. e.g. someone from far, like from Kampala, can come and see that the machine can display such information, and can tell many people that they can come - that our eGranary - that our library would be known all over the world, the country, and even outside the country. (Interview November 24, 2008)

It is clear from these data, collected at four research sites, that both students and teachers were highly invested in eGranary because eGranary expanded the range of identities available to them, in both the present time and in their imagined futures. Despite some of the challenges they faced, our data suggest that users' cultural capital and social power increased as they became more digitally literate and proficient with eGranary, and digital technology more broadly.

The African Storybook and digital identities

My research on identity and the African Storybook initiative was conducted with Espen Stanger-Johannessen, then a PhD student at UBC (Stranger-Johannessen & Norton, 2017, 2019) and the late Juliet Tembe, a former PhD student (Norton & Tembe, in press). The research was focused in the Arua district of northwestern Uganda and the Mbale area of eastern Uganda, where we worked with elementary school teachers, teacher educators and librarians. The case study of a teacher called Monica in the Arua area is illustrative of the relationship between identity and technology in this particular African community. My research with Stranger-Johannessen set out to address to what extent Monica was invested in the African Storybook, how Monica's investment provided insight into her identity as a language teacher, and what implications this had for classroom practice. The 2015 model described earlier in the chapter (Darvin & Norton, 2015) provided a useful framework within which to analyse Monica's changing identity and her investment in the African Storybook.

We found that Monica and other teachers were invested in the African Storybook for a number of important reasons, associated with the economic, cultural and social capital afforded by the initiative. With reference to economic capital, the website provided useful material resources for the teachers' large classrooms, particularly with respect to the promotion of mother tongue maintenance for the local children, who were predominantly speakers of Lugbarati. As Monica said,

> People had already phased Lugbarati out of Arua Hill. Now since this project came, I now had materials to be used. So the material was in the computer, so that, that thing made me now to think of teaching Lugbarati for the children. So I began now from there. And this time they can read now in Lugbarati. (Interview, October 27, 2014)

With reference to cultural capital, the African Storybook encouraged both teachers and students to become multilingual writers, and to be recognized publicly for their work. For Monica, the focus on stories validated her own stories and gave her an opportunity to be recognized as a poet. As she said:

Monica: It has made me to become a poet now. Because I have given for you two poems, I still have there three poems, and I have some stories which has made me to think more and more, such that I also be remembered in future by other people. [laughs]

Espen: That's great. And now you are writing.
Monica: I want to struggle all the time to, to do something. I used to not
           have time for those stories, but since I have known—the what?—
           the importance of using the stories, it has now made me to become
           creative, which I was not.
           (Interview, October 27, 2014)

It is important to note it was only when her creative potential was recognized in a public forum that Monica identified herself as a poet, and began to use poems in her teaching. The following extract provides a window on the excitement Monica felt at the opportunity to write a poem called 'Yiyia', translated into English as 'Mosquito, Mosquito', and upload it to the African Storybook website:

> When I see my name in there [online], ah! [excited] I'll be very happy. I wanted my name to appear such that people, people come, I mean, people begin to look for me. Who is this woman who writes this story? But when they reach here they will want to know who Monica is. (Monica, Interview, November 27, 2014)

Monica's own stories and language repertoires were seen by her as meaningful and valuable aspects of education. Her bilingualism and her knowledge of traditional stories (and poem styles), as well as her knowledge about diseases associated with mosquitos, were valued cultural capital encoded in the local language and English. The affirmation of such resources positioned Monica as a capable, knowledgeable teacher with a repertoire of cultural resources relevant to classroom practice. Such enthusiasm was shared by other teachers we interviewed in Arua. As Judith noted, 'I feel very happy. Because other people can go and read it somewhere' (Interview, November 19, 2014). Milly was equally enthusiastic: 'Very interesting! [laughs] It's interesting to see your stories with your names appearing in the web. It's interesting, I like it' (Interview, November 26, 2014).

Also important is the expansion of Monica's social capital and social networks, which was integral to her investment in the African Storybook. Going to Kampala, staying in a hotel, and receiving training enabled her to make new friends and learn about computers, and afforded the time for reflection on theories of reading, literacy and language, and their practical application in the classroom. As she noted:

> African Storybook Project has given a lot to me. At first I was computer illiterate. I've learned how to use computer through that project. I've now got friends. I have friends to whom I can talk through the project. I can now read something, I can now download stories, I can now do—try to do something to search in computer is the—the what? —the importance of African Storybook Project. (Interview, October 27, 2014)

Further, Monica's newly acquired skills and experience with the African Storybook earned her an invitation to run a workshop for teacher candidates at the nearby Arua Primary Teachers' College. The opportunity to teach adults, including those who once trained her, enhanced her social capital, as she notes in the following extract:

> It went on well. We trained them for two days. The first day was for year twos, and the second day was for year one. It has now exposed us! [cheerfully] I can now talk on, in front of these people, which I used to not to do. I wish it could continue. But I also learned a lot. It has made me learn a lot! (Interview, October 27, 2014)

With an enhanced range of identities, Monica shared the knowledge she had gained with her peers, as well as her former instructors, and 'can now talk on, in front of these people'. Whereas most teachers struggled to find the time to teach the African Storybook stories due to the content specifications and themes of the curriculum, Monica embraced the stories to teach English and local language literacy, inspired by a broader interpretation of the curriculum. In this way she was able to claim legitimacy as a language and literacy teacher, use time more efficiently, and still have the liberty to teach the stories that she saw as pedagogically rich.

Challenges

Notwithstanding enthusiasm for the affordances of digital technology, our research found that there were limitations associated with access to and use of eGranary, the African Storybook and digital technology more broadly. Teachers felt frustrated that they did not have their own personal computers, that their digital skills were limited, that electricity supply was intermittent, and that there was a lack of digital projectors in their workplaces. At the local level, for example, the sites into which most eGranary systems were placed had little socioeconomic infrastructure, no electricity, and no running water. Teachers at Sebatya noted with disappointment that eGranary 'Works only on electric power', and is 'useless without electricity.' It was sometimes only with solar power that the eGranary was able to operate, and even this resource was often unreliable. As the student Theo at Kyato noted,

> Power is still a problem, because we just use the solar system and then sunshine takes sometimes long without shining, and it rains for two and three days. So if it rains and then to me there is no power. So we just need more solar panels just to connect the power to the computers. (Interview, November 24, 2008)

Lauryn Oates, drawing on her research in the Gulu district, noted that teachers had experienced problems with the installation of eGranary onto the laptop computer, and that problems were exacerbated when technical support was not available:

> [The technology assistant] needs to be on hand to get the program going each time the lab opens, or if there is a power outage and things need to be restarted. Sometimes he is away from the lab or busy, which is a problem if users can't start up the program easily on their own. (email to Norton, February 25, 2010)

Oates also noted in her research that there is a need for more material with an African perspective, while teachers at Sibatya noted that information on the eGranary could be a little overwhelming. As one teacher said:

> [The eGranary] has too much information, some of which we might not need... right? For our purposes. So we're looking at the possibility of looking for those sensitive topical issues which we need for our own particular [course work]. (Interview, August 2009)

At Kyato community library, we also became aware of a darker set of practices associated with eGranary, which could not possibly meet local demands for its use. The students often made reference to the fact that only one eGranary was available, but that hundreds of students and many teachers wished to use it. As Williams noted in her journal on 13 October 2008:

> EGranary has created mild chaos in the library. Order in the court! Big crowds have started to cause a lot of disturbance (to me and Dan especially) and distraction. Will next discuss establishing order around the computer. Rules and signup sheets perhaps? Yes!

With reference to the African Storybook, the data highlight the challenges that some African teachers encountered as they tried to navigate the African Storybook within the context of ideological assumptions about the power of English and the curricular demands of administrators and policymakers. Apart from practical challenges of electrical power, bandwidth and time pressures, teachers had to confront complex assumptions about mother tongue usage, on the one hand, and teacher evaluation practices on the other, which affected teachers' investment in the African Storybook initiative.

While teachers like Monica in Arua recognized the value of the mother tongue in the multilingual context of the school, which is well established in the literature (Trudell, 2013), it was the discourse of English that dominated expectations at the grassroots level, notably among parents, and to some extent among teachers. As Monica noted:

> At first when they introduced thematic, we were teaching in Lugbarati. Every learning area was handled in Lugbarati, except English. So they found there were lots of challenges—the what? —the parents didn't like us to teach their children in Lugbarati. At home they speak Lugbarati, so they have sent their children here in order to learn English. So they

decided in their PTA meeting no teaching of Lugbarati in Arua Hill. It is now this RTI which has brought teaching in Lugbarati only this year. It used not to be there. (Interview, October 27, 2014)

While Lugbarati was a valued resource for the majority of students, who spoke it as a mother tongue, English was the medium of instruction from Grade 4 onwards, and thus seen to be paramount for the students to learn and develop in the earlier grades. Teachers were thus torn between government policy in the early grades, which supported mother tongue instruction, and pressures from parents, who were concerned about the transition to English medium in Grade 4, a concern that has been well documented in our other research projects in the Ugandan context (Abiria *et al.*, 2008; Tembe & Norton, 2008). As Monica said,

> The pressure from outside is when we don't follow the outside, the government policy. And from the school is from the parents. 'We want you to do this, and this time you are teaching our children vernacular and you do this.' It's just there. (Interview, October 27, 2014)

The power of English is also promoted by assessment practices in Ugandan education, a challenge in many other African contexts, where high-stakes tests are in the medium of English, despite support for mother tongue instruction (Early & Norton, 2014; Rea-Dickins *et al.*, 2009).

Another challenge for the African Storybook was that the stories were not perceived to be directly connected to the Ugandan curriculum. As one teacher, Santurumino, noted:

> And it is our weakness that we have not taken the books for the children. Because we mostly dwell on the coverage of the syllabus. And those ones—they may not give us time to —no—reading separately is not there on the curriculum. So, once you include reading lesson, you have already gone out of curriculum. ... Mostly when we teach, we teach what the curriculum specifies for us. But we add reading on top of that. ... The scheme [plan for the term] is fully filled with what is on the syllabus. Because of this one, it causes us only to teach the syllabus continuously because we want to finish its coverage. So that is the greatest challenge. (Interview, November 26, 2014)

Curricular goals in Ugandan education are reinforced by the practice of teacher supervision. Government appointed inspectors, as well as the school leadership, are required to approve the teachers' lesson plans and schemes of work. The teachers in our research were anxious about the outcomes of these inspections, and the extent to which their lesson plans were consistent with school and government policy. This led to mixed investments with regard to the African Storybook, as teachers were centrally concerned with the 'fear' of supervision.

> It is those ones who are teaching the real subjects, the real learning areas, who are getting problems in using the stories. Because when they will be, when in terms of supervision, at times they get the curriculum, at times

they get the books. Maybe they fear that area which they are—they are fearing—the what?—the supervisions. So they don't pick—the what?—the stories which appear. (Interview, October 27, 2014)

It was evident from our findings that the potential of eGranary, the African Storybook and digital technology more broadly, needs to be recognized and embraced by administrators, policy makers and parents if teachers are to be fully invested in digital innovations, and students are to reap the full benefits of these innovations.

Concluding comments

In his seminal article, 'The language factor in development goals', Ayo Bamgbose (2014) draws attention to the role of language in socioeconomic development, arguing persuasively that language is the 'the missing link' in global policy initiatives for development, and can aid in communication and information dissemination, transfer of technology, education and good governance. He notes in particular that meaningful development must aim for the full realization of human potential and an optimal utilization of a nation's resources. The most important findings from our long-term research program in Uganda suggest that students and teachers are key human resources in African society, and that their talents need to be harnessed with creative and supportive policies and practices (Makalela, 2009, 2015, see also Makalela, this volume). To this end, an understanding of the intriguing relationship between identity, investment and technological innovation needs to be better understood.

In our research program, we found that the value of eGranary and the African Storybook was associated with a wide range of functions in Ugandan schools and communities, all of which had implications for the identities and investments of both students and teachers. As the students using eGranary developed valued digital skills and the ability to serve as trainers to other members of their communities, their identities shifted, and they gained increasing cultural capital and social power. Similarly, for teachers using the African Storybook, the expanded range of identities as poets, writers, trainers and global citizens increased their investment in the African Storybook, and enhanced their identities as teachers. It was clear that the African Storybook encouraged both teachers and students to become multilingual writers, and to value the multiple languages in their homes and communities. Further, 'to be known' by others was a common theme across both the eGranary and African Storybook projects, for both students and teachers, and is associated with increased cultural and social capital on the part of users. At the same time, the limitations of eGranary and the African Storybook were associated partly with limited material resources in Ugandan society, and partly with ideological practices associated with language policy, curriculum development and teacher supervision.

In African contexts in which classroom resources are in short supply, and where large class sizes might compromise effective learning and teaching, technological innovations like eGranary and the African Storybook can provide valued pedagogical support, with the capability of improving multilingual literacy education and promoting African languages. The knowledge gained from these technological innovations, as well as the new literacies developed, may also enhance what is socially imaginable to students and teachers. In our research, we found that student hopes for advanced education, professional careers, study abroad and other opportunities became part of their imagined identities. Teachers, similarly, explored a wider range of identities and expressed desires for improved professional opportunities. As the students and teachers gained greater access to both information and technology, they eagerly sought to shift the boundaries of their worlds, to learn more about Uganda, Africa and the international community, and to make meaningful connections with a wider world. Indeed, it was clear that the students and teachers were invested in digital innovations to transform both themselves and their place in the world.

References

Abiria, D.M., Early, M. and Kendrick, M. (2013) Plurilingual pedagogical practices in a policy constrained context: A Northern Ugandan case study. *TESOL Quarterly* 47 (3), 567–590.

Andema, S., Kendrick, M. and Norton, B. (2013) Digital literacy in Ugandan teacher education: Insights from a case study. *Reading & Writing* 4 (1), 8 pp.

Anderson, B. (1991) *Imagined Communities: Reflections on the Origin and Spread of Nationalism* (Rev. edn). New York: Verso.

Bamgbose, A. (2014) The language factor in development goals. *Journal of Multilingual and Multicultural Development* 35, 646–657.

Blommaert, J. (2010) *The Sociolinguistics of Globalization*. Cambridge: Cambridge University Press.

Bourdieu, P. (1977) The economics of linguistic exchanges. *Social Science Information* 16 (6), 645–668.

Bourdieu, P. (1991) *Language and Symbolic Power*. Harvard University Press.

Burbules, N.C. and Torres, C.A. (2000) *Globalization and Education: Critical Perspectives*. New York, NY: Routledge.

Cummins, J. (2000) *Language, Power and Pedagogy: Bilingual Children in the Crossfire*. Clevedon: Multilingual Matters.

Darvin, R. and Norton, B. (2015) Identity and a model of investment in applied linguistics. *Annual Review of Applied Linguistics* 35, 36–56.

Early, M. and Norton, B. (2014) Revisiting English as medium of instruction in rural African classrooms. *Journal of Multilingual and Multicultural Development* 35, 674–691.

Kanno, Y. and Norton, B. (2003) Imagined communities and educational possibilities: Introduction. *Journal of Language, Identity, and Education* 2 (4), 241–249.

Makalela, L. (ed.) (2009) *Language Teacher Research in Africa*. Alexandria, VA: TESOL.

Makalela, L. (2015) Translanguaging as a vehicle for epistemic access: Cases for reading comprehension and multilingual interactions. *Per Linguam* 31 (1), 15–29.

Mutonyi, H. and Norton, B. (2007) ICT on the margins: Lessons for Ugandan education. *Language and Education* 21 (3), 264–270.

Norton, B. (2013) *Identity and Language Learning: Extending the Conversation* (2nd edn). Bristol: Multilingual Matters.

Norton, B. (2014) eGranary and digital identities of Ugandan youth. In K. Sanford, T. Rogers and M.Kendrick (eds) *Everyday Youth Literacies: Critical perspectives for new times* (pp. 111–127) Singapore: Springer.

Norton, B. and Early, M. (2011) Researcher identity, narrative inquiry, and language teaching research. *TESOL Quarterly* 45 (3), 415–439.

Norton, B., Stranger-Johannessen, E. and Doherty, L. (2020) Global storybooks: from Arabic to Zulu, freely available digital tales in 50+ language. *The Conversation*. See https://theconversation.com/global-storybooks-from-arabic-to-zulu-freely-available-digital-tales-in-50-languages-127480

Norton, B. and Tembe, J. (in press) The African Storybook, multilingual literacy, and social change in Ugandan classrooms. *Applied Linguistics Review*. See https://doi.org/10.1515/applirev-2020-2006.

Norton, B. and Welch, T. (2015) Digital stories could hold the key to multilingual literacy for African children. *The Conversation*, May 15.

Norton, B. and Williams, C. (2012) Digital identities, student investments and eGranary as a placed resource. *Language & Education* 26 (4), 315–329.

Oates, L. (2012) ICT, multilingual primary education and classroom pedagogy in Northern Uganda. Unpublished PhD thesis, University of British Columbia, Vancouver.

Prinsloo, M. (2005) New literacies as placed resources. *Perspectives in Education* 23 (4), 87–98.

Rea-Dickins, P., Yu, G. and Afitska, O. (2009) The consequences of examining through an unfamiliar language of instruction and its impact for school-age learners. In L. Taylor and C. Weir (eds) *Language Testing Matters: The Social and Educational impact of Language Assessment,* (pp. 190–214). Cambridge: CP.

Snyder, I. and Prinsloo, M. (Guest Eds) (2007) The digital literacy practices of young people in marginal contexts. *Language and Education: An International Journal* 21 (3).

Stranger-Johannessen, E., Doherty, L. and Norton, B. (2018) The African storybooks and storybooks Canada: Digital stories for linguistically diverse children. *Language and Literacy* 20 (3), 121–133.

Stranger-Johannessen, E. and Norton, B. (2017) The African Storybook and language teacher identity in digital times. *Modern Language Journal* 101 (S1), 45–60.

Stranger-Johannessen, E. and Norton, B. (2019) Promoting early literacy and student investment in the African storybook. *Journal of Language, Identity, and Education* 18 (6), 400–411. doi: 10.1080/15348458.2019.1674150.

Street, B. (ed.) (2001) *Literacy and Development*. New York: Routledge.

Stromquist, N.P. (2002) *Education in a Globalized World: The Connectivity of Economic power, Technology, and Knowledge*. Maryland: Rowman & Littlefield.

Tembe, J. and Norton, B. (2008) Promoting local languages in Ugandan primary schools: The community as stakeholder. *Canadian Modern Language Review/La Revue Canadienne Des Langues Vivantes* 65, 33–60.

Trudell, B. (2013) Early grade literacy in African schools: Lessons learned. In H. McIlwraith (ed.) *Multilingual Education in Africa: Lessons from the Juba Language-In-Education Conference* (pp. 155–161). London: British Council.

Tuhiwai Smith, L. (1999) *Decolonizing Methodologies: Research and Indigenous Peoples*. Dunedin: University of Otago Press.

UNESCO (2000) *The Dakar Framework for Action. Education For All: Meeting our collective commitments*. Paris: UNESCO.

UNESCO (2014) *Education for All Global Monitoring Report 2013/14*. Paris: UNESCO.

UNESCO (2016) *Global Education Monitoring Report, 2016.* Paris: UNESCO

Warschauer, M. (2010) Digital literacy studies: Progress and prospects. In M. Baynham and M. Prinsloo (eds) *The Future of Literacy Studies* (pp. 123–140). Basingstoke: Palgrave Macmillan.

Weedon, C. (1997) *Feminist Practice and Poststructuralist Theory.* Cambridge, MA: Blackwell.

Welch, T. and Glennie, J. (2016) Open educational resources for early literacy in Africa: The role of the African Storybook Initiative. In F. Miao, S. Mishra and R. McGreal (eds) *Open Educational Resources: Policy, Costs and Transformation.* Paris: UNESCO.

Williams, C. (2009) E-Granary, digital literacy, and the identities of Ugandan students. Unpublished MA Thesis, University of British Columbia.

Appendix: Open Access Resources for Language Teachers, Children and Parents

The African Storybook: https://africanstorybook.org/

The African Storybook is an open access digital initiative that provides illustrated storybooks for early reading in the languages of Africa, as well as English, French and Portuguese. Developed by the South African organization, Saide, the African Storybook is hosted on an interactive website that enables users to read, create, download, translate and adapt stories. The initiative addresses the dire shortage of children's storybooks in African languages, crucial for children's literacy development. As of May 2020, there were over 1300 stories with over 6000 translations, in over 190 African languages.

Storybooks Canada: https://storybookscanada.ca/

Storybooks Canada is a free open educational resource that promotes literacy and language learning in homes, schools and communities. It makes 40 stories from the African Storybook available with text and audio in English, French, and 28 of the most widely spoken immigrant and refugee languages of Canada. Users can toggle between different linguistic translations of the same story, to enhance comprehension, language learning and literacy development. Stories can be downloaded in multiple formats for ease of use and distribution. The site includes pedagogical resources for teachers and open access publications for researchers. Storybooks Canada was developed by a team at the University of British Columbia, Canada.

Global Storybooks portal: https://globalstorybooks.net/

Modelled on the open access Storybooks Canada (https://storybooks-canada.ca/) digital site, the Global Storybooks portal customizes multiple global languages for use in countries and regions across five continents.

The country-wide sites, from Storybooks Afghanistan to Storybooks Zambia, draw on open access illustrated stories from the African Storybook. There is also an Indigenous Storybooks site (https://indigenousstorybooks.ca/). As of March 2021, there were over 50 sites on the Global Storybooks portal, including Storybooks African Languages. The Global Storybooks portal was developed by a team at the University of British Columbia, Canada.

7 Networked Poetics: WhatsApp Poetry Groups and Malawian Aesthetic Networks

Susanna Sacks

Introduction

On 18 July 2016, hundreds of students marched through the University of Malawi's flagship Chancellor College. They were protesting the government's announced fee hike of 400%, which would have prevented most students from continuing their education. The students blocked the main tarmac road leading into the college and chanted a direct threat to the Malawian government: 'tinapha Bingu ifeyo / apolisi anapha Chasowa' (We killed Bingu ourselves / the police killed Chasowa). In two lines, the students reminded the ruling party of their power by claiming responsibility for the death of the late president, and indicted the government's human rights record by recalling suspicions surrounding the 2011 death of student activist Robert Chasowa. Through their chants, the students rewrote the nation's recent history while addressing a broader anglophone audience: written on posters and ringing through the crowd came chants of 'Fees must fall,' and the verbal link '#FeesMustFall.' The protesters' discourse echoed student protests that had shut down universities in South Africa the year before and had spread internationally as #FeesMustFall, as Robyn Baragwanath (2016), Pundy Pillay (2016) and others have documented. Through the hashtag, the protestors positioned their movement within a youth-oriented, digitally inflected, pan-African future.

The protests were organized in part through WhatsApp, a digital messaging platform linked to mobile phones that allows users to share text, image, audio and video messages with individuals and groups at relatively low data costs. Over the past decade, as mobile infrastructure has improved, WhatsApp has become an increasingly important part of digital communication in Malawi: students and teachers use it to expand the classroom; poets use it to share and critique work; and protestors use it to discuss their grievances. Its flexibility has made it influential across Africa, from South Africa to Rwanda to Ghana, in each case promising to improve transnational and multilingual communications (cf. Makalela, this volume; Niyibizi *et al.*, this volume; Norton, this volume). In southern Africa, the digital platform influenced the movement's rhetoric as well as its form: unlike many places where #FeesMustFall has spread, Malawi has barely 15% internet penetration rates, and among the lowest social media penetration rates on the continent (World Bank 2017). Rather than act as a literal link, the hashtag became an affective link, a poetic line drawing together the community it addressed, even without technological intervention, and gesturing towards a broader imaginary of the international community.

The hashtag participates in a form of global, networked poetics that allows users to mark their affective connections across nations and movements. I draw on Roman Jakobson's ([1960] 1999) use of 'poetic' to indicate the formal characteristics of communication, or 'the message for its own sake.' Jakobson argued that poetry, as a form, was characterized by its emphasis on the use of specific verbal signs. I would add that the hashtag – as a short, memorable phrase linking a host of conversations – similarly relies heavily on poetics for its impact. Hashtags and digitally circulated chants represent the rise of networked poetics, a component of the networked public sphere. Digital media, as Zeynep Tufecki has argued (2017), have shaped everyday experiences such that even those publics drawn together without recourse to digital networks are, nonetheless, shaped in their wake. Contemporary poetry is pre-mediated, created in response to and with a view of digital networks. Moreover, WhatsApp and other digitally mediated forms of address offer alternative forums for poetic production. Networked poetry is, thus, an implicitly public and political form, establishing communities, claiming rights and performing the nation for a transnational audience.

In this chapter, I examine how social media publication has influenced poetic forms and literary communities in Malawi. Poetry has long held a political and social role in Malawi, as in much of southern Africa, offering a language through which individuals in a community recognized one another's and accomplishments, telling collective histories and establishing norms of behavior. I therefore draw on Howard Becker's model of 'art worlds' to evaluate how cultural, social and technological milieus shape poetic practice. Indeed, Becker (1982) notes that, while poetry may seem a solitary pursuit, 'this appearance of autonomy is likewise superficial. Poets depend on printers and publishers […] and use shared traditions for the background against which their work makes sense and for the raw materials with which they work' (1982: 14). Poets simultaneously respond to long literary traditions and broad artistic communities, and to the shifting exigences of digital aesthetics. I investigate how poetry's social role manifests today, when community organization increasingly relies on social media platforms like Facebook and WhatsApp, and when communities themselves are increasingly diffuse and mobile, centered around a range of urban areas. In particular, I focus on the role of WhatsApp groups in the formation and maintenance of poetry communities. Understanding how this works requires a broader view of the art worlds that shape literary production, including poetry's political role, its position on digital media, and the communities form around it. The chapter begins therefore with an overview of the historical position of poetry in Malawian politics; situates this history in relation to contemporary poetry WhatsApp groups; offers an example of how WhatsApp supports viral circulation of particular poetic forms; and considers the implications for the use of poetry in protest.

Historical Background

In Malawi, as in much of southern Africa, poetry has long been used to imagine and critique forms of political organization. As Lupenga Mphande (2007) has noted of praise poetry among the Tumbuka in Malawi, Tanzania and Zambia, 'Memory is considered a collective phenomenon of the individual, and private memory is viewed suspect. Narratives about the chief's heroic deeds may refer to deeds of individuals, but these deeds are always depicted as collective' (2007: 387). Poetic narratives invest the individual in the communal, creating a public through collective claims to belonging. As artists build on recognizable forms, they address new communities, marking potential counter-publics in moments of political struggle. Nationalist poetic forms such as *izibongo* offered a rhetoric of affiliation through which marginalized voices could claim political power, and through which political power could be consolidated. These forms were adopted by anti-colonial activists and political leaders, who, as Mphande notes, 'appropriated and deployed the performance skills of song singers and praise poets for political expedience' (2007: 377). This chapter focuses on the contemporary reverberations of poetry's political force in order to investigate how new media publication influences its form and its publics.

Malawi's first president, Hastings Kamuzu Banda (r. 1963–1993), co-opted legacies of praise poetry to craft a political image in line with his desire to return to an imagined, neotraditional Malawi (Chirambo, 2001). As John Lwanda has detailed, dissident singers and poets turned these exact forms against the regime, to critique Banda's turn to censorship. In the 1970s, for instance, official songs declared:

A Kamuzu aja adenena wokha	Kamuzu has said this himself
Limani nsawa	Plant peanuts
Ndipo mudzalemera	And you will be rich

And popular singers responded:

Nyumba ndinali nayo koma inagumuka	I had a house, but it fell down.
Chakudya ndinalo nacho koma chinadithela	I had food but it is gone.
	(qtd. in Lwanda, 2008)

These songs were both popular in the late 1970s, but offered opposing visions of the citizen's position in the nation: one enriched by the country's autocratic leader, the other ruined by his regime. Singers and poets had to carefully craft their lyrics to evade censorship, finding creative ways to express their complaints and address a discontented national public.

Following the introduction of multipartyism in 1993, print poetry moved away from political topics in favor of more 'universal' themes, such as religion, patriotism, and morality. The 'newspaper poetry' which has come to dominate over the last three decades prescribes an ideal life: respect your parents, study hard, worship God, and your life will come out well (Kishindo, 2003). However, for most of Malawi's youth, following these prescriptions has not yielded the promised life: the country's economic circumstances, with an official unemployment rate of over 20% and 17% of all funds coming from foreign aid (World Bank, 2017a), have weakened the links between higher education and a well-paying job.

In response to the popularity of newspaper poetry, much of the politically critical poetry since multipartyism turned to the stage. Performance poets comment on current events and bring up topics which have not been endorsed by Malawi's publishing houses. Poetry performances and radio shows featuring poetry in English and Chichewa flourish. Where musical performance requires instruments and many people, and written poetry is unlikely to be read, performance poetry provides an inexpensive and accessible avenue for mass communication. In this same time, an increasing focus on digital publication has opened wider, predominantly local and Southern audiences for African writers across the continent. Poetry slams, open mics and fan bases are maintained through digital networks on WhatsApp and spread through recordings published on YouTube.

The interactive capabilities of WhatsApp – which allow users to define communal expectations, respond to one another's work, and create collaborative poems – represent a mobile alternative to the face-to-face poetry and writing workshops which remain popular in Malawi. Unlike Facebook, which – as Elvis ResCue and G. Edzordzi Agbozo find – presumes monolingual users (this volume), WhatsApp's ability to foster both vertical and horizontal translangauging support the multilingual experiences of its users, as Epimaque Niyibizi, Cyprien Niomugabo and Juliet Perumal found (this volume). The platform's limited linguistic coding may, ironically, enable a wider range of multilingual literatures. WhatsApp creates a collaborative poetics of the everyday: as one group debated the best soft drinks in October, a poet posted a piece that began

'Ndakulira frozy / iwe ndi number 1' (I am crying for [the soft drink] frozy / that's my number 1'), and another tagged the poem #FantaMustFall, a play on the #FeesMustFall protests that had recently shut down the national universities. WhatsApp makes poetry part of everyday conversational rhythms and situates it in the language of the digital. I therefore turn to analyze the influence of WhatsApp, which is the most popular platform for poetry organizing in Malawi, on poetic communities and literary form.

The Structure and Style of Malawian Poetry Groups on WhatsApp

As poetry appreciation, production, and promotion have grown among Malawian youth over the past five years, poetry communities have become increasingly dispersed, both across the country and internationally. Poets must coordinate across large distances regularly. In this context, WhatsApp has emerged as a primary site of poetic coordination. While in-person events and meetups help establish poetic networks, a growing number of WhatsApp groups are working to maintain dispersed communities. These networks keep poets in Zomba connected with colleagues 360 miles north in Mzuzu; with arts organizers in Zimbabwe; and with scholars in the global North. Moreover, because it is a private platform, WhatsApp allows poets to share work that may be shunned in public venues: one poet, for instance, wrote about the taboo topics of suicidality and AIDS, in a piece that begins:

Zatha Zonse	Everything is finished
Misonzi ya wawawa	The tears of the swarms
Matenda osakata	Chronic diseases
Ululu othodwetsa	Painful ease
Tsopano nidpumule	Now leave me to rest.

Although the poet frequently writes about controversial topics in public platforms, this particular poem has not, as far as I can tell, been published. Instead, it generated conversation and new poetry on WhatsApp itself, where community members labeled it a 'dirge' and applauded with clapping emojis. As an encrypted messaging platform, WhatsApp provides a sheltered space for debating frequent claims by established poets that the youth have nothing to add; a closed community for developing new poetic genres; and a forum for discussing their practice.

As poets move between cities, make international connections through festivals and social media, or leave the country for months or years at a time, WhatsApp groups allow them to maintain and build connections across national and local bounds. The connections WhatsApp draws mirrors those of extant social networks. The application allows users to connect through phone numbers, and it does not have a searchable data-base, so it cannot connect strangers. Instead, it solidifies offline connections. Moreover, the groups are private and require an administrator to add each new member directly. Rather than the endlessly expanding network imagined in Facebook groups and Twitter channels, each new member of a WhatsApp group is connected, like spokes on a wheel, to the central administrative group, establishing inward-facing social networks. This structure makes the groups a sanctuary within which emerging poets can test out ideas that are in conversation with, yet removed from, published and recorded poetry.

WhatsApp reconfigures the form aesthetic networks can take, and thus the form poetry itself can take. In Malawi, this has meant that aesthetic networks are increasingly divided along class, generational, and linguistic lines, rather than geographic ones. Additionally, the platform grants administrators the power to approve users and dismiss transgressors. This control provides users a template for proper styles and responses, but implicitly constrains the poetry and discourse of each group. The shared understanding of their roles transforms participants into an audience, who, in Karin Barber's terms, 'make the meaning of the text "whole" by what they bring to it. In many performance genres, this co-constitutive role is made palpable by the audience's visible and audible participation' (2007: 137). To maintain the speed of real-time collaboration, the groups establish close-knit personal connections that create expectations of direct responses. Although WhatsApp's poetry is not performed bodily or in front of a live audience, the speed of reception and response directly engages the audience in its composition, as does the feedback that follows.

Even as they resemble writers' workshops in their function, WhatsApp groups' formal structure facilitates a dramatic shift in the way poetry is produced and revised. WhatsApp poems tend to reflect the platform's presumptions of real-time reception and the poets' connections to performance and music. On 10 February 2017, for instance, one poet wrote: 'For a while I stopped writing / Stopped fighting for a cause / That only you n me understand, word [...] Word stands bold, when the wild is loose inside me, word delivers my tame / All the same, word, its you and me… for life…word.' The poem's irregular line lengths suggest the conversational rhythms typical of slam poetry; its punctuation offers spaces for breath and thought; and its language evokes the wordplay typical of spoken word. But where a live performance might elicit simple applause, the poem on WhatsApp is open to direct feedback. In this case, audience members offered positive critiques, calling the poem 'too deep'; interpretive analysis, asking about the speaker; and recirculation, sharing it on other platforms.

These groups are quietly, almost invisibly, transforming a nation's poetry. WhatsApp's ability to connect users internationally expands poets' potential interlocutors, changing writers' focus from national to global conversations. Its norms of interactivity encourage more dialogic poetry. To trace these transformations more closely, I examine the specific interactions of two, very different, but broadly typical, poetry WhatsApp groups: the Lilongwe Living Room Poetry Club (LLRPC), a group organized around a weekly open mic in Lilongwe, and Sapitwa Poetry's Artists (SPA), a group organized around a poetry website (www.sapitwapoetry.com). Observations are based on messages collected between 19 September and 29 December 2016, during which period the groups generated 2440 and 3134 messages, respectively. The two groups had similar rates and numbers of participations – with 189 and 254 members respectively, and an average participation rate of 26.9% and 24.8% – in the observed period. Stylistically and thematically, though, the two groups mark extreme ends of the five poetry WhatsApp groups I interacted with in Malawi. On LLRPC, members write almost exclusively in English, have chats focused on in-person events, and rarely share poetry. In SPA, on the other hand, members write in Chichewa slightly under half the time, have conversations focused on disseminating information, and share or critique poetry in nearly a quarter of conversations. Together, these two groups represent the range of affordances WhatsApp creates for poetic participation in Malawi: from linking in-person groups during the off season to providing entirely new venues for online groups, supporting collaboration across geographic space and temporal distance.

Creating Poetry Communities on WhatsApp

WhatsApp's always-on character creates potential links between all users at all times. Group members expect regular participation on the platform, and because of this, the groups include a much wider range of conversations than occurs at in-person events, from sharing jokes and news to debating cultural norms. Of those messages that focused on poetry, most offered straightforward support over critical feedback. For instance, when a participant in SPA posted a poem entitled 'Intense Affection,' three people responded within minutes: one with fire emojis, another complimenting the 'Zabwino [very good] heavy' poem, and the third claiming 'wayambapo...' [you've gotten started]. Some groups debate current issues in the poetry scene, asking what it means to be poets in this cultural moment, what counts as poetry, and what poets should be doing. But the WhatsApp groups functioned as general venues drawing together individuals invested in one another's well-being. In addition to poetry-specific discussions, members share and discuss regional news, sage or humorous advice, and broader issues.

The groups are part of a broader aesthetic ecology. They help sustain artistic activity through cooperation with a wide range of networks and platforms, as reflected in the different conversation and feedback patterns between the two groups. The Living Room Poetry Club is a group with weekly, in-person meetings, where poets share poetry and receive feedback, founded by anglophone poet Q. Malewezi. Sapitwa Poetry, on the other hand, is a website that publishes poems for personal downloads by anonymous fans, founded by Chichewa poet Robert Chiwamba. Correspondingly, members of the SPA WhatsApp group tended to share poems and discuss current events more regularly than members of LLRPC did. The SPA WhatsApp group thus became a virtual open mic, a space to share and receive feedback on early work, from applauding comments like the common flame emoji to more critical responses asking for clarification or critiquing word choice.

WhatsApp networks serve the purpose Heather Inwood (2014) has ascribed to in-person events in China, 'giving geographic shape to poetry communities and generating aesthetic developments, one-off incidents, and long-running sources of content that have in some cases irrevocably changed the course of contemporary poetry' (2014: 115). WhatsApp groups create translocal networks invested in the simultaneously digital and embodied experience of a poetic community. However, earlier divisions have not necessarily been erased. Instead, the platform's near-exclusive emphasis on written commentary has underscored and deepened linguistic divides in the country's poetry scene. In Malawi, Chichewa and English are the two most common languages, frequently used as lingua francas to the detriment of nationally minor language including Chitumbuka and Chiyao. Yet Chichewa use is slowly fading, or blending with English use, as more young people – who are officially educated solely in English beginning in secondary school (Mchombo, 2017; Nagarajan *et al.*, 2018) – enter Malawi's poetry scene. Moreover, because WhatsApp's language settings rely on those of the mobile phone, its use implicitly relies on an Anglocentric infrastructure. This infrastructure has encouraged an increasingly Anglocentric poetry scene and aesthetic networks, even though a large portion of the country's population speaks little or no English, and indeed, attendance tends to be much higher at Chichewa poetry events.

Language use is of particular concern for Malawian poets, relatively few of whom regularly use multiple languages in their poetry. Each of the 15 Malawian poets I interviewed framed their language choice in terms of the sacrifice entailed. Yankho Seunda, who writes primarily in English, told me that, 'Our challenge is getting people to realize that poetry is a thing that everyone can relate to. [...] Most people relate to local poets, because it's in the vernacular, they don't have to struggle to understand the meaning behind it' (2016). In contrast, Robert Chiwamba, who writes in Chichewa, was concerned that 'it is hard, even for the Chichewa language, to go and recite in other countries. It's only for the English guys, and we are now encouraging them.' To have their voices heard, both literally and figuratively, poets need an attentive audience who can understand their language as well as their allusions. Malawian poets, many of whom say they feel alienated from the people they want to engage, risk figuratively losing their voice if their messages are not taken up. Their language choice marks their choice of audience, their particular poetic community and the possibility for remediation. It connects the individual poet to a broader audience, projecting or limiting their voice in particular directions.

While none of the groups I worked with used one language to the exclusion of the other, differences in language use between WhatsApp groups nonetheless marked demographic changes. These differences reflected larger shifts in Malawian literary production, which is increasingly moving towards English and Anglophone writing. SPA and LLRPC, each of which is made up predominantly of young poets based in and originally from urban areas, represent this shift and its attendant anxieties remarkably well. On LLRPC, English dominated almost all conversations, with only occasional, stand-alone interjections in Chichewa. On SPA, in contrast, language changed with conversation, so that responders would continue in whatever language the initiator used, and language shifts marked topic shifts: on 25 October 2016, for instance, one poet switched from Chichewa to English to mark a shift from discussing a recently posted poem to advertising an upcoming event; the next day, the group switched from English to Chichewa when they moved away from sharing memes about the dangers of cell phones to joking about an ongoing debate on Facebook.

The difference in language use can be accounted for in the groups' poetic investments and origins. Sapitwa Poetry Artists is organized by Robert Chiwamba, who founded the site in part to promote Chichewa poetry (Chiwamba, 2016). Lilongwe Living Room Poetry Club, in contrast, founded by the poet Q. Malewezi, who writes and performs primarily in English. Although Malawezi mentors younger poets in both English and Chichewa (Malewezi, 2015), the Living Room Poetry Club has remained a predominantly English event: on the three occasions I attended in August and September 2016, chat and commentary moved smoothly between languages, but over 85% of the poetry performed was in English.

In this sense, online chats mirrored their lived equivalents, ingraining patterns established or promoted in face-to-face interactions even as they mediated group behavior and enabled group formation between those interactions. However, the poetry produced on and for WhatsApp follows the logic of the platform itself: closed, connective and collaborative. The allusions are highly specific. Responses are rapid. Pieces are short and easy to read. Though poets rarely repeat each other's work directly, they often use the platform's built-in 'reply' function to quote one another and clarify who they are responding to. The platform opens texts to constant commentary and remediation, through near-instant editing, copying and sharing. In this sense, the text becomes itself dialogic, created within a potentially interactive framework. WhatsApp groups enable newly collaborative genres and allow poets to address a broader audience.

As more and more young poets capitalize on WhatsApp's connective capacities, the networked poem remaps the connections upon which the country's poetry relies. As Mark Andrejevic has argued (2013), the technological platform reshapes literary genres and aesthetic networks more broadly: 'If the traditional notion of the individual genius/author/creator comes under pressure in an era in which the collaborative, networked character of creation – and its reliance on previous creations – comes to the fore, it is noteworthy that, from the perspective of e-commerce, the work of authorship is, in a sense, transferred from the individual creator to that of the application to perform' (2013: 133). The platform has entered the process of poetic production and thus, along with the author and her respondents, the very authorship of poetry.

The Collective Poetry of WhatsApp

Despite the groups' differences, the poetry they produced was similar – using varied line lengths and a conversational tone and rhythm – as was their approach to critique. In part, these similarities reflect the platform's particular affordances and constraints. However, their emergence also reflects the fact that each group constitutes one part of a series of overlapping networks that make up the broader Malawian poetry art world. Howard Becker's model of art worlds illustrates the importance of these overlapping networks, which require the cooperation of many actors to produce collective aesthetic productions and sensibilities. Becker writes, 'Every art world uses, to organize some of the cooperation between some of its participants, conventions known to all or almost all well-socialized members of the society in which it exists' (1982: 42). Those conventions simultaneously facilitate and constrain aesthetic production and reception. WhatsApp groups rely on these broader conventions, but they are also themselves venues for developing and enforcing emergent poetic conventions. Along with the conventions for proper behavior they enforce – no swearing, no gossiping, no fake news – they innovate conventions for poetic production and responses.

In each group, when participants posted the texts of their poems, at least three people responded with accolades, complimenting the author on the piece or representing their embodied reading experiences with emojis of clapping hands and crying faces. Readers pointed to specific elements of pieces they liked – individual words, or overall senses – and debated if a piece was more interesting or funny, sad or serious. If too many poems received only accolades, someone would speak up, decrying the lack of genuine feedback and insight. After a few relatively quiet weeks, one user commented:

> When I was about to join this group a few months ago I was told that the people here discuss everything poetry and assist each other to become better. But honestly, I have not seen any of that happening here. I am not a pro. but I know there are people here who have the ability to dissect poems and show you where you need to improve on or where nothing needs to be changed. Should we say everything posted here is too perfect and needs no critique? I know we all have lives to attend to and can't be here full time, but seriously what's the point of being a member of a group where silence can go for up to entire day at a time?

Her complaint – which presumed, first, that the group would work together to improve one another's poems, and second, that group members would be active most days – suggested a broader, collective understanding of the group's purpose and rhythm. Others agreed, noting, 'Mwina anthu amaopa kukhumudwitsana. Komano [Maybe people are forgetting how to criticize. However,] the group is cold now…not as it used to be…everyone for himself it seems,' and 'I feel like people, we don't love this anymore.' The proclamations of doom marked the group's failure to live up to its promises and poetic expectations, speaking to a shared understanding of what the group was meant to achieve and fulfill.

Still others jumped in to suggest that the group get 'back to business' and host a 'poetry cycle tonight.' Each of the group's 55 participants understood what a 'poetry cycle' entailed. When they decided on a theme of 'Silence,' 10 participants contributed stanzas in order, building a poem about 'Silence' together. The poem included stanzas in Chichewa and English, and one left blank, to visually represent silence. A few days later, Chiwamba organized a new cycle of poetry competitions, akin to one he had held six months before, where poets would submit works to him, which he would then anonymize and share with the group, who would vote for their favorite poems and poets to continue. The participants' collective participation in the cycle, and the poems they produced for one another, implied that the group shared a common language for and expectations of poetic participation, and members regularly step in to correct failures.

Such collective participation in poetic production, and in the production of group norms, works on WhatsApp because its groups are small – limited, in February 2016, to 256 members – and closed, meaning that each member must have a direct, personal connection to one of the group's administrators to be invited. The presumption of broader social connections also moderates the sort of content members are expected to share, which can vary from group to group. While members of LLRPC rarely expect criticism, poets do expect direct responses to their poems, and the group has a similar model for creating collaborative poems. In between their weekly meetings, or during the rainy season when in-person meetings happen less frequently, group members rely on the WhatsApp group to maintain connections and continue their poetry-oriented socializing. During one joking interlude in October 2016, a new member made fun of the group name (which refers to the bar where they meet), commenting, 'Now write abt the deading room.' Together, the participants suggested poetic alternatives to the 'living room,' such as:

> I used to live. I existed in love. I cut off my poetry supply. Now I suffocate in the deading room.

Or

> the dead suck out all that is… in the deading room …

And later,

> This invitation to enter, too tempting for my soul, but sitting in here, the flow of rhythm, the lingering melody, this tune of a song of wickied (sic.) evil masters, and lovers parade. I dance in this deading room, on tombstones of beautifully crafted verses, that lie unpublished.

Unlike SPA's poetry cycles, which feature lineated stanzas of consistent length, LLRPC's collective poetry evokes poetic improvisation. Stanzas are written in full paragraphs, with line breaks implied by ellipses and dashes. In lieu of the deliberation suggested by lineation, the punctuation suggests pauses for breath and thought. Many of the contributions are highly repetitive, including one that begins: 'For the love of the room of love, the love the room the love the room.' The repetition creates a rhythm that carries into the rest of the lines, while evoking the breathing room necessary for improvisation, manifesting the relationship between thought, breath and word.

Building on vernacular poetic forms, which encourage call-and-response style collaboration, digitally facilitated poetic production supports new poetic forms like the poetry cycles described above, as well as digitally popular forms like slam poetry. The poetry of these two groups – one focused on critique and the other on accolades, one on the production of poetry and the other on its reception – encapsulates each group's purpose, its rules and norms, and its leadership. It also speaks to the capacity of WhatsApp as a platform to host poetic collaborations, and to shape groups that want, write, read and share them. As a messaging platform, WhatsApp grants no post or individual a clear status above or below any other. Tracing conversations, and separating the threads of a multi-conversational group, is challenging at best. In this seeming messiness – the lived sociality of the WhatsApp group, nested among so many other conversations unique to each user's social world – each WhatsApp group carves out its own poetics, its own expectations, its own civility, so that a poetry cycle that crosses linguistic and modal boundaries signifies within the social boundaries of the group.

WhatsApp groups' capacity for connecting mobile communities, for establishing aesthetic norms, and for developing poetry's networked character is consistent with broader trends online: as Karin Barber (2017) explains, 'electronic media greatly expanded the potential public initially opened up by the press. [...] This broad, all-encompassing address to an unknown, dispersed and heterogeneous audience required a new kind of textual transparency' (2017: 161, 164). Even though WhatsApp's publics are, in fact, private, its ability to connect users internationally expands poets' potential interlocutors, creating closed circuits within a potentially infinite network. It opens texts to constant commentary and remediation, through near-instant editing, copying, and sharing. In this sense, the text becomes itself dialogic, created within a potentially interactive framework. The communities created on each platform cross over onto each other, and into face-to-face networks, creating transmodal aesthetic networks which span digital platforms, live performance and print mediation. The collaborative, participatory, and urgent ethos of social media platforms conjures the collective effervescence of performance and spectatorship. Although they lack the physical co-presence important to performance genres, they presume a shared intellectual and emotional co-presence, one which requires listening – even if it is the distracted listening of a linked, hashtagged public.

Online Poetry in Performance

The shift in poetry's production, onto the informal but highly regular interactions of WhatsApp, has engendered a rise in forms of poetry that speak to social media's emphasis on interactivity, immediacy, and authenticity – a shift often typified by the rise of slam poetry, a form characterized by highly rhythmic yet conversational speech with an emphasis on wordplay and sound and on the performance of marginalized identities. Such poems spread through live performances, through WhatsApp groups, and through their publication on YouTube and on websites such as the local Malawian poetry site SapitwaPoetry.com. While these platforms open up apparently global – or at least broadly regional – audiences and acclaim, that comes only after poets gain recognition among highly local communities the Living Room Poetry Club. Only with local support can poets' work gain traction in the transnational spaces of YouTube and Facebook. In some cases, though, this movement is direct, and shockingly fast. In late 2015, Q. Malewezi posted to Facebook requesting names of promising young poets to join him on his album launch tour, which would culminate in a performance at Lake of Stars, the country's largest arts festival. Fans of Phindu Banda, who was then a student and had just begun performing, commented to suggest her name (P. Banda 2016). Through their contact on social media, she went on to work and perform with Malewezi, launching a national presence from a few very small-scale local successes.

The poem Phindu Banda presented at that year's Lake of Stars evoked trends of heightened rhythms and repetition with variance that reflect the rise of slam poetry forms in Malawi. Her poem begins quietly, but as it progresses, her volume picks up and her tempo rises, building on the familiar rhythms of the slam poem. It begins:

> This is a nothing poem
> Written by
> A nothing poet
> For a nothing nation with nothing to show the next generation
> These / are nothing letters
> Molded into nothing words
> Joined together to form nothing sentences
> To highlight your nothing prison sentences

The poem's urgency and clear political message, together with the word-play and repetition, imbue the text with a sense of emotional immediacy. Because of the circulation of this form across languages and media, audiences could recognize the poem when they heard it, even though they may not have prepared for it in advance. They learned from Phindu Banda's cues how to respond, and, by the end, they sighed and cried in time with her rhythm, creating a collective poetic engagement. The poem lays bare conventional narratives about Malawi – that imagine it as an impoverished, backwards, 'nothing' country. But she resists those narratives to declare instead the power of youth to reimagine the future – a rhetoric that grows, in part, out of her time as a student at Chancellor College, during the 2016 university crisis.

(Digital) Protest Poetry

Ironically, little poetry was written about the university crisis at the time: in conversations, many poets cited fears of informal blacklisting and lingering concerns about censorship, decades after official censorship laws had been repealed. Instead, the chants themselves became the poetry of the moment, developing political rhetoric and aesthetic urgency to establish communal protest practices. In chants, performance poetry's immediacy, repetition, and audience engagement meld with the urgency and populism of digital media to encourage alternative literary and poetic expressive forms – forms which may exceed the sort of thing usually recognized as poetry.

As students massed together on campus, physically occupying the space they risked being financially forced out of, their collective chanting created a rhetoric which united their supporters against the policy change. Through their chants, they built on poetry's rhythms and performance's interactivity to tell a youth-centered story of Malawi's failures, and its hopes. One of the most popular chants, for instance, was 'timcheka-cheka Mutharika' ('We will chop down Mutharika'). It laid the blame for the fee hike at President Peter Mutharika's feet and suggested that they, as students, would determine the country's future. The chant is structured as a call and response: one student projects his voice above the shouts and drumming of his co-protestors and shouts, 'timcheka-cheka' – we will cut him up – and others confirm the subject of their rage, 'Mutharika.' A threat to the president's body, understood as a vow to cut him down politically, became a way to confirm group commitment, to shape group identity through a shared poetic and political rhetoric. The 'we' of these chants declares a collective agency against which, it was posited, established political structures could not stand.

The chant, as poetic speech-act, enacts its promises, drawing together the community into a single speaking body. The collectively chanted 'we' produces a counterpublic whose existence cuts against Pres. Mutharika's power to frame national narratives. As 'tinapha Bingu ifeyo / apolisi anapha Chasowa' calls attention to the state's failures, 'Timcheka-cheka Mutharika' imagines a future in the present moment. Collective chanting grants the speakers affective power where, politically and materially, they have very little. The immediate future tense of 'timcheka', combined with the historical memory of 'tinapha…', produces an alternative narrative of Malawi's national structure and political circumstance.

While these chants suggest that the protest was primarily an internal critique of Malawian governance and representation, other chants like 'Fees Must Fall' marked students' attention to a transnational community of protest and poetic production. These symbols of transnational engagement made the protestors' actions legible to an international audience, and they were deployed strategically, typically appearing during press-heavy moments like when Jill Biden, then-Second Lady of the United States, tried to visit the campus. Thus, while the protests were primarily grounded, reported on and promoted through broadcast outlets, they built on strategies of social media movements, incorporating hashtags and populist, poetic forms in their claims to address a potential global and digital audiences.

Conclusion

As social media platforms come to dominate poetry publication, the audience addressed through them is shifting the nature of poetic form, and of the broader communities it interpellates in turn. However, the poetic communities and audiences this chapter considers are exceptional in Malawi: educated, urban youth communities with regular access to digital communications. Most audiences of performance in Malawi remain offline, without recourse to digital commentary or responsiveness and yet affected by it. And, as Bonny Norton argues (this volume), lingering associations of digital technologies with the global North, and in particular with Anglocentric discourse, may further limit both the producers and the audiences of these works. Digital poetry publication is thus a double-edged sword: at once opening up a wider, broadly regional or diasporic audience to more artists and allowing dissident communities to organize, and yet changing the art that is widely available – and placing it at the mercy of largely unknowable corporations like Facebook, which owns WhatsApp. Nonetheless, such publication supports new, regionally specific channels of distribution that have disrupted commonplace ideas about the role of poetry in everyday life, integrating a form that had been reserved for the schoolroom into everyday discourse.

References

Andrejevic, M. (2013) Authoring user-generated content. In C. Chris and D.A. Gerstner (eds) *Media Authorship*. New York: Routledge.

Banda, P. (2016) Personal interview. 1 October 2016.

Baragwanath, R. (2016) Social media and contentious politics in South Africa. *Communications and the Public* 1 (3), 362–366.

Barber, K. (2007) *The Anthropology of Texts, Persons and Publics*. Cambridge University Press.

Barber, K. (2016) *A History of African Popular Culture*. Cambridge University Press.

Becker, H. (1982) *Art Worlds*. Berkeley: University of California Press.

Chirambo, R. (2001) Protesting Politics of 'Death and Darkness' in Malawi. *Journal of Folklore Research* 38 (3), 205–227.

Chiwamba, R. (2016) Personal interview. 23 July 2017.

Nagarajan, G., Gonzalez, E. and Hur, A. (2018) Malawi National Reading Program Baseline Assessment. USAID.

Inwood, H. (2014) *Verse Going Viral: China's New Media Scenes*. Seattle: University of Washington Press.

Jakobson, R. (1960) Linguistics and poetics. Reprinted in A. Jarworski and N. Coupand (eds) *The Discourse Reader*. New York: Routledge.

Kishindo, P. (2003) Recurrent themes in Chichewa verse in Malawian newspapers. *Nordic Journal of African Studies*, 327–353.

Lwanda, J. (2003) Mother's songs: Male appropriation of women's Music in Malawi and Southern Africa. *Journal of African Cultural Studies* 16 (2), 119–141.

Lwanda, J. (2008) Poets, culture and orature: A reappraisal of the Malawi political public sphere, 1953–2006. *Journal of Contemporary African Studies* 26 (1), 21–101.

Malewezi, Q. (2015) Personal interview. 26 July 2015.

Mchombo, S. (2017) Politics of language choice in African education: The case of Kenya and Malawi. *International Relations and Diplomacy* 35 (4), 181–204.

Mphande, L. (2007) If you're ugly, know how to sing: Aesthetics of resistance and subversion. In H. Maupeu and K. Njogu (eds) *Songs and Politics in Eastern Africa* (pp. 377–401). Dar es Salaam: Mkuki na Nyota Publishers.

Pillay, P. (2016) Financing universities: Promoting equality or reinforcing inequality. In S. Boysen (ed.) *Fees Must Fall: Studies Protest, Decolonisation and Governance in South Africa*. Johannesburg: Wits University Press.

Seunda, Y. (2016) Personal interview. 29 July 2016.

Tufekci, Z. (2017) *Twitter and Teargas*. New Haven, CT: Yale University Press.

World Bank (2017) Individuals Using the Internet (% Population) – Malawi. See https://data.worldbank.org/indicator/IT.NET.USER.ZS?locations=MW (accessed 31 May 2020).

World Bank (2017a) Unemployment, total (% of total labor force) (modelled ILO estimate) – Malawi. https://data.worldbank.org/indicator/SL.UEM.TOTL.ZS?locations=MW (accessed 18 Feb 2021).

Part 4

Language Change

8 Human–Agent Interaction: L1-mode Intelligent Software Agents Instructing Nigerian L2 Speakers of English During Assembly Tasks

Abdulmalik Yusuf Ofemile

The Nigerian language teacher education context contends with large classes, few teachers and inadequate teaching and learning facilities. These encourage tertiary institutions to adopt blended systems that extend classrooms using learning technologies within dual modes of education combining full-time with open and distance learning. This in turn, extends boundaries of discourse to contexts where speakers of English as a second language (EL_2) take instructions from Computer-Assisted Language Learning (CALL) technology (DuoLingo) and use intelligent personal assistants (Siri) designed for English as first language (EL_1) contexts. There is the need to understand communication occurring between EL_1-speaking software agents and EL_2 listeners in multilingual contexts. This chapter reports a scoping study that used spontaneous facial actions to understand patterns of marked nonverbal listenership behaviours of multilingual EL_2 speakers taking instructions from EL_1-mode devices. Ten EL_2 speakers were tasked with assembling two Lego models within 15 minutes per iteration using vague verbal instructions from a computer interface (EL_1-mode agent instructor) and one human instructor using his own voice. The interface used three voices – two synthesised voices and one human recording by a voice actor. A 5-hour long multimodal corpus was built and analysed for nonverbal listenership behaviours. Results indicate that participants displayed some listenership behaviours only when interacting with agents, others with the human instructor while some were common to both. Participants were able to nonverbally express positive, negative and neutral attitudes towards instructors. In doing this, they drew from their knowledge of nonverbal sense-making in Nigerian languages to create semiotic mergers with English using nonverbal translanguaging strategies. Semiotic mergers resulted in locally culturised multimodal facial actions used to indicate their comprehension or incomprehension of instructions. The chapter outlines implications for English Language teaching and theories of listenership in multilingual EL_2 blended learning contexts.

Introduction

This chapter reports a scoping study that tries to understand communication occurring between English as first language (EL_1)-speaking software agents and English as a second language (EL_2) listeners in Nigeria where digital technologies intersect multilingualism to enhance the vitality of English language teacher education (E-LTE).

Nigeria has about '519 living languages' (Simons & Fennig, 2018) where Hausa, Igbo and Yoruba are most widely spoken with English as second language. While Nigerian languages share some roles with English in national life, English remains the language of instruction, governance, commerce and general interaction among Nigerians.

The national policy on education (FGN, 2013) aims to develop in English language teachers four communicative language skills, make them confident and competent users of English language for diverse purposes and well-equipped to teach English language and literature in schools. Concurrently, the national ICT Education policy (FGN, 2011) proposes an integration that will move teacher-competence beyond basic literacy towards using technology to facilitate quality improvement and transformation in educational delivery. These policies aim is to transform teachers from knowledge doyens to facilitators and passive students to active participants in learning and knowledge construction.

Interaction contexts are changing rapidly from being solely Human–Human Interaction (HHI) to Human–Agent Interaction (HAI). Agents are described as highly inter-connected computational components capable of acting autonomously and intelligently (Jennings *et al.*, 2014). Agents include intelligent personal assistants (IPAs) like Amazon's Alexa, Apple's Siri; and instructors/advice-givers (sat navs and map applications, automated checkouts in supermarkets). While most of these agents afford users robust verbal and written interaction, they provide limited nonverbal and monolingual–English interaction.

The Nigerian interaction context is further disrupted by the Covid-19 pandemic. This is leading to a notable increase in individual and group interaction with digital devices where interlocutors negotiate meaning-making choices while translanguaging during interaction. Translanguaging is derived from Makalela's concept of Ubuntu translanguaging (Niyibizi *et al.*, this volume) and operationally defined as the manner in which interlocutors concurrently use more than one nonverbal resource to communicate, build knowledge and contextualise meaning during interaction.

The author's UK study indicated that speakers of EL_1 reacted in different ways to EL_1-mode software agents' vague instructions and language use. The study concluded that agents should be adaptive to user context since no one size fits all. It recommended that the study be replicated in other contexts of English language use to improve our understanding of HAI. Following these, a scoping study was carried out in Nigeria that aimed to understand communication occurring between EL_1-speaking software agents and EL_2 listeners in Nigeria.

These critical contextual, linguistic and technological diversities in Nigeria may enable us to understand how digital technologies intersect multilingualism to engender marked multimodal nonverbal listenership behaviours during interaction. Such user behaviour may enable us to assess how multilingual EL_2 speakers make sense of interactions with EL_1-mode devices. Sense-making is a process by which interlocutors gather information, gain an understanding of the information and then use the understanding to give meaning to their collective experiences and finish a task (Weick *et al.*, 2005). Sense-making may signpost user readiness for an increased use of smart multilingual digital technology in teaching and knowledge construction in emerging contexts.

Related Literature

Simulated agents

This chapter uses the contexts of HAI/HHI to assess how multilingual EL_2-speakers make sense of interactions with EL_1-mode software agents and EL_2-mode instructors. As outlined earlier, a simulated agent was used in the study and it has the following characteristics.

Firstly, the agent's personal identity is linked to affordances incorporated into it by designers and given by voices used to issue instructions similar to Apple's Siri that can offer verbal interaction across platforms (Kiseleva *et al.*, 2016).

Secondly, it uses object-oriented application frameworks to define its behaviour and interaction patterns. An object-oriented framework is technology used for reifying software design and implementation at reduced costs with greater efficiency and specialisation (Fayad & Schmidt, 1997). These frameworks enable simulated agents to have goal-oriented behaviour because they are designed at task level to exhibit specific behaviours in specific contexts (Lin *et al.*, 2015). Specialisation makes it impossible for them to function in other contexts; for example, trust agents (that sell ideas e.g. mobile phone top-up voice) cannot function as agent-instructors in business contexts (e.g. self-checkout) or vice-versa.

García *et al.* (2000) suggest that simulated agents react to input with regulated spontaneity because their internal state modulates this reactive behaviour and structures external behaviour. For example, Siri's designer intended it to interact verbally with users thus, programmed it to recognise voices, understand only Euro-Asian words that are required for it to fulfil tasks it supports and give appropriate feedback. Similarly, the agent in this study takes in keyboard-based commands (clicking start button) and returns appropriate speech-based output (voicing first assembly instruction).

These characteristics are normalised internally in the agent's personal identity and linked to its verbal capabilities, which may make users categorise agents as having a particular linguistic or vocal property. This is linked to the notion that agents conforming or not conforming to human expectations may inform researchers on how users socially position agents during interaction(Clark *et al.*, 2016).

Nigerian Teacher Education Context

The E-LTE context in Nigeria comprises different languages, interaction modes and instructional methodologies with technology opening up new possibilities that create a hybrid interaction context. A diversity framework is used to analyse the meshing and interweaving of diversities in Nigeria's E-LTE context. The diversity framework as a social construct recognises and engages varieties of differences and similarities among people and entities using Appiah *et al.*'s (2018) dimensions such as culture, nationality, education, language, education, work style, work experience, job role and function, thinking style and personality type.

As an operational framework, diversity in Nigeria is originating, integrative and modal. Deng (2008) describes diversity as the plurality of identity groups that inhabit individual countries. Originating diversity is created by the mere existence of 519 linguistic groups in Nigeria. Integrative diversity is deliberately created from originating diversity using the federal character principle enshrined in Section 14 subsections 3 and 4 of Nigeria's 1999 constitution. This principle stipulates that, in the composition of government and its agencies, people from all sectional and ethno-linguistic groups must be represented (FGN, 1999). This ensures that students and staff come from different ethno-linguistic backgrounds, thus creating multilingual E-LTE cohorts.

Modal diversity refers to the multiplicity in curriculum delivery modes that enable Nigerian tertiary institutions to cope with large classes and inadequate facilities. Relatedly, learning in these institutions is becoming more blended because it combines traditional learning approaches with technology-driven learning. It also combines various media, tools, resources in an e-learning environment and mixes several pedagogic approaches in a flexible manner (Tomilson & Whittaker, 2013).

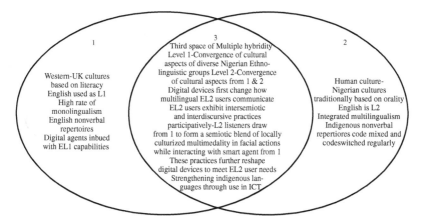

Figure 8.1 The hybrid context of Interaction in E-LTE

Nigerian E-LTE classrooms are hybrid spaces (Figure 8.1) of interaction based on Bhabha's 1994 theory of hybridity. The theory postulates that when two cultures meet at the borderline of multicultural interaction, a new culture is born within a hybrid space (Bhabha, 2015). The first level of hybridity occurs among humans when people from diverse Nigerian ethno-linguistic groups meet in E-LTE classrooms.

Another level of hybridity is created when EL_1-mode devices meet with multilingual EL_2 users in E-LTE classrooms (circle 3, Figure 8.1) because they represent different cultures. First agents are manmade from literate cultures, while EL_2 users are humans from oral cultures. Research suggests that oral and literate cultures contrast in thought, expression and organization of human experience. Oral cultures are additive, subordinative, aggregative, analytic, redundant, concise, based on tradition, unconventional, close to human experience, more abstract and situated within the context of struggle. In contrast, literate cultures are less agonistic, tone empathic, participatory, objectively distanced, with strong focus on the present and past situational frames of reference and engender more conceptual thinking (Ogbondah & Siddens III, 1999: 3–5).

Using Figure 8.1 to illustrate Nigerian E-LTE context, circle 1 represents literate cultures such as the UK where English is L1 with a high rate of monolingualism and rich repertoires of nonverbal English language. EL_1-mode devices come permeated with aspects of literate cultures and capabilities that generate a distinct computerised interactional culture (Figure 8.1). Circle 2 represents cultures that are predominately oral with emphasis on spoken words and high multilingual capacity in foreign and indigenous languages.

Following Bhabha (2015) and Ogbondah and Siddens III (1999), it is argued here that these cultural dissimilarities imply that interlocutors from these contexts possess distinctive interactional competences. Thus, when human-EL_2-oral interactional culture meets EL_1-literate agent inter-actional culture, a third-hybrid interactional culture (Level 2 hybridity) is born and this encounters Level 1 hybridity to create multiple hybridity within the hybrid space (circle 3) which is the intersection of digital tech-nologies and multilingualism in E-LTE contexts.

The diversity framework clarifies the background for examining inter-action and convergence levels between digital technology and EL_2-user multimodal translanguaging practices with a focus on what Baynham *et al.* (2015) referred to as dynamic processes and practices that illustrate the varieties of discursive practices multilinguals employ to conceive and build meanings during interaction.

Listenership Through Multimodal Facial Actions

In assessing how multilingual EL_2 users perceive EL1-mode agent identities and make sense of interactions, it is useful to understand the role of listenership using multimodal facial actions in interaction. Listenership is '...the active, responsive role that listeners have in conversation' (O'Keeffe *et al.*, 2007: 142). By implication, listeners participate actively in any discourse, even when they are not talking using backchannels, and it is a behaviour expected of them by speakers.

Knight (2009) citing Yngve (1970) explains that backchannels are lis-tener responses during one-way communication that can be verbal or non-verbal expressions such as facial actions. And White (1989) posits that backchannels imply that there are two channels of communication used by speakers and listeners. Speakers use the main channel while listeners use backchannels to interject speakers without claiming the floor. Functionally, backchannels are used to maintain conversation flow, indi-cate listener agreement with speakers, show listeners paying attention to speakers, and information uttered is of interest to listeners and may be evaluative (Tsuchiya, 2013).

For the purpose of this chapter, backchannels are spontaneous facial actions. Spontaneous facial actions are '... unmodulated emotional facial expressions that are congruent with an underlying emotional state' (Hess & Kleck, 1997: 271). This means that spontaneous facial expressions often align with associative expressions like voice, gesture or posture showing fluency in communication.

Spontaneous facial actions are used for assessing listenership because faces have gargantuan sending capacity. Ofemile *et al.* (2018) report that in 1969 Paul Ekman and Wallace Friesen developed the concept of sending capacity as a means of evaluating information sending capabilities of human body parts. Ofemile *et al.* (2018) further explain that Ekman and Friesen established that in comparison to other human body parts, faces possesses the highest sending capacity because they have shortest trans-mission time, complex musculature that allows for multiple discriminable stimuli pattern display and greatest visibility except when covered by hair, sunglasses, masks or veils.

From a social semiotic perspective, it is argued that facial actions are multimodal because they meet all of Bezemer and Jewitt's (2010) multi-modality-compliance benchmarks. Firstly, nonverbal listenership draws on a variety of composite modes including facial actions, gestures and proxemics. Facial actions also draw on complementary communication modes namely, eyebrows, eyes, gaze, mouth, head and posture, all of which contribute to meaning making during interaction. Furthermore, listener facial actions like other forms of communication modes have been shaped through cultural, historical and social uses to fulfil social functions.

Secondly, communication occurs within a social context and meaning is derived from and about that context. Bezemer and Jewitt (2010) posit that the meaning of multimodal signs is located in the social origin, moti-vations and interests of interactants in specific interaction contexts. For example, the length and direction of a gaze, intensity of furrows on fore-heads, width and shape of listeners' lips are all resources for contextual-ised meaning making during interaction.

Thirdly, meaning derived from every mode is always inter-woven across co-present and cooperating modes in interaction contexts. Thus, the face in conjunction with other body parts combine to communicate, while every part of the face – eyebrows, eyes, gaze, mouth and head – cooperate to convey meaning congruently.

As per taxonomy, facial actions are fundamentally related to emotions categorised as basic, non-basic, emotional attitudes, moods, eye and lip actions and microexpressions. Facial actions can be different due to indi-vidual differences, but basic ones are universal because they are present in every human population, have evolved within man to deal with vital life tasks and are easily recognisable (Ekman, 2007) as anger, disgust, sad-ness, fear, happiness, surprise and neutral expressions (see Table 8.3 later in text).

Non-basic emotions are produced from a mixture of basic emotions because facial muscles are amply complex to display a blend of emotions (Ekman, 1997) such as a smug. The blending process involves one emo-tion merging into another to produce a new one in a manner similar to articulation of diphthongs where one vowel runs into another to sound as one (Ofemile et al., 2018).

Emotional attitudes often involve more than one emotion being elic-ited and are more persistent than basic emotions during interaction (Ekman, 2007). Attitudinal reactions like frowns may indicate listeners' willingness to accept or reject a message nonverbally in ways that are dif-ferent from emotions, yet can be used to indicate peculiar preferences, affective disposition, intrapersonal stances and communicative strategies (Ekman, 1997; Ofemile, 2018).

Ekman (1997) and Miller (2014) posit that people can control facial actions because of social pressures and the very behaviour expected in each context is concealed so, people manage to deliberately give off emotions that do not reflect their true feelings. However, when humans are experiencing emotions, the physiology takes over such that even when they try to mask their true feelings, the genuine feelings usually leak out as microexpressions. Microexpressions flash on and off the face so quickly that they are usually missed; nevertheless they constitute the greatest source of information leakage from human faces (Ekman, 2007).

This chapter holds that facial actions project our emotional state, which is constantly changing due to events in our surroundings as mediated by our understanding, disposition and environmental factors. This affirms Ogbay and White's (this volume) assertion that emotion is critical in determining how messages are framed during interaction. Therefore, it is vital to understand how and why EL$_2$ listeners' spontaneous facial actions as discrete and semiotic mergers project their viewpoints during interaction.

The Nature of Human–Agent Interaction

As interaction contexts rapidly shift from being solely HHI to HAI, the nature of human interaction in diverse settings of HAI/HCI requires understanding and has been investigated by Nass, Reeves and others using the Computers are Social Actors (CASA) paradigm later elaborated as Media Equation (M-E) theory. CASA paradigm holds that during interaction people treat computers and computerised spaces as real people and spaces (Nass *et al.*, 1994) based on three premises.

The first is that people applied social norms and notions of self and other to computers, responded socially to computers and do not see computers as channels of social interaction with programmers. Secondly, CASA suggests that, basic human communication devices are powerful because of their control and influence over people and events while social responses such as facial actions are automatic because they are naturally ingrained in us which agrees with Ekman's (2007) assertion that facial actions are present in every culture. Thirdly, HCI/HAI is social–psychological and many theories from psychology, sociology, linguistics and other fields of study are also relevant in HCI/HAI (Nass *et al.*, 1997).

As a progression from CASA, M-E holds that social rules guiding interactions with people can apply equally to HCI; therefore, Reeves and Nass (1996) argue that an 'individual's interactions with computers, television, and new media are fundamentally social and natural, just like interaction in real life' (Reeves & Nass, 1996: 5) 'Social' refers to the tendency to treat media as if you were working with another person, while 'natural' refers to the propensity to treat media as if you were dealing with a normal physical environment. The medium becomes invisible and humans are oriented to its socialness or what is been seen (Reeves & Nass, 2014). For example, people have identified themselves as teammates with computers, and perceived computers as having personalities similar to humans, whereas even small changes in creating these perceived personalities could elicit social behaviours from users (Nass & Lee, 2001; Nass & Moon, 2000).

Following these, it is expedient to understand how EL_2 listeners use spontaneous facial actions to indicate their comprehension or incomprehension of instructions, perceptions and attitudes towards instructors' performative identities during interaction.

Methodology

As outlined earlier, the study reported endeavoured to understand communication occurring when EL_1-speaking software agents instruct EL_2 listeners using these research questions:

RQ1   Do participants give nonverbal feedback (facial actions)?
RQ2   Are there differences in user perception of instructor characteristics across the voice cline, e.g. human versus simulated agent?

The steps outlined in the following section were taken to answer these questions.

Agent design and human instructor choice

A simulated agent was created on a computer interface instead of a real agent for the study because it provides users with experiences similar to that which actual agents provide (Clark *et al.*, 2014). There are three ranges of voice progression in the continuum: synthesised, human-like and human voice (Figure 8.2). Synthesised voices include Cepstral Lawrence (CL)[1] and Giles from CereProc (CP).[2] While recorded human voice was provided by a professional voice actor (HR) hired from http://voicebunny.com, the human instructor (HV) used his natural voice.

The three agent voices were male, had a southern RP English accent, and were aged between 45–60 years old. In creating the synthesised speech instructions, text files were inputted into a text-to-speech program (Text2SpeechPro) and exported as .wav files. For the human recording, a

Figure 8.2 The voice continuum

voice actor recorded the same text which was edited into individual .wav files using Audacity.[3]

HV is a 45-year-old male EL_2 speaker with a Nigerian accent that is generally understood by Nigerians. HV was used for this study because he is an experienced teacher of English, teacher trainer and a PhD researcher in a Nigerian university. Instructors provide natural and familiar interaction envisaged in real-life HAI and HHI contexts since participants are used to taking instructions in various contexts.

Participants and Task

Purposive sampling was used to select EL_2 speakers as target population in order to understand how they will respond to vague instructions during interaction. Ten participants were self-selected from among student-teachers of English at the FCT College of Education Zuba-Abuja, Nigeria for this study. There were five males (50%) and five females (50%) aged between 18–24 years old. These students passed English at credit level in School Certificate/GCE examinations and have studied English in higher education for two years. Using Cambridge University's (2013) guide to the Common European Framework of Reference for Languages (CEFR) descriptors, participants are classified as independent speakers of English.

Task assignment was randomised to make sampling counterbalanced when allocating slots, voices, tasks and timings to participants because it is straightforward, simple, eliminates clustered selection (Dörnyei, 2007) and balances population and corpora without researcher bias.

Participants were provided with two Lego models in two separate tasks and were briefed that they will construct the models using verbal instructions from a simulated agent on a computer interface and/or HV within a 15-minute time limit per task. Participants ask for instructions (by pressing the Start button in HAI or giving thumbs up sign in HHI). Participants can ask for a repeat of the same instruction by pressing repeat button in HAI or raising their forefinger in HHI, but they cannot ask for previous instructions. These conditions were imposed to discover self-propelled behaviours in participants.

Participants were given consent forms to indicate agreement and willingness to participate in or withdraw from the experiment followed by demographics forms for personal details. The first model was given to them and after 15 minutes or when they completed model assembly, depending on which comes first; the second model was given to them.

Data Collection

A clear record was obtained of interactions observed for measurements using two digital video cameras (Knight, 2009) that recorded interactions from two angles – face and side (Figure 8.3).

Figure 8.3 Side and front camera views of interaction

Figure 8.4 Front camera views of interaction

Using two cameras enables recording of individual sequences of body movements and different positions of participants during task. This allows for analyses of synchronised videos and examination of coordinated movements across each view (Knight, 2009). However, power outage damaged one camera, leaving only one to record interactions (Figure 8.4). While this provided only one view, it ensured that all recordings were acceptably clear.

A 5-hour-long multimodal corpus was built and analysed from these interactions. ELAN-EUDICO Linguistic Annotator[4] and CLAN[5] (Computerized Language ANalysis) software were used to manage and annotate the corpora for facial actions using adapted schemas, coding systems and hierarchies (Ekman *et al.*, 2013; Feng & O'Halloran, 2013).

Data Analysis

Annotating multimodal facial actions

Data analysis combines two processes. The first is designing an annotation scheme to make the multimodal data useful and searchable. The annotation coding scheme combined and extended insights from Ekman and

Friesen (2003), Ekman *et al.* (2013) and Matsumoto and Willingham (2009) and others contained in the analysis. The second process focuses on developing a 'thick description' (Dörnyei, 2007) of emerging nonverbal behaviours using the annotation scheme to identify specific facial actions (see Table 8.4 later in text), annotation tiers, values and their descriptions.

Since holistic transcription is unmanageable, Harrison (2014) suggests that researchers normally decide on a system of annotation and coding that is oriented towards specific communicative functions such as speakership skills. Therefore, this annotation is geared towards spontaneous facial actions as the multimodal communicative listenership modes that listeners displayed during interaction.

The Facial Action Coding System (FACS) of Ekman *et al.* (2013) is used to identify all functional anatomic facial muscle movements or Action Units (AU), and to measure relaxation or contraction of each muscle, while Matsumoto and Willingham's (2009) protocols are used to map head and eye positions.

Using social semiotic understanding, annotation levels (Table 8.1) used to measure facial actions displayed include eyebrows, eyes, gaze head and mouth in relation to other body parts because they are physically placed on the listener's face, unlike gestures that can occur outside the interlocutor's body as seen in stance or deictic gestures.

Dragoi's (2015) anatomy of facial muscles (Figure 8.5) guides the annotation scheme to indicate muscles responsible for each AU which are coded and linked to facial muscles as outlined in Table 8.2.

The annotation scheme includes lips and eye movement in relation to facial actions and task completion. These on their own may not project emotion but they enable observers to make better judgements. Bell (2015) describes lips as puckering, protruding and pouting and posits that lip-licking action has stronger forms including biting, swallowing or compressing lips.

Specific movements and positions of faces relate to given impressions in normal interaction because there is an association between specific facial muscles and specific emotions (Ekman *et al.*, 2013). More than one muscle can be grouped into an AU or a muscle may be divided into separate AUs based on duration, intensity and asymmetry (Ekman, 2003) of facial actions as shown in Table 8.3.

Intensity of expression is classified as A = trace; B = slight with C = pronounced articulation as the default where AUs are shown without labels, e.g. AU1 = pronounced; AU1B = slight; AU1C = a trace.

Table 8.1 Annotation levels for listener multimodal facial actions as semiotic modes

Modality	Semiotic mode/ Expression type	Listener facial actions displayed
Facial actions	Eyebrows; eyes; gaze; mouth; head	Within-listener during assembly task

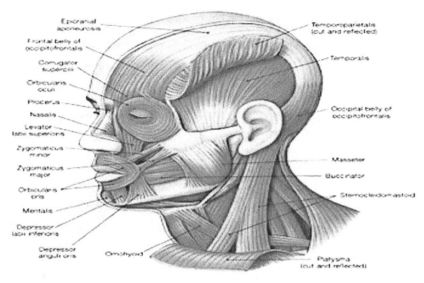

Figure 8.5 Muscles for facial expression
Source: Dragoi (2015).

Table 8.2 Facial action annotation scheme

Annotation group	Facial action	Action Unit number/ code	Muscular basis
	Neutral face	AU0	
	Inner brow raiser	AU1; AU1B	frontalis (pars medialis)
	Outer brow raiser	AU2	frontalis (pars lateralis)
	Brow lowerer	AU4; AU4B	depressor glabellae, depressor supercilii, corrugator supercilii
	Upper lid raiser	AU5; AU5B	levator palpebrae superioris, superior tarsal muscle
	Cheek raiser	AU6; AU6B	orbicularis oculi (pars orbitalis)
	Lid tightener	AU7; AU7B	orbicularis oculi (pars palpebralis)
	Pulls or tighten lips towards each other	AU8; AU8B	the orbicularis oris muscle
	Nose wrinkle	AU9; AU9B	levator labii superioris alaeque nasi
	Lip corner puller	AU12; AU12B; R12A	zygomaticus major
	Dimpler	AU14; R14A	Buccinator

Continued

Table 8.2 Facial action annotation scheme (*Continued*)

	Lip corner depressor	AU15; AU15B	depressor anguli oris (also known as triangularis)
	Lower lip depressor	AU16; AU16B	depressor labii inferioris
	Chin raiser	AU17	mentalis muscle
	Lip stretcher	AU20	risorius w/ platysma
	Neck tightener	AU21	platysma
	Lip funneler	AU22	orbicularis oris
	Lip pressor	AU24	orbicularis oris
	Lips part	AU25	depressor labii inferioris muscles
	Jaw drop	AU26	masseter; relaxed temporalis and internal pterygoid
	Mouth stretcher	AU27B	pterygoids, digastric muscle
	Dimpler	R14A	Buccinator
	Lip bite	AU 32	
	Swallowed/ compressed lips	AU8B	orbicularis oris
	Glabella lowerer	AU41	Separate Strand of AU4:depressor glabellae (Procerus) muscle
	Inner eyebrow lowerer	AU42	Separate Strand of AU4: depressor supercilii
	Eyebrow gatherer narrows eyes	AU44; AU44B	corrugator Supercilii (Darwin's muscle of difficulty)
	Wink	AU46	orbicularis oculi
	Head downward movement	AU54	
Intensity of facial action	Trace Slight Pronounced or maximum	A B C	
Eye/Ocular motor movement	Saccade – Left Saccade – Right	AU61 AU62	Lateral rectus and Medial rectus muscles; AU46 orbicularis oculi muscle

Source: Adapted from Ekman et al. (2013); Matsmoto & Willingham (2009); Dragoi (2015).

Table 8.3 Ekman's basic emotions

EMOTION	Action Units
Happiness	6 + 2
Sadness	1 + 4 + 15
Surprise	1 + 2 + 5B + 26
Fear	1 + 2 + 4 + 5 + 7 + 20 + 26
Anger	4 + 5 + 7 + 23
Disgust	9 + 15 + 16
Contempt	R12A + R14A

However, when information provided by the face contradicts that provided by other behavioural modalities, Ekman and Friesen (2003) suggest that researchers should look for the regularity of these discrepancies and how subjects mitigate them. As per HCI/HAI, we seek for information sources from the context. These conventions provide a framework for systematic practical analysis of multimodal facial actions emerging from interaction.

Describing Multimodal Facial Actions

This is the second stage of data analysis where thick description occurs in three stages viz, linguistic annotation and segmentation, classification, then establishing interactive, communicative and task functions of facial action (Ofemile, 2018).

Linguistic annotation involves first describing neuro-biological processes generating facial actions. Biological processes involve facial muscles or AUs responsible for an expression using Ekman *et al.*'s (2013) FACS illustrated in Figure 8.6.

Facial muscles responsible include AU6 + AU12 + AU7 cheek raiser, lip puller and lid tightener.

Figure 8.6 Identifying AUs responsible for a felt smile

Neurological processes relate to the five senses that elicit emotions through stimulation (Mixdorff *et al.*, 2017); for example, when people relish touching, seeing, hearing, smelling, tasting or experiencing something they smile.

The next step involves classifying facial actions. Such categorisation creates systematic typologies called facial actions families with defined characteristics (Ekman, 2007). Each family has child and sibling subgroups that are identifiably distinct in their manner of execution and communicative functions (Tables 8.4, 8.5 and 8.6).

Table 8.4   Representative samples of spontaneous listener facial actions displayed along the continuum

Listener facial actions

REF	A-POSITIVE	B-NEUTRAL	C-NEGATIVE	D-OTHERS
1				
2				
3				
4				
5				
6				

Table 8.5   Corpus of spontaneous listener facial actions

Table REF	Facial action family	Child	Sibling buckets	Action Units (AU)	Interactive function
B1	Basic facial actions	Neutral	Neutral	AU0	Indicates relaxed composure, multitasking and turn-taking initiation
B4, 5			Neutral face down	AU0 + AU54	cognitive processing
B3			Neutral concentration on task	AU0 + AU8	concentration on task
B6			Neutral hard	AU0 + AU44	Difficulty in cognitive processing
B2			Neutral concentration on instruction	AU0	Indicates cognitive processing of on-going instruction
A5-6		Smile	Felt smile	AU6 + AU12 + AU7	Indicates positive interaction with instructor, task and self
A1			Nervous smile	AU12	Making the best of a bad situation
A2-4			Tight-lipped	AU6 + AU6B + AU12B	Positive mask for real feelings
C2		Disgust	Disgust	AU9 + AU15B +AU16B +AU44B (strand of AU4)	Indicates feeling of aversion towards self-efforts or interaction experience

Linguistic segmentation and categorisation also include descriptive arrangement and discussion of the most frequent linguistic and multi-modal bundles considered as indicators of agreement and variation in listenership behaviours (Field, 2008). Moreover, identifying emerging relationships is useful for rule setting (Ekman, 2016). Thereafter, classification focuses on understanding listeners' communicative practices and what stimulates communicative behaviours during interaction.

A second rater analysed and annotated videos of randomly selected interactions using the annotation scheme (Tables 8.1–8.3) in order to provide another perception of listener facial actions and ascertain inter-rater reliability following Clark *et al.* (2016) and Kita *et al.* (2007).

Table 8.6 Corpus of spontaneous listener facial actions

Table REF	Facial action family	Illustration Child	Sibling Buckets	Action Units (AU)	Interactive function
D6	Non-basic blends	Whuck!	Whuck! Moment	AU13 + AU24 + AU34 + AU55 (tilt's head left)	A mixture of surprise, astonishment, incredulity, shock (eye-action), confusion and difficulty in cognitive processing; disruption of cognitive processes as listener concentrates on instructor input (puffy pout). A locally culturized facial action created from Nigerian eye-action and English head movements suggesting nonverbal translanguaging
C4, C6	Emotional attitudes/ moods	Frown	Frown	AU44 + AU46 + AU24 + AU21 + AU41 + AU17 + AU15	Suggests concentration while processing instructions or assessing action taken
D1		Workman face	Work face	AU9 + AU15 + AU16	Indicates listener's exertion of force under pressure during tasks
D3- 4		Tense mouth and lip action	Compressed lips	AU8	Indicates concentration, cognitive processing, anxiety, nervousness, mood shift, change of heart
Fig 8		Emotional build-up	Frustration process	(AU0 + AU4B + AU1);(AU0 + AU44 + AU69); (AU9B + 15B + 16B)	Indicates listener's burden as their ability to deal with specific challenges diminishes as they give up on task completion

Table 8.6 Corpus of spontaneous listener facial actions (*Continued*)

Fig 9	Nonverbal private talk		Sideways head nods	AU5+AU52 + AU51 + (AU44B + AU46B + AU24B + AU21B +AU41B + AU17B + AU15B)	A sign of negation in Nigerian cultures used here to suggest listener self-recognition of their incomprehension of instructions during interaction –nonverbal codemixing suggesting translanguaging
D5			Pouty face	AU17 + AU25, AU21 + AU22 + AU23	Potentially used for concentration or self-comfort
5	Eye action		Eye closure	AU7 + AU9 + AU12 + AU43B + AU56B (slight tilt left)	Indicate listener's degree of self-belief or certainty and ongoing cognitive processes regarding their comprehension of instructions/appropriacy of task execution
C1	Microexpressions	Basic hot spots	Anger	AUB4B + AU5 + AU7B	Emotional leakages indicating true emotions depending on context
C2			Disgust	AU9B + AU15B + AU16 + AU44B	same as C2 above with lesser intensity
C5			Sadness	AU1B + AU15B + AU20B + AU6B	May indicate inability to achieve a set interaction goal

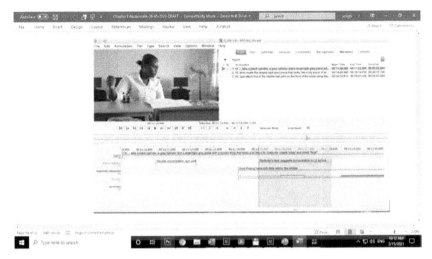

Figure 8.7 ELAN annotation interface

The second rater, a PhD researcher, was trained, given some practice for two days and used ELAN with already marked interactions (Figure 8.7) to analyse 10 randomly selected interactions.

Results

The results show that multimodal communication occurs between EL_1-speaking software agents and EL_2-listeners when digital technology intersects multilingualism. The results are presented under two integrated research questions focusing on spontaneous facial actions EL_2 listeners display, and why and how these compare along the voice continuum.

RQ 1. Spontaneous facial actions displayed

The spontaneous facial actions displayed include basic, non-basic blends, emotional attitudes, eye actions and microexpressions classified in columns A, B C and D in Table 8.4 and outlined in Tables 8.5–8.6.

Basic facial actions displayed include neutral face, smile and disgust. Neutral face (AU0) is expressionless with all muscles relaxed (Ekman & Friesen, 2003). However, the results suggest that listeners' faces are never expressionless because of involvement in task and information processing. Participants displayed five forms of neutral expressions (Table 8.4) as follows. B1's facial muscles are completely relaxed. B2's eyes look away from both instructor and kit layout suggesting that he is trying to process repeated instruction.

B3's face is expressionless, but her hands are engaged indicating that she is multitasking- concurrently joining assembly pieces and listening to instructions. B4 is assessing work done while B5 is examining assembly pieces selected. B6 is leaning forward given by AU 54 – head down (Ekman, 2007) with eyes focused in space just as people do when they want to have a better listening position and comprehension. Although B6's hands are idle, the partially furrowed forehead drawn together by a separate strand of AU44 known as Darwin's muscle of difficulty or eyebrow gatherer (Ekman, 2007) suggests determination or confusion.

Participants displayed felt, nervous and tight-lipped smiles elicited by positive stimulation including amusement, delight, contentment, satisfaction, beatific experiences, relief from pain, pressure or tension (Ekman, 2016; Ofemile, 2018).

The felt or Duchenne smile (A5 & A6) occurs when AU6 raises the cheek, gathers skins around the eyes inwards, narrows eyes apertures and produces crow's feet wrinkles; AU12 pulls lips sideways exposing teeth and AU7 tightens eye lids, raising the lower eye lid to create wrinkles below lower eye lids.

Nervous smile (A1) aka miserable smile (Ekman & Friesen, 2003) is deliberately produced for a short period and may be superimposed on a negative expression. Muscles responsible include AU6 raising the cheeks, AU12 pulling down lip corners and AU54 producing downward head movement.

Tight-lipped smile (A2, A3, A4). The lips are stretched tight across faces in straight lines with teeth unexposed (Ekman & Friesen, 2003). Muscles responsible include AU6B slightly raising the cheeks without visibly reducing eye apertures or creating very visible crow's feet around the eyes. AU12B slightly pulls lip corners and creates some wrinkles.

The Whuck! Moment is a non-basic blend combining surprise-astonishment-incredulity-shock (D6) with pouty mouth. AU1 produces wide open eyes and AU2 raises the inner and outer brows (Ekman, 1997). When people pout AU17 and AU25 contract the chin together, AU21 stretches the neck, while AU20 stretches lower lip muscles (Givens, 2010; Ofemile, 2018). AU22 funnels the lips making the pout more prominent and shaped to that used in whistling. Children pout in sadness, frustration and uncertainty while adults pout when disagreeing with comments or trying to make sense of conversations (Givens, 2010). Pouting suggests that D6 is either cognitively processing instructions or self-comforting during interaction.

Listeners also displayed emotional attitudes as moods – frown, workman face, compressed lips and frustration as a transition of emotions. Ekman (2007) describes a frown (C4, C6) as an emotional attitude produced primarily by eyebrows furrowing using AU44 brow gatherer aka the 'muscle of difficulty' because, frowning occurs with many kinds of mental or physical difficulties (Ekman, 1997). AU46 lowers eyelids as done in a wink and could be executed with the neck jerking forward. Other muscles involved include AU24 lip pressor and AU21 producing a slight wrinkling of the neck's surface skin in an oblique direction (Standring & Borley, 2008), AU41 creating a horizontal wrinkle across the nose's bridge, AU17 raising the chin and AU15 depressing lip corners.

Workman's face (D1) is perceived as disgust blending with contempt and anger; however, it occurs as a result of physical force exerted when assembling models similar to people who clench their teeth or press their lips when lifting very heavy things or pulling things apart in Ekman's (1997) study. This is produced by AU9 nose wrinkler, AU15 lip corner depressor raising the upper lip, AU16 lower lip depressor raising the lower lip making it protrude while lid tightener slightly pulls lip corners.

Compressed lips action (D3-4) is produced by in-rolling and narrowing lips to a thin line position in which they are visibly tightened and pressed together. This occurs when AU8 pulls the lips towards each other (Ekman, 2007) In assembly tasks, lip compression may indicate cognitive processing as pondering, thinking or feeling uncertain about instructions.

Emotion building up as frustration (Figure 8.8) occurs in our lives as a response to opposition and from our perception of resistance to the fulfilment of a given goal (Jeronimus & Laceulle, 2018). Frustration observed in Figure 8.8 could be caused by task difficulties due to participant's incomprehension of instructions. It occurs in three stages characterised by four features. Stage1 Initiation – the participant's germinal encounter with instruction and task: the two curved arrows indicate how shoulders hunch over-inwards, while the neutral face-AU0, eyebrows drawn down(AU4B), lips slightly turned down (AU12-sadness) suggest that she has met blockages in the assembly process. Stage 2 Unsuccessful intensive comprehension efforts – posture changes with a shoulder shrug in two concurrent movements sideways-outwards (bidirectional arrow) and downwards (slanted arrows) as she heaves a sigh of resignation, neutral

Figure 8.8 Emotional build up

Figure 8.9 Sideways head nods left–right–left as self-recognition of self-errors

face concentration-AU0, eyebrows straightened-AU44 with eyes pinned on task-AU69. Stage 3 Frustration manifests fully: lips turned down in micro-disgust (AU9B + 15B + 16B) as she abandons the task.

Nonverbal private talk indicated by sideways head nods (Figure 8.9) occurs with three movements using the following muscles; 1 = AU51 – head turn left; 2 = AU52 – head turn right; 3 = AU51 – head turn left again.

Montazeri *et al.* (2015) discovered that people use nonverbal private talk for self-regulation which helps them to plan, monitor and guide activity in demanding situations such as assembly tasks in unidirectional interaction contexts. In addition, left–right–left sideways head nods (Figure 8.9) as a composite communicative action is used by Nigerians to indicate negation, disagreement with a co-interlocutor's view and self-recognition of one's errors or inability to do the expected during interaction. The participant (Figure 8.9) uses sideways head nods with a frown to indicate self-recognition of his incomprehension of instructions and consequent task errors.

Eye actions identified include eye opening and closing (D6 & D2). D6 has already been explained as an aspect of Whuck! Moment where it indicates surprise incredulity or astonishment. The muscles responsible for the eye closure include, AU7 lid tightener in tandem with a relaxed AU43B (levator palpebrae superioris) to partially close the eyes creating a squint. While AU12 pulls lip corners rightwards, AU9 wrinkles the nose and AU56B slightly tilts the head left to give the peeping look. Research suggests that communicative eye closures (D2) provide information about the sender's mind regarding their level of self-belief in ongoing interactions (Vincze & Poggi, 2011). Hence, eye closure communicates D2's self-confidence and attempts to correctly interpret and execute assembly instructions.

Microexpressions are consistent and represent the externalisation of a person's true feelings at a particular time and context. Microexpressions observed among participants include anger, disgust and sadness. Ekman (2007) suggests that anger and fear often occur together with fear preceding anger thus, they have similar features however, anger galvanises people to action (C4). Although, participants tried to remain calm, anger leaks out probably due to perplexity (Ekman & Friesen, 2003) during interaction. C4 displays micro-anger realised by AU4B – brow lowerer, AU5 – upper lid raiser, AU7B – orbicularis oculi muscle or lid tightener, AU20B –lip stretcher making lips thinner provides clues to anger.

Disgust is characterised by lowered brow, raised upper lip, flaring nostrils, and (sometimes open) mouth curved downwards. Micro-disgust (C3) is prominently displayed on lower side of the face in the one-sided disgust with the mouth bending rightwards. Micro-disgust is realised when AU15B –lip corner depressor raises the upper lip, while AU16B lower lip depressor raises the lower lip making it protrude with relaxed eyelids. In contrast, C2 displayed full disgust using AU44 a separate strand of AU4 brow lowerer to narrow the eyes, AU9 to wrinkle the nose, AU5 lowers upper lid, AU7 tightens lids, while AU15 and AU16 depress upper lip corners, and lower lip respectively.

C5's slightly turned down lips signal emotional leakage of sadness. Muscles responsible include AU1B -inner brow raiser, AU15B – lip corner, AU20B – mouth stretcher and AU6 – cheeks raiser (Ekman, 2007).

RQ2 inferred listener attitudes towards instructors

When instructors engage listeners, facial actions may project listener attitudes signalling their comprehension or incomprehension of instructions. Listener attitudes towards interaction might be reliably detected and measured through facial actions, which are also distinguishable as positive, neutral or negative (Meadors & Murray, 2014; Mehrabian, 2007). Listeners displayed 302 facial actions reflecting these attitudes towards instructors during interaction (Figure 8.10).

Positive facial actions include felt, slight and tight-lipped smiles, representing 13% of the distribution. Neutral includes neutral, neutral concentration-instructions, neutral concentration-task, neutral intense, neutral face-hard, neutral face-down and workman face representing 66%. Negative facial actions comprise 21% and include disgust, slight

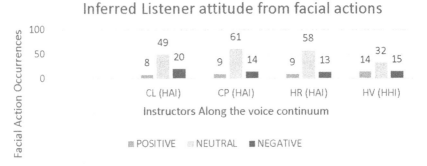

Figure 8.10 Inferred listener attitudes from facial actions

disgust micro-anger, micro-sadness, compressed/swallowed lips, micro-sadness, frown and nervous smiles.

The dominance of neutral facial actions suggests that participants were not judgmental towards instructors or interaction rather, they were concentrating on tasks, cognitively processing instructions or simply indifferent. Neutral face may also suggest that listeners are stoic by nature so can maintain blank faces during interaction; however, this is beyond this study's scope.

The next attitude inferred is negative with 16% suggesting that participants had issues with interaction that generated anger, disgust and sadness; however, they successfully made the best of a bad situation, as hinted by nervous smile. In addition, participants displayed more negative facial actions during interaction with CL than HV, CP and HR in that order. The results reinforce the view that people are attracted to co-interlocutors that share same characteristics with them, which reaffirms Lee and Nass' (2003) finding that in matched conditions participants perceived agents to be more socially attractive and trustworthy.

However, negative responses suggest that participants' incomprehension and attitudes are individualistic and depend on instructor fluency and consistency in instructions delivery. For example, HV displays a higher-level disfluency than HR and other agent voices while CP and CL placed more demand on listeners' cognitive processing possibly attributable to the non-human quality of synthesised voices.

Positive emotions such as enjoyment is culturally and contextually defined (Ekman, 1997). The felt smile is a positive face suggesting that participants enjoyed and liked their interaction, established bonds with instructors (Pease & Pease, 2004) or just found agents' voices funny. However, nervous smiles may indicate participants' need to cover errors or incomprehension with smiles as self-defence mechanisms because Malik (2010) found that in several cultures, people smiled when they are unhappy or in adverse circumstances as a face-saving strategy while tight-lipped smile has been found to be used by people to hide their true feelings. Following these, this chapter holds that positive facial actions suggest that participants comprehended instructions and enjoyed interacting with instructors except in circumstances when they had to employ nervous smiles. Specific results suggest that participants enjoyed interacting with HV and the human-like voice recording (HR), while synthesised voices (CP; CL) were the least enjoyable.

In addition, listeners' blended emotional responses, i.e. locally culturised semiotic mergers of emotions, indicate their capacities to mentally adjust to changes in interaction in novel ways. Increasing build-up of negative attitudes leads to a breakdown in communication due to frustration as seen in Figure 8.8. Following these, this chapter holds that the ability to create and use instruction execution strategies is potentially linked to listeners' adaptive use of comprehension skills during interaction.

Implications

As per meaning making, participants effectively used multimodal facial actions to execute Halliday's (1978) ideational, interpersonal and metafunctional meanings. Clearly, listeners in both HAI and HHI have been able to use multimodal facial actions as pragmatic markers indicating their comprehension and incomprehension of verbal instructions. Listeners thus used facial actions as multimodal meaning-making modes to interpret their experiences and tell us something about their interaction (ideational meanings).

Spontaneous multimodal facial actions also accomplished interpersonal functions by providing EL_2 multilingual listeners with strategies for guiding co-interlocutors in their interpretation of listener nonverbal feedback as structured text even though EL_1-mode agents could not attend to them during interaction.

In addition, listeners used participatory intersemiotic and interdiscursive linguistic practices to create multimodal facial actions as meaningful and contextualised linguistic texts indicating how they organise nonverbal language. Simpson (2016) explains that intersemiotic linguistic practices describe switches between spoken and written; visual and verbal language; as well as non-linguistic signs, e.g. spontaneous multimodal facial actions. Interdiscursive linguistic practices describe language use that occurs when unfamiliar discourse is negotiated in hybrid interaction contexts; for example, when listeners ask instructors to repeat new instructions to aid their comprehension and task execution. Participants created blends from Nigerian and English nonverbal repertoires concurrently by codemixing Nigerian eye-action with universal head movements to articulate Whuck! Moment; codemixing facial actions to indicate nonverbal private talk, negation (D6, Table 8.4) and emotional build-up (Figure 8.8). These indicate how EL_2 listeners used linguistic practices to locally culturize blended facial actions as examples of nonverbal translanguaging practices that are deep-rooted to multilingual nonverbal repertoires and orient users to meanings created by the expressions themselves.

These meaning-making strategies imply that for E-LTE to effectively harness the power of digital technology for improving learning, multilingual communication and interaction in Nigeria, interaction with digital technology should involve using multiple strategies and communication modes (verbal and nonverbal, audio-visual and multimedia) to enhance user comprehension. Additionally, the development of E-LTE content and pedagogy should be user-driven with a strong focus on high-quality, meaningful and culturally responsive multimodal materials for teachers and students.

It is argued that effective use of multimodal facial actions during tasks implies that nonverbal multilingualism cannot be discountenanced, but rather should be utilised to enhance the vitality of E-LTE. Consequently, there is a need for such multilinguistic behaviours to be factored into ICT4-E policies, language planning and theories that will account for organisation and management of such behaviours in blended E-LTE contexts where EL_2 speakers interact with EL_1-mode agents.

For digital technology to adequately support multilingual practices in Nigeria, adaptable software agents may be the most feasible for interaction because they can be socially reshaped to meet user needs in various contexts. Social reshaping of technology enables digital devices to understand indigenous and culturized nonverbal repertoires which, according to Bamgbose (2011), bridges the digital divide between Nigeria – a developing country – with the developed world. Bamgbose (2011) also posits that using African languages in technology is a powerful means of language empowerment. For example, the search engine Google came to Nigeria as a monolingual English-only platform, but was socially reshaped to meet Nigerian user needs by becoming multilingual with Hausa, Igbo, Yoruba, and Nigerian Pidgin added as operational languages. This update enhanced the status of Nigerian languages and reduced negative perceptions of multilingualism as an impediment to effective communication. Google's transformation supports Bamgbose's (2011) and Prah's (2017) assertions that multilingualism has an enormous advantage which can be utilised in our collective African interest because multilingualism enhances cross-linguistic communication.

Similarly, intelligent software agents in cross-cultural encounters require skills to perceive user cues and understand culturally sensitive nonverbal behaviours. This is achievable by intellectualising Nigerian languages and using linguistic data from multicultural contexts to drive design in the areas of nonverbal skills perception by agents. Prah (2017) argues that intellectualisation will effectively enable our languages to develop scientific and technological capacity, rational, logical approaches and analytical techniques. Intellectualisation involves using Nigerian languages to build linguistic data as input for programmers developing algorithms that energise EL_1-mode agent's awareness of implicit linguistic differences and development of appropriate responses for multilingual interaction in Nigeria. These enhance EL_1-mode agents' communication and intercultural interaction skills in addition to preserving the Nigerian languages employed.

Conclusions

This chapter evaluated user-interaction with software agents in hybrid contexts where digital technology intersects multilingualism. Analysis stimulates interest on the impact of user multimodal facial actions as medium of assessing HAI/HHI. Although digital technology has impacted on language use and interaction, it requires social reshaping to meet user needs. Socially reshaping technology increases potentials for intellectuali- sation of Nigerian languages, enhanced support for multilingual prac- tices, useful interaction with adaptable software agents, and development of user-driven materials, pedagogy and policies that enhance the vitality of E-LTE in Nigeria. Further research could assess interactions between humans and agents in the wild such as the use of software agents in con- texts outside laboratories to provide opportunities for investigating mul- tilingual practices in real-life contexts.

Notes

(1) See https://www.cepstral.com
(2) https://www.cereproc.com
(3) More information http://www.audacityteam.org
(4) https://tla.mpi.nl/tools/tla-tools/elan/download/
(5) http://childes.talkbank.org/clan/

References

Appiah, E.K., Arko-Achemfuor, A. and Adeyeye, O.P. (2018) Appreciation of diversity and inclusion in Sub-Sahara Africa: The socioeconomic implications. *Cogent Social Sciences* 4 (1), 1521058.

Bamgbose, A. (2011) African languages today: The challenge of and prospects for empow- erment under globalization. In Selected proceedings of the 40th annual conference on African linguistics (pp. 1–14). Somerville eMA MA: Cascadilla Proceedings Project.

Baynham, M., Bradley, J., Callahan, J., Hanusova, J. and Simpson, J. (2015) Language, Business and superdiversity in Leeds. Birmingham: Translation and Translanguaging Project. See http://www.birmingham.ac.uk/generic/tlang/index.aspx (accessed 2 December 2016).

Bell, S.S. (2015) Reading body language, read body language of men and women. See http://readingbodylanguagenow.com/readingbodylanguageofbitinglips/(accessed 5 May 2015).93.

Bezemer, J. and C. Jewitt (2010) Multimodal Analysis: Key issues. In L. Litosseliti (ed.) *Research Methods in Linguistics* (pp. 180–197). London: Continuum.

Bhabha, H.K. (2015) *Debating Cultural Hybridity: Multicultural Identities and the Politics of Anti-racism*. London: Zed Books.

Cambridge University (2013) *Introductory Guide to the Common European Framework of Reference (CEFR) for English Language Teachers*. Cambridge: Cambridge University Press.

Clark, L.M., Bachour, K., Ofemile, A.Y., Adolphs, S. and Rodden, T. (2014) Potential of imprecision: exploring vague language in agent instructors. Proceedings of the second international conference on Human-agent interaction (HAI '14) (pp. 339–344). New York NY, USA: ACM. doi: http://dx.doi.org/10.1145/2658861.2658895.

Clark, L.M., Ofemile, A.Y., Adolphs, S. and Tom, R. (2016) *A Multimodal Approach to Assessing User Experiences with Agent Helpers*. ACM Transactions on Interactive Intelligent Systems (TIIS).

Deng, F.M. (2008) *Identity, Diversity, and Constitutionalism in Africa*. Washington D.C.: United States Institute of Peace Press.

Dörnyei, Z. (2007) *Research Methods in Applied Linguistics: Quantitative, Qualitative, and Mixed Methodologies*. Oxford: Oxford University Press.

Dragoi, V. (2015). Ocular Motor Control Section3: Motor Systems. In J. H. Bryne, Neuroscience Electronic Textbook (p. Chapter 8). Retrieved 12 14, 2015, from http:// neuroscience.uth.tmc.edu/s3/chapter08.html.

Ekman, P. (1997) What we have learned by measuring facial behaviour. In P. Ekman and E. Rosenberg (eds) *What the Face Reveals: Basic and Applied Studies of Spontaneous Expression Using the Facial Action Coding System (FACS)* (pp. 469–486). Oxford: Oxford University Press.

Ekman, P. (2007) *Emotions Revealed: Recognizing Faces and Feelings to Improve Communication and Emotional Life*. New York: Macmillan.

Ekman, P. (2016) What scientists who study emotion agree about. *Perspectives on Psychological Science* 11 (1), 31–34.

Ekman, P. and Friesen, W.V. (2003) *Unmasking the Face*. Cambridge: Major Books.

Ekman, P., Friesen, W.V. and Ellsworth, P. (2013) *Emotion in the Face: Guidelines for Research and an Integration of Findings*. New York: Pergamon Press Ltd.

Fayad, M. and Schmidt, D.C. (1997) Object-oriented application frameworks. *Communications of the ACM* 40 (10), 32–38.

Federal Republic of Nigeria-FGN (1999) Constitution of the Federal Republic of Nigeria (As amended). Lagos: Federal Government Printer.

Federal Republic of Nigeria-FGN (2013) *National Policy on Education* (6th edn). Abuja: NERDC Press.

Federal Republic of Nigeria-FGN (2011) *ICT Competency Framework for Teachers in Nigeria*. NCCE Abuja: NCCE Press.

Feng, D. and O'Halloran, K.L. (2013) The multimodal representation of emotion in film: Integrating cognitive and semiotic approaches. *Semiotica* 197, 79–100. doi: DOI 10.1515/sem-2013–0082.

Field, J. (2008) *Listening In the Language Classroom*. Cambridge: Cambridge University Press.

García, C.G., Pérez, P.P. and Martínez, J.N. (2000) Action selection properties in a software simulated agent. Mexican International Conference on Artificial Intelligence (pp. 634–648). Berlin Heidelberg: Springer.

Givens, D.B. (2010) Center for Nonverbal Studies. D.B. Givens (ed.) See http://center-for-nonverbal-studies.org/tensemou.htm (accessed 18 October 2015).

Halliday, M.A.K. (1978) *Language as Social Semiotic: The Social Interpretation of Language and Meaning*. London: Edward Arnold.

Harrison, S. (2014) *Methods of Gesture Analysis: Describing Gesture Forms and Interpreting Their Meanings*. Intercampus Mobility Grant, UNUK (pp. 1–42). Nottingham: University of Nottingham, UK.

Hess, U. and Kleck, R.E. (1997) Differentiating emotion elicited and deliberate emotional facial expression. In P. Ekman and E. Rosenberg (eds) *What the Face Reveals: Basic and Applied Studies of Spontaneous Expression Using the Facial Action Coding System (FACS)* (pp. 271–286). Oxford: Oxford University Press.

Jennings, N.R., Moreau, L., Nicholson, D., Ramchurn, S., Roberts, S., Rodden, T. and Rogers, A. (2014) Human-agent collectives. *Communications of the ACM* 57 (12), 80–88.

Jeronimus, B.F. and Laceulle, O.M. (2018) Frustration. In V. Zeigler-Hill and T. Shackelford (eds) *Encyclopedia of Personality and Individual Differences* (pp. 1–8). Cham: Springer.

Kiseleva, J., Williams, K., Jiang, J., Awadallah, A.H., Cook, A.C., Zitouni, I., ... Anastasakos, T. (2016) Understanding user satisfaction with intelligent assistants. *Proceedings of the 2016 ACM on Conference on Human Information Interaction and Retrieval* (pp. 121–130).

Kita, S., Özyürek, A., Allen, S., Brown, A., Furman, R. and Ishizuka, T. (2007) Relations between syntactic encoding and co-speech gestures: Implications for a model of speech and gesture production. *Language and Cognitive Processes* 22 (8), 1212–1236.

Knight, D. (2009) A multi-modal corpus approach to the analysis of backchanneling behaviour. University of Nottingham, School of English. Unpublished PhD thesis.

Lee, K. and Nass, C. (2003) Designing social presence of social actors in human computer interaction. *CHI Letters*, 289–296.

Lin, H., Guo, F., Wang, F. and Jia, Y. (2015) Picking up a soft 3D object by 'feeling' the grip. *The International Journal of Robotics Research* 34 (11), 1361–1384.

Malik, A.A. (2010) The secrets of body language. *Arifanees Management*. Retrieved 05 2015, from SlideShare: http://www.slideshare.net/arifanees/secrets-of-body-language

Matsumoto, D. and Willingham, B. (2009) Spontaneous facial expressions of emotion of congenitally and noncongenitally blind individuals. *Journal of Personality and Social Psychology* 96 (1), 1–10.

Meadors, J.D. and Murray, C.B. (2014) Measuring nonverbal bias through body language responses to stereotypes. *Journal of Nonverbal Behavior* 38 (2), 209–229.

Mehrabian, A. (2007) *Nonverbal Communication*. New Brunswick and London: Aldine Transaction.

Miller, J. (Director) (2014) Top Documentary Films – The Secrets of Body Language [Motion Picture]. See https://www.youtube.com/watch?v=HTb7XQGKp-g

Mixdorff, H., Hönemann, A., Rilliard, A., Lee, T. and Ma, M.K.H. (2017) Audio-visual expressions of attitude: How many different attitudes can perceivers decode? *Speech Communication* 95, 114–126.

Montazeri, M., Hamidi, H. and Hamidi, B. (2015) A closer look at different aspects of private speech in SLA. *Theory and Practice in Language Studies* 5 (3), 478–484.

Nass, C. and Lee, K.M. (2001) Does computer-synthesized speech manifest personality? Experimental tests of recognition, similarity-attraction, and consistency-attraction. *Journal of Experimental Psychology: Applied* 7 (3), 171–181.

Nass, C. and Moon, Y. (2000) Machines and mindlessness: Social responses to computers. *Journal of Social Issues* 56 (1), 81–103.

Nass, C., Moon, Y. and Green, N. (1997) Are machines gender neutral? Gender stereotypic responses to computers with voices. *Journal of Applied Social Psychology* 27, 864–876.

Nass, C., Steuer, J. and Tauber, E.R. (1994) Computers are social actors. CHI Conference (pp. 72–78). Boston, Massachusetts: ACM.

Ofemile, A.Y (2018) Listenership in human-agent collectives: a study of unidirectional instruction-giving. Being a PhD thesis submitted to the University of Nottingham, UK. Unpublished.

Ofemile, A.Y, Agu, I.E. and Agu, E.C (2018) Watch and listen to my face: The potential for facial communication in human-agent interaction. *African Journal of Social Sciences and Humanities Research* 1 (1), 124–154.

Ogbondah, C., and Siddens III, P. J. (1999). Defining Traditional Forms of Communication in Nigerian Culture within the Context of Nonverbal Communication. Paper presented at the Joint Meeting of the Central States Communication Association, St. Louis, MO, April 7–11, 1999. Retrieved from http://www.eric.ed.gov/PDFS/ED429324.pdf

O'Keeffe, A., McCarthy, M. and Carter, R. (2007) *From Corpus To Classroom: Language Use and Language Teaching*. Cambridge: Cambridge University Press.

Pease, A. and Pease, B. (2004) *The Definitive Book of Body Language: How to Read Other's Thoughts by their Gestures*. Buderim, Australia: Pease International.

Prah, K.K. (2017) The intellectualisation of African languages for higher education. *Alternation Journal* 24 (2), 215–225.

Reeves, B. and Nass, C. (1996) *How People Treat Computers, Television, and New Media Like Real People and Places*. New York: CSLI Publications and Cambridge University Press.

Reeves, B. and Nass, C. (2014, January 29) The Media Equation. (E. Griffin, Interviewer) See https://www.youtube.com/watch?v=26BclMJQUwo.

Simons, G.F. and Fennig, C.D. (2018) In G.F. Simons and C.D. Fennig (eds) *Ethnologue: Languages of the World* (21st edn). Dallas, TX: SIL International. See from http://www.ethnologue.com.

Simpson, J. (2016) Translanguaging in the contact zone: Language use in superdiverse urban areas. Working Papers in Translanguaging and Translation (WP. 14). Birmingham, UK. See http://www.birmingham.ac.uk/generic/tlang/index.aspx

Standring, S. and Borley, N.R. (2008) *Gray's Anatomy: The Anatomical Basis of Clinical Practice* (40th edn). London: Churchill Livingstone.

Tomilson, B. and Whittaker, C. (2013) *Blended Learning in English Language Teaching: Course Design and Implementation*. London: British Council.

Tsuchiya, K. (2013) *Listenership Behaviours in Intercultural Encounters*. Amsterdam, The Netherlands; Philadelphia, USA: The Benjamins Publishing Co.

Vincze, L. and Poggi, I. (2011) Communicative functions of eye closing behaviours. *Analysis of Verbal and Nonverbal Communication and Enactment. The Processing Issues* 393–405.

Weick, K.E., Sutcliffe, K.M. and Obstfeld, D. (2005) Organizing and the process of sensemaking. *Organization Science* 16 (4), 409–421.

White, S. (1989) Backchannels across cultures: A study of Americans and Japanese. *Language in Society* 18 (1), 59–76.

Conclusion: Digital Technology and African Multilingualism

Introduction

The dawn of the 21st century, and the fourth industrial revolution (Industry 4.0) in particular, has no doubt brought about unprecedented challenges and opportunities in revolutionizing ways of being, knowing and acting in the world. This well-documented double-edged sword of the information age catapulted by technology and digitization is best described in the mnemonic: VUCA, which characterises the 21st-century environment as **volatile, unpredictable, complex and ambiguous** (see Makalela, this volume). In this fast-paced world, the nations of the world are challenged with the dialectic of developing an agility competence to balance chaos and cohesion simultaneously and/or to manage disruption for innovation. Indeed, our vulnerability and exposure of injustices and inequalities were brought into a sharp light by the unprecedented COVID-19 pandemic that forced all governments to be heavily dependent on ICT. Although the COVID-19 infections rates were much lower in most of the African countries, except South Africa, it is worth noting that the rate of response was largely inadequate due to limitations of access to technology and health communication systems that were not readily made available in African languages. As a consequence of communication failure, disruption of economic and education activities was among the highest in the world (Kapata *et al.*, 2020).

Following the COVID-19 disruptions, it has increasingly become vital to assess the relationship between technological advances and African languages. It can be argued that apparent absence of African languages on the internet and a media of digital communication is a challenge that reduces efforts to build African knowledge societies and foster sustainable development. An all-important key question stands out: Is it possible for Sub-Saharan Africa to reach high levels of modernity without the full use of African languages? Whereas advances in technology may potentially leapfrog people into the technology of economic opportunities and foster cultural and linguistic development, this assumption is not wholly true if the language question is not addressed (Brock-Utne *et al.*, 2019). To unravel the complex interface between African languages and technological solutions that are mainly developed in the West, this book sought to take a stock of this dialectic by exploring the impact of digital technological advances and offering insights at length on linguistic diversity and multilingualism in the African societies.

Linguistic Dominance and Literacy

One of the themes that stand out in this volume is the interface between technology and language dominance. There is no doubt that many European languages are used as key languages for official purposes in Africa. This phase of what Phillipson (2012) once referred to as linguistic imperialism began with the Berlin Convention of 1884 and continued throughout the colonial period which lasted with the end of the Second World War (Ricento, 2015). The post-colonial African states inevitably carried on with these language practices in positions of prestige such as education, government and technology (Alexander, 1989; Bamgbose, 2014; Brock-Utne, 2015). Several chapters in this volume dwelt on the issue of language dominance and maintenance as crucial since English and European languages do dominate as internet languages (Gunkel, 2000). Research is replete with the findings that the use of exogenous languages in African countries have been for a long time been associated with limitations to accessing knowledge and invariably keeping the people uninformed and barely literate (Batibo, 2014; Brock-Utne, 2018; Makalela, 2018a; Prah, 2009). In this connection, the concern about access to technology as reported in this book is doubled by the use of foreign languages as technology lingua-francas, which are not well positioned for the creation and transmission of indigenous knowledge. The chapters are couched on the need for Africa to resolve the political, educational, economic and technological matters by using African languages digitally – something that includes website creation in African languages and African data-processing specialists training. Without massive progress on the digitization of African languages, the risk of double marginalization (i.e. by language and technology) looms large in the foreseeable future.

Epistemic Access and Identity Positions via Technology

Technology, like language, predisposes epistemic access and identity positions of the users. This means that a language typology predicates particular ways of knowing, making sense of one's world and self (Mignolo, 2012; Ndlovu-Gatsheni, 2020). For example, it has been established that African languages of *Bantu* origin are reader- or hearer-responsible languages that value an indirection way of making sense where textual coherence is outside of the text. Conversely, many languages of Indo-European origin follow the maxim of straight to the point where textual coherence is inside the text. With regard to the former, circumlocution becomes a rhetorical organizing strategy for meaning making whereas in the case of the latter, information is organized in a hierarchical efficiency that orders topic sentences, supporting sentences and a concluding sentence in a linear and predictable fashion as evidenced in the preferred paragraph structure (Makalela, 2019; Motlhaka & Makalela, 2016). It is therefore curious how these differentiated epistemic beliefs are negotiated as African languages embrace technological advances that were initially carried over in Western lingual francas. This book cautions against the assumptions about world views carried by technological solutions to development problems in Africa as value free and context independent. To this end, it is instructive that technology-generated knowledge bias may place African countries in a position where they passively become consumers of foreign cultural values (see, for example, Alzouma, 2005; Batchelor & Lautenbach, 2013). It remains a developmental question on whether the culture and identities of the indigenous people can be infused with foreign content so that this content is sensitive and relevant to the local environments. Several authors (this volume) framed the notion of identity and cultural constructs as a matter of concern even as Africa gravitates towards digitization. Key philosophical questions are around what and how people come to know and how their identities are affected by technological knowledge that is found to be at odds with their livelihoods and ways of acting. When framed in this light, African languages are core intermediaries in moving people into the world of economic opportunities and decolonization of knowledge.

As we show in some of the chapters, we have used the African value system of Ubuntu (African humanity) to unearth the issues of complexity and a methodology of parallel but complementary co-existence. The chapters brought about several interlocking themes that include the prevalence of digital media spaces, degree of use, migration of cultural practices into the digital ecological systems, giving agency to muted voices, linguistic decolonization, sustenance of indigenous knowledge system and novel ways of meaning making in a multilingual Sub-Saharan African region. These themes were undergirded by an all-important question: whether these rapid technological advances benefit the previously marginalized languages and people or whether perpetuate the forms of disadvantage (digital colonization).

Closing Gaps through Digital African Multilingualism

It is axiomatic and reiterated in the preceding chapters of this volume that African languages are not on the same level as languages of wider communication such as English and French when it comes to digital technology integration (e.g. Alzouma, 2005). Not surprisingly, the medium through which digital participation is carried out reflects a digital divide between the global North and global South, on the one hand, and between dominant languages from the West and marginalized languages in Sub-Saharan Africa, on the other hand. However, there is a glimpse of hope in that African language usage in the digital spaces shows that more progress has been made compared use of these languages within the traditional print environment. As vehemently argued (this volume), the digital platforms serve, therefore, as enablers for the African languages to be used in public spaces and conversational forums that were historically reserved for lingua francas such as English, French and Portuguese. Compared to linguistic and ethnic separation forged in the past, African languages are now used more fluidly, disrupting some of the colonial and ethnic boundaries and at the same time affirming speakers' plural identities and indigenous ways of knowing that are particular to the local contexts. These Digital African Multilingualism (DAM) patterns signal a milestone that digitalization of African languages is effective repository to meeting the 21st-century needs of its users. When framed in this light, digitization of African languages becomes a precursor for closing the gaps of language in domains of prestige such as education and government media of communication where English and French are still de facto the main languages (Brock-Utne, 2015; Prah, 2009). Norton (in this volume) presents a compelling case that digital stories in African languages advances African languages by affirming speakers' identities and cultivating imagined identities, which develop through emotional investment. Here, we see the value of digital technology in breaking the cycle of disadvantage and opening up more possibilities for closing the gaps.

The next highlight is that social media platforms such as Wazzup have an enabling effect on using languages in versatile ways. Contrary to conservative views, social media planforms are found to be effective in enhancing rapport and social integration. For example, the lessons from Rwanda showed that exponential use of Wazzup groups by the youth provided opportunities for full expression of their identities through use of a range of languages that overlapped each other (Niyibizi, Niyimugabo and Perumal in this volume). The users' ability to give input and output in different languages during the interactions is an affirmation of a local multilingual competence named translanguaging (García, 2009; Makalela, 2016). It is noteworthy that this discourse practice has been normalized as reflective of harmonized social relations in a country where new friendships, relationships and cultural border crossing are established across a wider spectrum of the communities that were traditionally divided along ethnic lines. We deduce from this experience that having multiple perspectives and developing multicultural understanding forms the core of a transforming nation and aligns with the key competencies of the 21st century such as one's ability to resolve tension and commit to trade-offs. It is in this connection that we claim (Makalela; Sachs; Ogbay & White in this volume) that digital technology is an enabler of the cultural competence of African societies and a gap filler in spaces where governzments failed.

Is also well established that social media platforms provide opportunity for economies of scale and affordances for creativity. A prototypical case is in Malawi where the users have found innovative ways of leveraging on hashtags to communicate widely and spread literary genres across a wider spectrum of communities (Sachs, this volume). In this way, there is an increased participation in the political and cultural dynamics of African countries where language had always been a barrier. Such a sensitive topic was expressed through Messenger as a transnational advocacy for political and social change for women outside and inside Eritrea (Ogbay & White, this volume). Here, the transglobal and multilingual discourses are carried out via semiotic resources such as video, emoticons, symbols, images, spoken and written word to make meaning and express identity, create solidarity among members, spur them into action and resolve conflicts. Digital technology is therefore an enabler for expression of diverse ideas, broadening participation in national and cross national dialogues and preserving endangered languages and multilingualism as a resource (Rowan, this volume).

The final point on DAM is the often reported concern that African languages are marginally used public spaces (Alexander, 1989; Prah, 2009) and that their extinction, as a result, is inevitable. Several chapters in this book show how technology has increased African languages to a status of languages of wider communication via social media platforms (ResCue & Agbozom, this volume; Ofemile, this volume). Equally, it was shown that these languages can also be used as vehicles for transborder connection between Africans in the region and in the diaspora to maintain heritage and indigenous philosophies (Rowan, this volume). In this way, the digital initiatives model promotes the vitality of African languages while at the same time contributing to the maintenance of multilingualism as a cultural competence and a heritage of the speakers. Put differently, digital technology has become a reservoir of indigenous African languages and new 'arbiter' for their continued existence and use among its speakers.

Does Digital Technology Decay or Develop African Languages?

Debates about the relationship between digital technology and African languages are incomplete without addressing the old-age question: *Does digital technology decay or develop African languages?* There has been a belief that technological inventions would erode the forms and structures of African languages as digital technology exposes them to borrowings from dominant languages such as English. We make a point in one of the chapters (Makalela, this volume) that languages have always been fluid and intersected in a continuous state of flux and mutual borrowing. The notion of a 'pure' language within the space of linguistic ecology remains a fallacy. It is instructive in the research findings reported in this volume that digital technologies have increased the domains and scope of use – something that constitutes progress or development. In particular, the sociolinguistic realities of the digital spaces have revealed 'digital trans-languaging' where there is mobility and fluidity of language forms that cross over traditional language boundaries. This form of translanguaging goes beyond concerns about maintenance of 'pure standards' and forms, and instead it extends to sustenance, which is about the survival of these languages in the future. Within a transformed space where there is an epistemological shift from what languages look like to what people do with the languages (a 21st-century competence), the digital technologies have brought hope for languages that were historically marginalized. Yet their evolution means that changes are inevitable.

Linguistic Decolonization Through Technology

As stated above, one of the main points made in this volume is the epistemological shift from what languages look like to what people do with the languages as explicated under the notion of translanguaging. This reconceptualization of languages interface is a response to historical displacement of African multilingualism as hermetically sealed units that are capable of being placed in boxes (Makalela, 2016; Makoni, 2003). To rehabilitate multilingualism in Sub-Saharan Africa, the notion of *Ubuntu translanguaging* is used to show the cultural competence of the African people where one language is incomplete without the other (Makalela, this volume). This horizontal view of multilingualism makes way for simultaneous cross pollination between African languages, on the one hand, and between African languages and Western-based lingua francas, on the other hand. Several chapters in the book revealed that this complex discursive regime is fully enabled and functional in the digital platforms (e.g. Niyibisi *et al.*, this volume). Taking a cue from Mazrui (2002) notion of horizontal counter-penetration as a decolonizing strategy, the intersection of vertical and horizontal multilingualism that finds resonance with Ubuntu translanguaging disrupts the establishment of colonial boundaries between languages and recreates new discursive ones with the idea of enriching educational experience, understanding and self-knowledge where meaning is the overriding principle for language use. This epistemological shift endorses an orchestra of chaos and disruptions co-existing to place African languages at the center of digitization in contemporary African societies. Partially aligning with complexity theory, which reflect on the state of continued disruption of elements that are not stable (see also

Makalela in this volume), this complex co-existence is grounded in the conception of discontinuation and continuation of Ubuntu translanguaging, which is defined elsewhere (Makalela, 2018b, 2019) as disruption of orderliness and simultaneous recreation of new discursive forms. Apart from offering a human turn on language, the universals of ubuntu translanguaging show complex identity configurations that characterize DAM and cultural identities of most multilingual African language speakers and in particular those with Bantu languages background.

Conclusion

Taken together, this book volume has expressed and demonstrated the interface between African multilingualism and digital technologies, which have exponentially proliferated the African linguistic ecology. In the fast-paced world where there is a constant disruption of orderliness and simultaneous recreation of new orders at the same time, it is crucial to ask questions around maintenance and sustenance of indigenous African languages, which remained marginalized throughout several stages of colonization. Because survival in the 21st century in general and the fourth industrial revolution in particular implicate adaptation to the context that is volatile, unpredictable, complex and ambiguous, migration of African languages into the digital linguistic ecology marks a positive stride for social transformation and their survival in future. One of the benefits of this migration is the opportunity for cross-linguistic and cross-cultural pollination, which disrupts colonial boundaries while at the same time rebuilding new forms of social cohesion among people who were historically divided along linguistic lines. Translanguaging, in this context, stands out as an empowering strategy to focus attention on what people do with the language rather than what the languages look like. Notwithstanding all the risks that come with digitization, there is a renewed hope infusion of African languages and technology to reflect ways of being, knowing and acting in the world. It is in this connection that we claimed: where the governments failed to promote use of African languages, technology shows promise.

References

Alexander, N. (1989) *Language Policy and National Unity in South Africa/Azania*. Cape Town: Buchu Books.
Alzouma, G. (2005) Myths of digital technology in Africa: Leapfrogging development? *Global Media and Communication* 1 (3), 339–356.
Bamgbose, A. (2014) The language factor in development goals. *Journal of Multilingual and Multicultural Development* 35 (7), 646–657.
Batchelor, J. and Lautenbach, G. (2013) Reaching out and connecting: pre-service teachers and their professional learning networks. ISTE International Conference on Mathematics, Science and Technology Education

Batibo, H.M. (2014) Plurilingualism in Southern Africa and the emergence of the Setswana language. *Boleswa Journal of Theology, Religion and Philosophy* 4 (2), 275–292.

Brock-Utne, B. (2018) Researching language and culture in Africa using an autoethnographic approach. *International Review of Education* 64 (6), 713–735.

Brock-Utne, B. (2015) Language, literacy and democracy in Africa. In L. Makalela (ed.) *New Directions on Language and Literacy Education for Multilingual Classrooms in Africa* (pp. 15–33). Cape Town: CASAS.

Brock-Utne, B., Halvorsen, T.A. and Vuzo, M. (2019) The school drop-out or rather 'push out' problem in the South and in the North. *World Studies in Education* 20 (2), 61–75.

García, O. (2009) *Bilingual Education in the 21st Century: A Global Perspective*. Miden, MA:Wiley/Blackwell.

Gunkel, D.G. (2000) The Empire Strikes Back: The cultural politics of the internet. In E. Bosah (ed.) *Cyberimperialism? Global Relations in the New Electronic Frontier*. Westport, CT: Praeger.

Kapata, N., Ihekweazu, C., Ntoumi, F., Raji, T., Chanda-Kapata, P., Mwaba, P. and Mfinanga, S. (2020) Is Africa prepared for tackling the COVID-19 (SARS-CoV-2) epidemic. Lessons from past outbreaks, ongoing pan-African public health efforts, and implications for the future. *International Journal of Infectious Diseases* 93, 233–236.

Makalela, L. (2019) Uncovering the universals of ubuntu translanguaging in classroom discourses. *Classroom Discourse* 10 (3–4), 237–251.

Makalela, L. (2018a) Community elders' narrative accounts of ubuntu translanguaging: Learning and teaching in African education. *International Review of Education* 64 (6), 823–843.

Makalela, L. (ed.) (2018b) *Shifting Lenses: Multilanguaging, Decolonisation and Education in the Global South*. Centre for Advanced Studies of African Society (CASAS).

Makalela, L. (2016) Ubuntu translanguaging: An alternative framework for complex multilingual encounters. *Southern African Linguistics and Applied Language Studies* 34 (3), 187–196.

Makoni, S. (2003) From misinvention to disinvention of language: Multilingualism and the South African Constitution. *Black Linguistics: Language, Society and Politics in Africa and the Americas*, 132–153.

Mazrui, A.M. (2002) The English language in African education: Dependency and decolonization. *Language Policies in Education: Critical Issues*, 267–282.

Mignolo, W. (2012) *Local Histories/Global Designs: Coloniality, Subaltern Knowledges, and Border Thinking*. Princeton University Press.

Motlhaka, H.A. and Makalela, L. (2016) Translanguaging in an academic writing class: Implications for a dialogic pedagogy. *Southern African Linguistics and Applied Language Studies* 34 (3), 251–260.

Ndlovu-Gatsheni, S.J. (2020) *Decolonization, Development and Knowledge in Africa: Turning Over a New Leaf*. Routledge.

Phillipson, R. (2012) Linguistic imperialism. *The Encyclopedia of Applied Linguistics*, 1–7.

Prah, K.K. (2009) Mother-tongue education in Africa for emancipation and development: Towards the intellectualisation of African languages. *Languages and Education in Africa: A Comparative and Transdisciplinary Analysis*, 83–104.

Ricento, T. (ed.) (2015) *Language Policy and Political Economy: English in a Global Context*. Oxford: Oxford University Press.

Index

African Storybook 119–122, 124, 127–133
Apps 99, 103, 108
Arabic 98, 102, 107
Assemblages 56, 58

Banda, Hastings Kamuzu 139–140
Banda, Phindu 150
Bilingual practices 58, 69
Blended learning 100

Chiwamba, Robert 144, 145, 147
Citizenship 114
COD Model 51, 54, 56
Code-meshing 34
Code-translation 33
Collective identity 65, 66
Comprehension 158, 165, 175, 177, 178, 180, 181, 182
Communiction power 100
Conflicts online 115, 116
Cultural assemblages 68
Cultural competence 3
Cyberspace 52, 53

Digital diaspora 99
Digital literacy 118, 119, 122
Digital media 56
Digital technology 68, 69
Digital translanguaging 3
Discourse practices 7

eGranary 119, 120, 124, 125–127, 129, 130, 132, 133.
English language 158, 159, 161
Emotion 108
Eritrea 100, 101, 111
Ewe 51, 54, 56

Facebook 52, 54, 55, 56, 69
Facial Actions 17, 157, 158, 162, 163, 164, 165, 167, 168, 171, 172, 173, 174, 175, 176, 180, 181, 182, 183
#FeesMustFall 137, 151

Ghana 54, 59
Global Storybooks 121, 122

Human-Agent Interaction 157, 158, 164
Hybridity 161, 162, 184

Identity 104, 118, 119, 122–124, 127, 132
Incomprehension 158, 165, 175, 178, 179, 180, 181, 182
Intangible culture 99, 106, 109
Investment 119, 122, 123, 127, 128, 130–132

Language ecology 98, 109
Language vitality 101
Lilongwe Living Room Poetry Club 143–144, 147–149
Linguistic assemblages 52, 53, 64, 65, 69
Linguistic continuum 11

Malawezi, Q 145, 149–150
Memory 110
Metadata 102
Methodological issues for analysing online data 104
Metro-languaging 32
Minority languages 51, 53, 56, 69
Mobile technology 3
Monolingual bias 4
multilingual repertoire 51, 59, 69
multilingualism 69
Multimodal 163, 168, 171, 176, 182, 183
Multimodal corpus 157, 167, 173, 174, 175

Network of Eritrean Women 99
Nigeria 158, 159, 160, 166, 182, 183, 184
Nonverbal listenership 157, 159, 163

Poly-languaging 30
Proverbs 99, 104, 105, 107, 108,

Repertoire 11

Sapitwa Poetry 143–145, 147–149
Seunda, Yankho 144
Social dynamics 26
Social media 23, 69
Social movement theory 65
Social networks 99, 108
Software Agents 6, 17, 157, 158, 159,
    165, 176, 183, 184

Storybooks African Languages
Storybooks Canada 121

Textual analysis 58
Translanguaging 69
Translocal language practice 35
Transnational language practice 34

Ubuntu translanguaging 5
Uganda 118–121, 123–125, 127,
    131–133
University of Malawi 137

Vertical and horizontal languaging 30

WhatsApp 137–138, 140

For Product Safety Concerns and Information please contact our EU Authorised Representative:

Easy Access System Europe

Mustamäe tee 50

10621 Tallinn

Estonia

gpsr.requests@easproject.com